IMAGES
of America

BROUSSARD

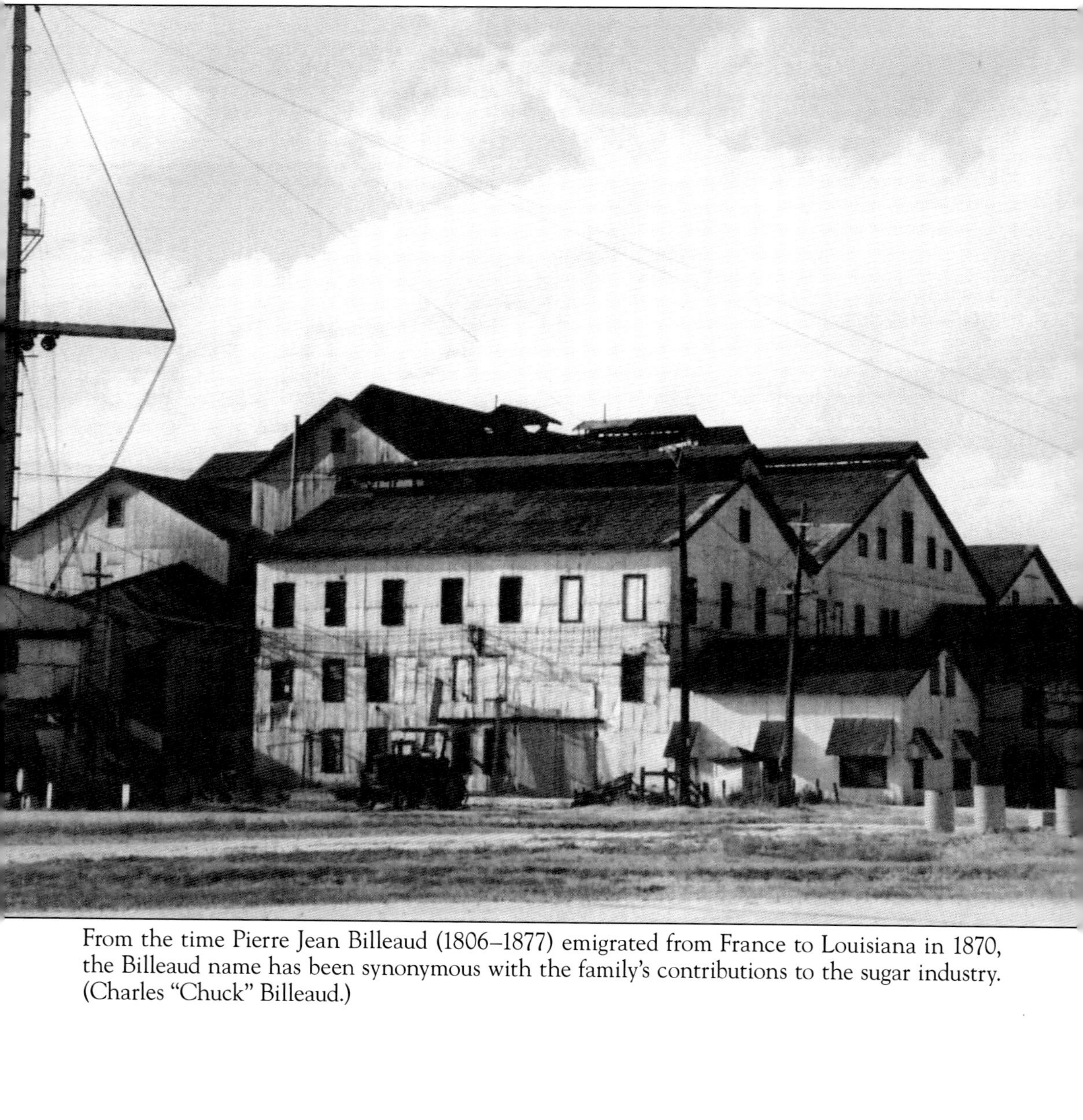

From the time Pierre Jean Billeaud (1806–1877) emigrated from France to Louisiana in 1870, the Billeaud name has been synonymous with the family's contributions to the sugar industry. (Charles "Chuck" Billeaud.)

On the Cover: St. Cecilia High School graduates of 1925 are pictured here with their teachers, nuns from the Order of Divine Providence that hailed from San Antonio, Texas. For 65 years, these sisters were responsible for supervising, guiding, and directing the pupils through a faith-based curriculum. More information can be found in chapter 4, "Public and Private Schools Emerge." (Lafayette Parish Clerk of Court Louis J. Perret.)

IMAGES
of America

BROUSSARD

Linda A. Meaux

ARCADIA
PUBLISHING

ISBN 978-1-4671-1501-8

Published by Arcadia Publishing
Charleston, South Carolina

Printed in the United States of America

Library of Congress Control Number: 2015945415

For all general information, please contact Arcadia Publishing:
Telephone 843-853-2070
Fax 843-853-0044
E-mail sales@arcadiapublishing.com
For customer service and orders:
Toll-Free 1-888-313-2665

Visit us on the Internet at www.arcadiapublishing.com

Claire Bernard Bonin lived a century of life filled with faith, family, and community, and gladly shared her vast wisdom and knowledge.

Contents

Acknowledgments

My vision began 16 years ago after reading *A Brief History of Broussard*, compiled in 1984 by J. Harold Hollier. Having amassed many tidbits of knowledge about Broussard's past through my husband's family connections to the community, I wanted to write a more in-depth history of the quaint village once known as Côte Gelée.

I sought to birth a visual panorama interspersed with eloquent speech to more fully understand the Acadie exiles, especially brothers Joseph "Beausoleil" and Alexandre Broussard's trials and tribulations when fighting against British troops and their ultimate emigration to Côte Gelée to settle the Acadians in a lush and fertile land. Moreover, I wished to learn what part Valsain "Valsin" Broussard played in the town growth of Broussard.

The Broussard Historical Society (BHS) proposed in 1982 to establish three historic districts—District A encompasses buildings and sites of local, state, or national historical significance in the Côte Gelée area, which is the town center; District B includes buildings and sites of local, state, or national historical significance located in the original incorporated area of the municipality extending the length of Main Street and a depth of two blocks on either side of this principal thoroughfare; and District C, which is an additional area of the original incorporation located northeast of District B. By 1998, the BHS was no longer active. Thanks go to Maxine Duhon for her continuing efforts towards that goal.

In addition, I would like to thank Robert "Bobby" St. Julien, retired educator and history buff, for facts rounding out the visual story. To Henry Langlinais and his sister Doris Larriviere, Ralph Racca and Sarah Guidry Racca, and James Gondron that shared daily workings on a dairy farm, thanks. In addition, Fr. Arockiam Arockiam, SVD, shared tidbits from St. Joseph Church parish history. Thanks also go to Broussard city councilwoman Gertrude N. Batiste for the calls and interviews conducted in identifying photographs.

Foremost, thanks go to Jennifer Armentor, whose technical skills and attention to detail kept the project running smoothly and on track. Mayor Charles E. Langlinais and the Broussard City Council lead the charge as Broussard enters the next century of growth and prosperity while keeping alive the spirit of our Acadian heritage.

INTRODUCTION

The city of Broussard, Louisiana, is located off Highway 90, a major transportation artery through the Gulf Coast. In addition, it is in two parishes, Lafayette and St. Martin, which is one of 22 parishes recognized on June 6, 1971, by the Louisiana State Legislature along with other parishes of similar cultural environments, as the Heart of Acadiana.

Broussard lies on a floodplain of one of the old meandering courses of the Mississippi River. The town's roots sprouted in 1765, a gift from Joseph "Beausoleil" Broussard, exiled sharpshooter and guerrilla fighter, and his followers, creating a wonderful legacy for generations to come with joie de vivre, food, music, culture, and arts. Its Francophone population of 9,382 oozes with Southern hospitality and charm, combining growth opportunities with cutting-edge 21st-century technology. In the year 2010, Broussard gained national recognition for its rapidly growing commercial expansions.

The State of Louisiana announced plans in 2014 to widen and construct a two-mile segment of I-49 South from north of Ambassador Caffery Parkway to Albertsons Parkway, the two main major arteries for commercial and residential building in the area. Work has begun on the project, and when completed, the entire section of infrastructure will have six lanes with frontage roads stretching to the neighboring Iberia Parish line.

Broussard, Louisiana, is the only city in Louisiana that does not have city property taxes, making it a great place to build, live, work, and play. Mayor Charles E. Langlinais's $17-million recreational project, St. Julien Park, will be located next to substantial acreage that will draw interest to restaurants, hotels, and retail businesses.

Set on a backdrop of 125-plus acres of rugged landscape, St. Julien Park took a substantial design effort to incorporate the rolling terrain into the final design plans. Phase 1 is underway and will offer a chance for youth and adults alike to play together in a state-of-the-art facility with the most up-to-date and safe equipment. It is likely that St. Julien Park will become a regional draw for competitive sports teams and their families. Patrick St. Julien lives across the road from the St. Julien Park, named after distant relatives, and he looks forward to watching his grandchildren play on the soccer and baseball fields. The Broussard brothers, Joseph "Beausoleil" and Alexandre, would be very proud to see how prosperous the once frozen hills of Côte Gelée have become.

The book would not be complete without mentioning the New Acadia Project (NAP) grassroots undertaking, a multidisciplinary, historical, and ethnographic initiative to fill a 10-year gap in history. NAP is based out of Louisiana Public Archeology Laboratories and is a cooperative between the University of Louisiana at Lafayette and NAP Steering Committee, headed by Mark A. Rees, PhD. Their goal is to locate some 64 Acadie graves they believe could be in the Jeanerette area near Fausse Point. Now, 250 years later, there is the possibility of finding the graves of Acadie émigré's Beausoleil, his brother, Alexandre, and other settlers who succumbed to yellow fever shortly after settling along the Teche Ridge in 1765.

This contribution to the Images of America series pays tribute to the spirit of the Acadians. However, despite Joseph "Beausoleil" Broussard's wits and skills, the Acadian resistance to the British failed. Through Beausoleil's exploits, his group of fighters held back the British along the Petitcodiac River until 1768. The British cleared Acadie, leaving the lush and fertile land bare. Beausoleil Broussard, Alexandre Broussard, Jean Basque, and Simon Martin delivered a petition to the British at Fort Cumberland on November 16, 1759, relinquishing the fight rather than face the prospect of starvation. Jean Basque and Michel Bourg led another group of starving Acadians to the fort a few days later. The Acadians that were sent to Halifax were freed in 1763 when the hostilities ended. After the Treaty of Paris, about 1,700 prisoners chose to remain in Nova Scotia.

The British drove the Acadians from their homes and deported them to foreign ports on both sides of the Atlantic; Beausoleil Broussard and his band of followers were in the second group of families escaping the first wave of deportation 250 years ago. They chartered a schooner in 1764 headed to Saint-Domingue in the Caribbean, then went up the mouth of the Mississippi River, intending to settle in Illinois. However, in November 1764, another enemy, tropical heat, fever, and epidemic plagues, wreaked havoc on the passengers, with only 200 Acadian survivors arriving in Louisiana in February 1765, having received permission to settle at Louisiana Poste des Attakapas.

Although French trappers, traders, and Indians lived in and around the Côte Gelée area prior to 1765, it was not until the exiled Acadians began arriving in southwest Louisiana at Poste des Attakapas that permanent settlement began. In April 1765, Beausoleil Broussard's group reached the Poste des Attakapas, one of two outposts divided by two districts west of the Atchafalaya Basin in south Louisiana. It consisted of a small store, chapel, and pitiful barracks for the 14 soldiers garrisoned in the area known today as St. Martinville.

Antoine Bernard d'Autrieve obtained a land grant in 1760 and contracted with eight of the Acadians to sharecrop cattle for a six-year tenure in exchange for land and half of the livestock increase. But when Beausoleil Broussard and his band got to d'Autrieve's land on the east side of Bayou Teche, their neighbors treated them as interlopers, although they had a voice as to where they would eventually settle. The leader earned the moniker Beausoleil for his and his people's round smiling faces and willingness to work.

Around the same time, Beausoleil Broussard received a commission with the Louisiana militia as commandant of the Acadians, to assist and direct Louis Audry, Louisiana's military engineer, with the continued settlement, as another 38 families, including Comeaux, Landry, Breaux, Girouard, Menard, and LeBlanc, settled into the area. These Acadians' descendants continue to influence Broussard's 21st-century development.

Three months shy of settling in Broussardville, Alexandre Broussard died in September 1765, a victim of the plague from the fever-ridden island from whence they migrated. His brother Beausoleil continued to direct and assist with the regrouping and settlement of the Acadians in Côte Gelée until his own death on October 20, 1765, a scant 13 days after Alexandre's. Valsin Broussard, a mail carrier and descendant of Alexandre Broussard, is given credit with the early development of Broussardville, later renamed Broussard.

In the early 1800s, the St. Julien and Billeaud families, French émigrés, began arriving in Louisiana, settling in the Côte Gelée area. Pierre Jean Billeaud, a wheelwright and blacksmith, immigrated from Bourgneuf, France, settling in Vermilionville, Louisiana, the present-day Lafayette, in 1840.

Billeaud passed on his skills to his youngest son, Martial François Billeaud, born in 1836, and he started his own forge and blacksmith shop, where the Acadiana Hotel now stands on Pinhook Road. Martial François Billeaud settled in Lafayette Parish in 1850 and by 1914 built the Billeaud Sugar Mill. He married Lucille St. Julien and leased land from his father-in-law, Gustave St. Julien, to grow sugarcane at a time when cotton was the major crop and sugarcane was just gaining popularity.

One

Beausoleil Brings Acadians to Côte Gelée

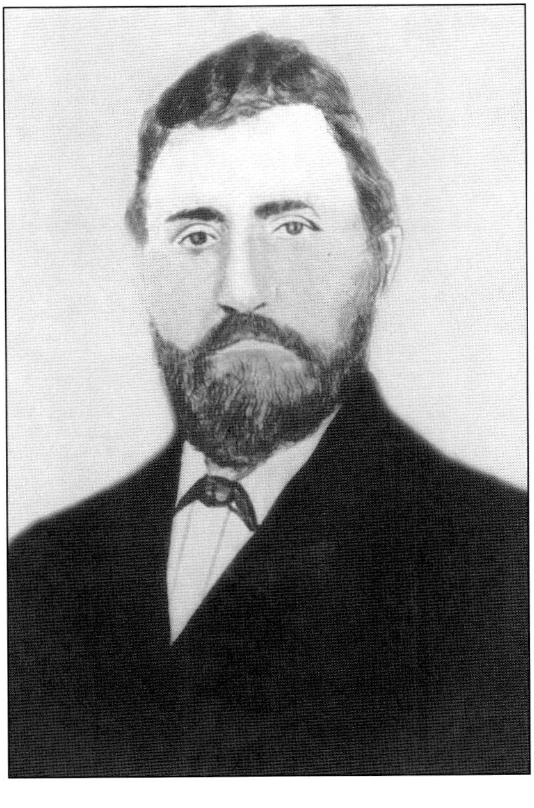

A monument in memory of Alexandre "Beausoleil" Broussard, founding father of Broussard, and his brother Joseph "Beausoleil" Broussard, was erected and is located on the grounds of Broussard City Hall. The monument honors the guerilla leader who stayed behind in old Acadie, Nova Scotia, fighting the British. He helped the Acadians move to the Côte Gelée area in 1765. Valsin Broussard (pictured), son of Don Louis Broussard and Anastasie Landry and a descendant of Alexandre Broussard, is credited for naming Broussardville. (Author's collection.)

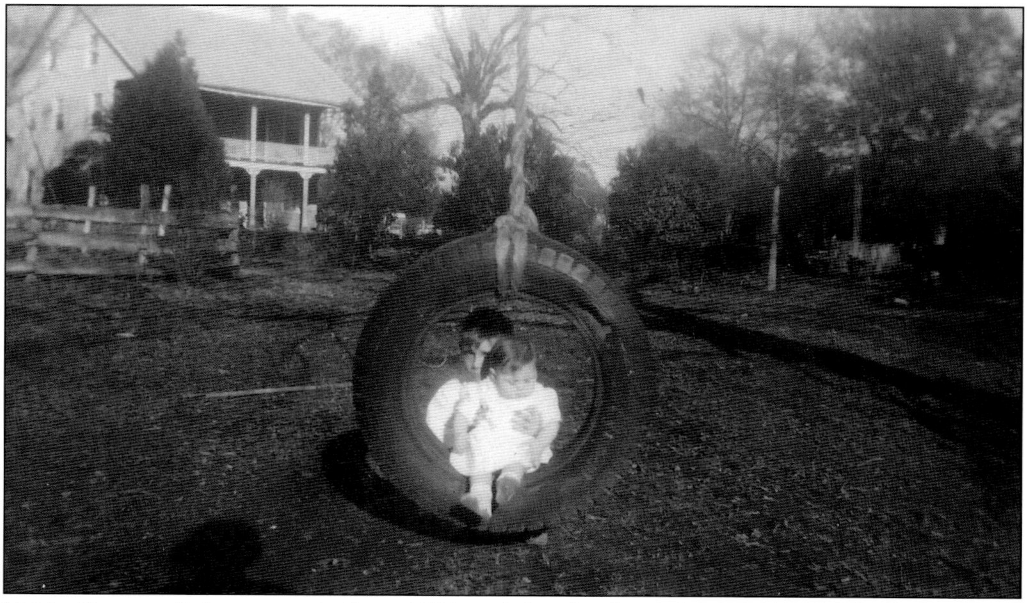

Valsin Broussard's home was built in 1876, with his family settling on that land soon after the Civil War. It is the oldest house remaining in Broussard and has enjoyed continuous occupation by Valsin's descendants, including granddaughters Nellie Bernard, Genevieve "Sweet" Bernard, and Adele Girouard. Pictured at the tire swing is an unidentified boy pushing Adele Bernard Hollier's daughter Emma Lee Hollier. Emma was the last child to be born in the Valsin and Emma Monte Broussard home. (City of Broussard archives.)

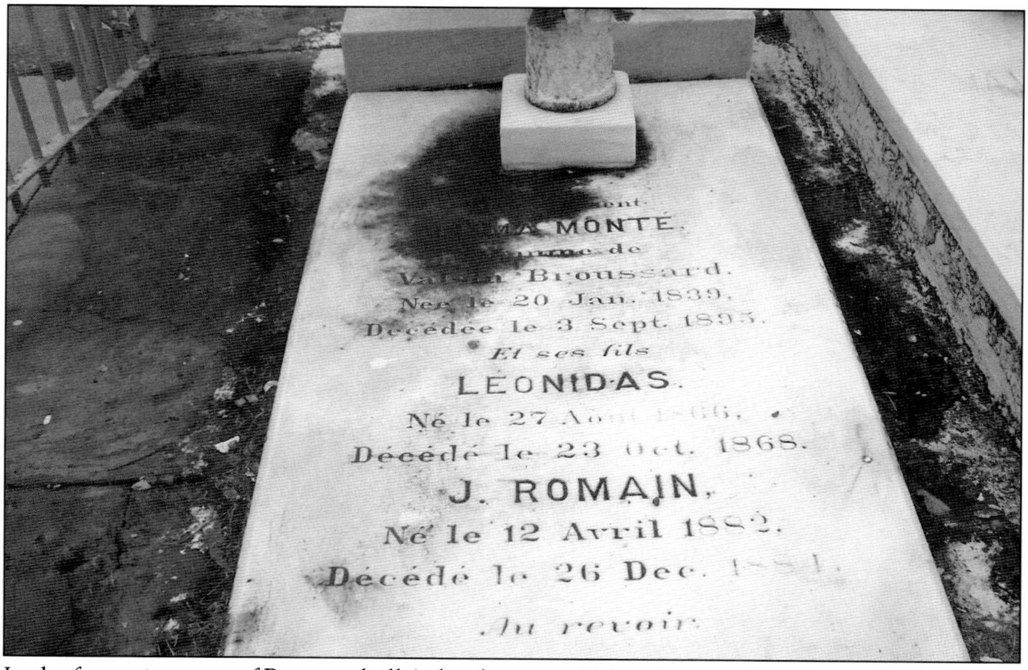

In the formative years of Broussardville's development, Valsin Broussard's surveyor drew out plans for land that was donated to build the Southern Pacific railroad depot, a bank, and the Sacred Heart Church parish cemetery, where Valsin Broussard and his wife, Emma Monte Broussard, sleep in eternal rest. (Author's collection.)

Little is known of Leonidas Broussard—just the dates of his birth, August 27, 1866, in Youngsville, and his death, October 23, 1868. He was the third of seven children born to Valsin Broussard, founding father of Broussard, and Emma Monte Broussard. (Lafayette Parish Clerk of Court Louis J. Perret.)

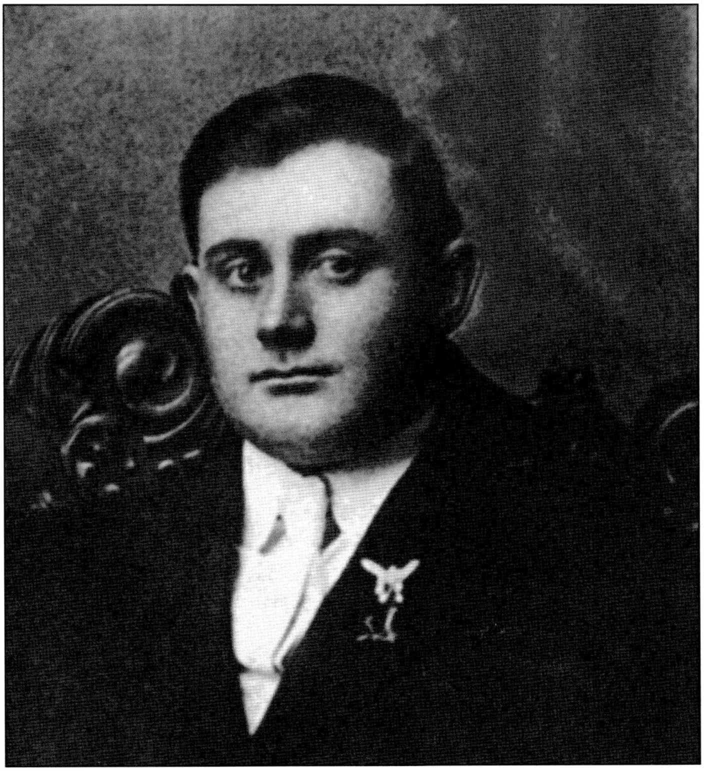

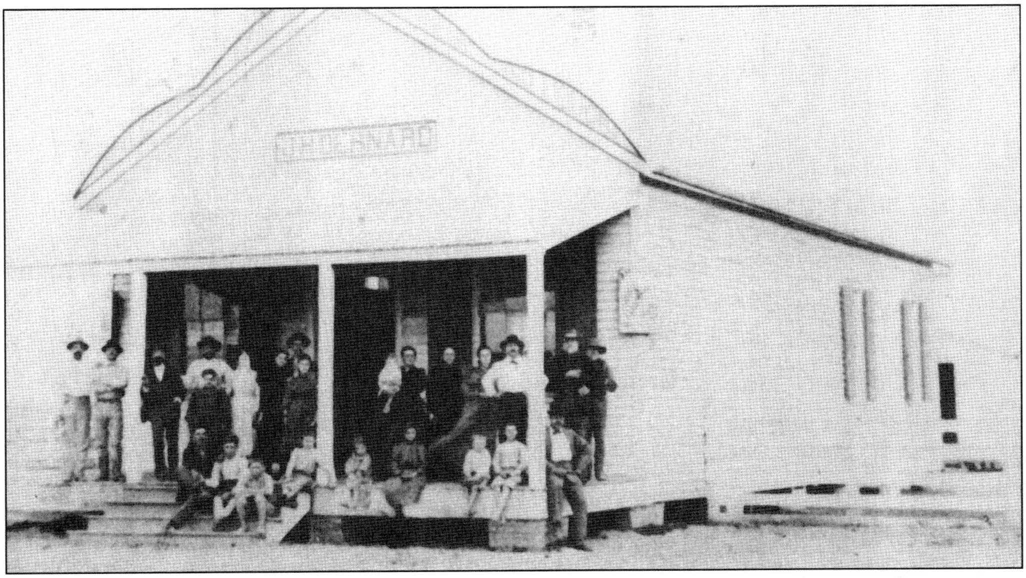

Jean Hazard Bernard owned and operated a general mercantile store on Highway 89 from 1891 to 1940. It was one of several in Broussard. The Bernard family reared nine children. Daniel Bernard, the third son, attended seminary and served as the parish priest in Arnaudville, Louisiana—later rising to rank of monsignor. (City of Broussard archives.)

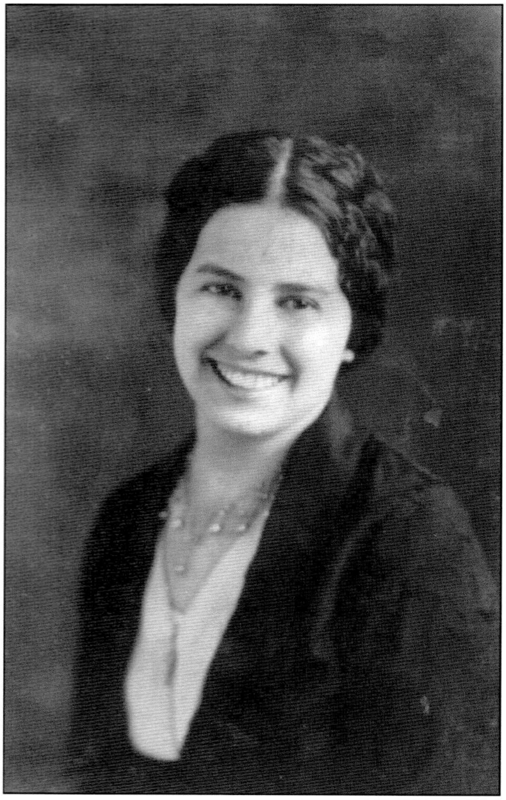

Claire Bernard Bonin, fifth daughter and the last of nine siblings, was born August 13, 1909, to Jean Hazard Bernard and Adonia Bernard Bonin of Abbeville, Louisiana. She lived in her family's 1890s home her entire life. In one of many interviews, she let it be known, "I was born, raised, married, widowed, and stayed in this house all my life, and will die here." She was known for her volunteer work with Sacred Heart Church Fair and St. Cecelia School as personal chauffeur for the nuns of the Order of Sisters of Divine Providence. Bonin died at the age of 104 on May 14, 2014. (Linda Bonin.)

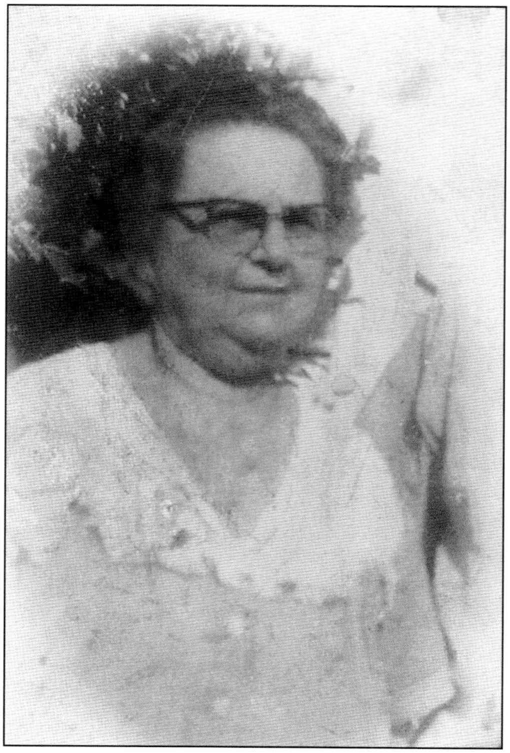

Nina Marie Bernard, the daughter of Guillaume Bernard and Clara Broussard, was one of Valsin Broussard's eight grandchildren. Nina Marie Broussard married Denis Bernard, and they reared a family of eight children. (Emma Lee Girouard Hollier.)

Carla Broussard, a daughter of Valsin Broussard and Emma Monte Broussard, is pictured here seated in the parlor of her ancestral home. The house is the oldest local residence in the National Register of Historic Places and has a continuous history of occupation by Valsin's many descendants. (Emma Lee Girouard Hollier.)

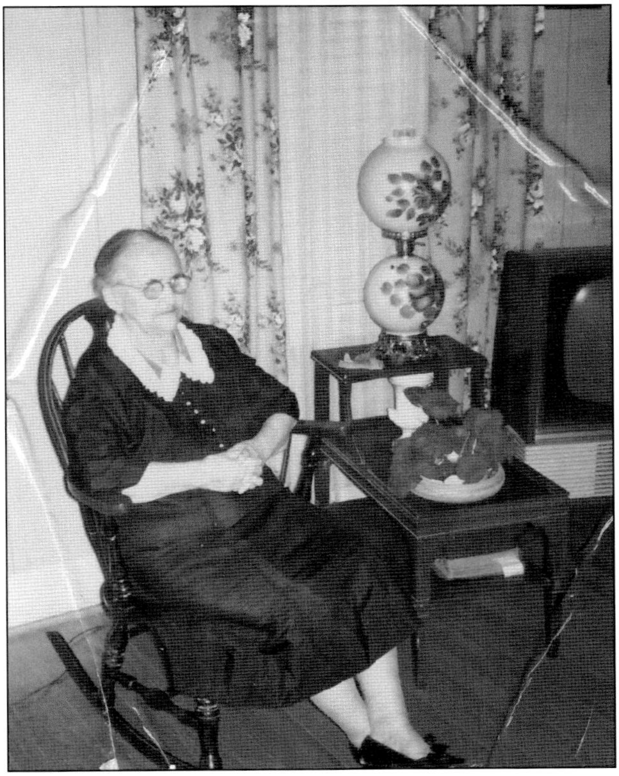

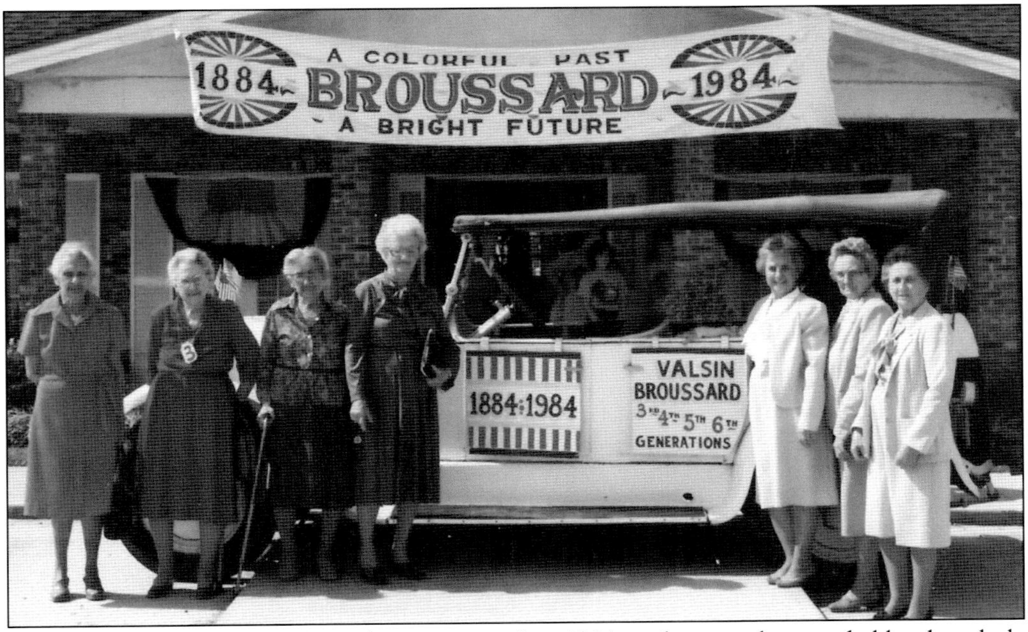

The town of Broussard celebrated its centennial in 1984, with a parade attended by the whole town. Pictured are the granddaughters of Valsin Broussard, a Civil War survivor recognized as the town's founding father. They are, from left to right, Bernadette Bernard, Loul Bernard, Nellie Bernard, Lydia Bernard, Adele Girouard, Lal Bernard, and Genevieve "Sweet" Bernard, a Broussard Middle School teacher. (Emma Lee Girouard Hollier.)

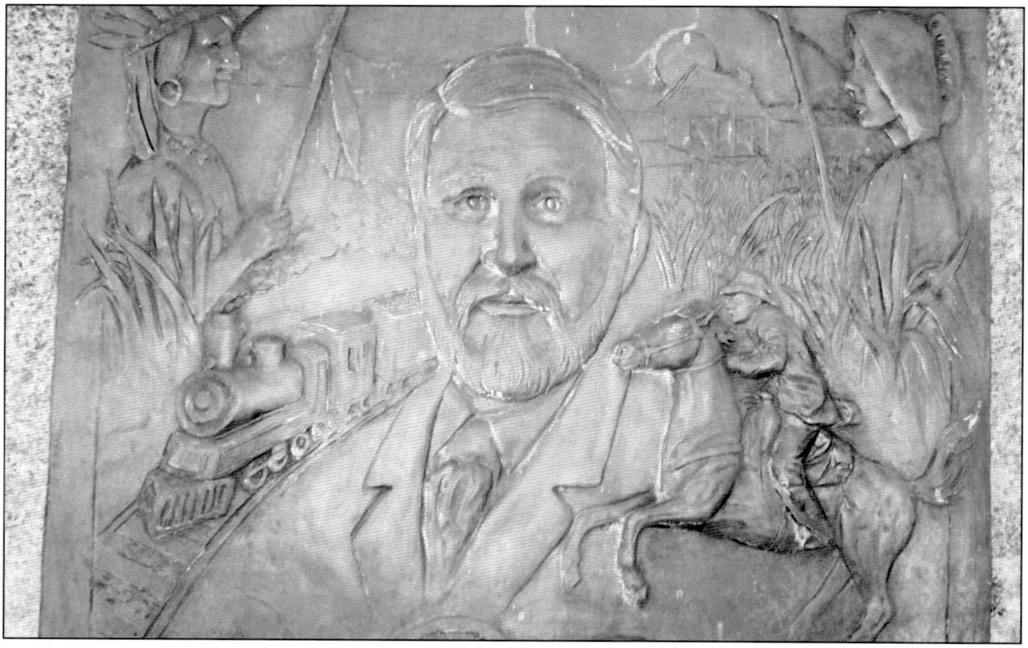

With help from local historians, Lafayette artist Patrick Soper and sculptor Celia Soper re-created a likeness for the Joseph "Beausoleil" Broussard monument erected on the grounds of Broussard Town Hall. The bronze bas-relief honors the memory of the guerrilla leader who fought the British and helped resettle the Acadians in Broussard. Beausoleil Broussard and his brother Alexandre Broussard died of yellow fever three months after settling into the Côte Gelée area. Valsin Broussard, their descendant, encouraged town growth by donating eight arpents of land, on which Sacred Heart Church and its cemetery are located. (Author's collection.)

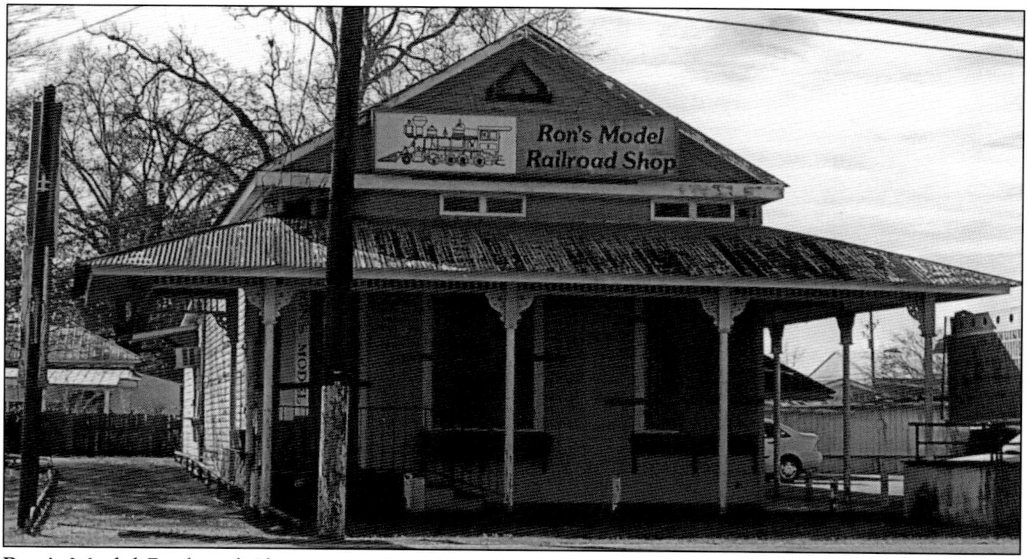

Ron's Model Railroad Shop, owned by Ron Brown Jr., is located at 106 East Main Street, in Broussard's historic district. Starting in 1980, this shop operated in a 100-year-old building for over a quarter of a century, bringing the joy of owning miniature trains to young and old alike. Ron's showroom was a place of wonder, set up to scale with village shops and trains that made the room come alive with the sound of bells, whistles, and clacking wheels. (Author's collection.)

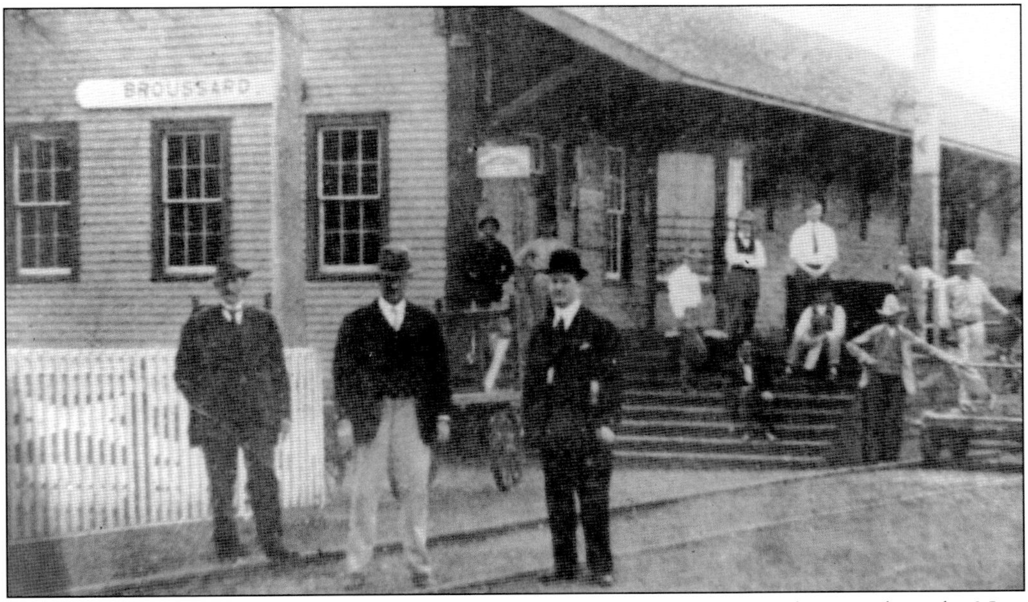

New prosperity was brought to the Broussard community before the Civil War, when the New Orleans, Opelousas, and Great Western Railroad Company was opened up to Lafayette in 1878. Work began on the western section in 1873 and was completed in 1881, thus opening a line from New Orleans though Broussard. This brought a financial boon to the Broussard area by facilitating transportation of agricultural produce. A group of nattily attired gentlemen is pictured here waiting for the train to come in. (City of Broussard archives.)

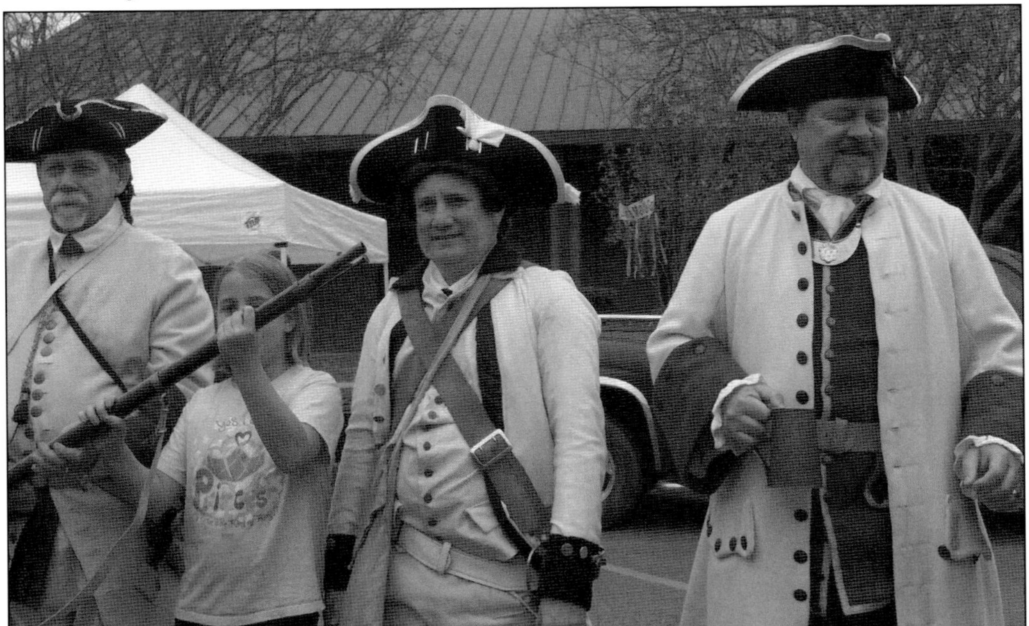
Several groups participate yearly in the reenactment of the Acadians arriving in Louisiana, which is held in St. Martinville. These men are dressed in typical 1760s militia uniforms: black, wide-brimmed hats with gold braid, white outer coats with huge black cuffs trimmed with gold braiding, and black pants and knee-high boots. (Author's collection.)

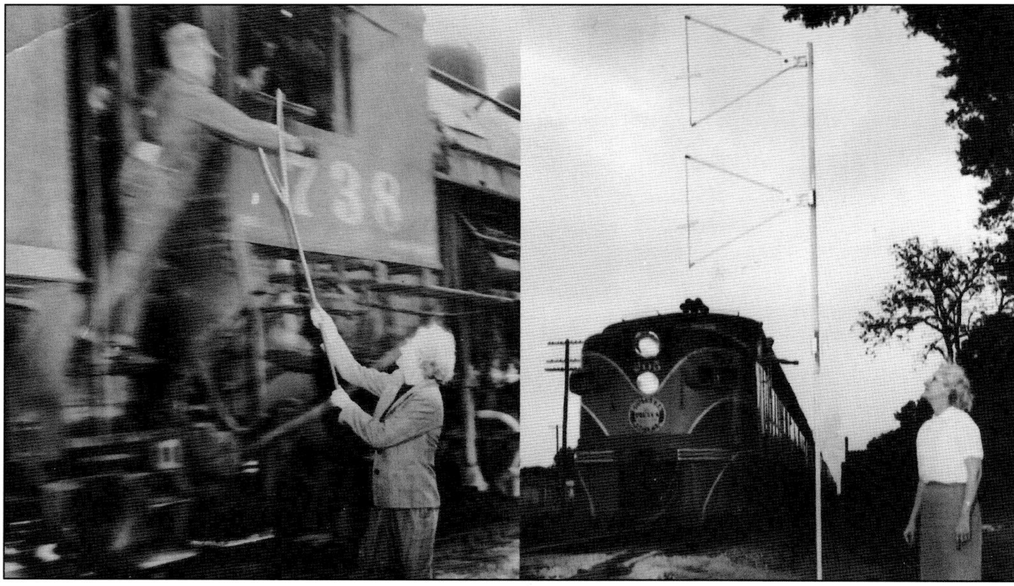

The Southern Pacific Railroad train with engineer C.C. Aultman, aboard No. 738, ran regularly through the town of Broussard. Thelma Toce (right), Broussard stationmaster, hands up order form 19 (a safety form) to the engineer. Engineers and conductors were required to sign order No. 31, including the agent's copy, in the depot office before the train could be cut loose. Thelma Toce is also pictured here waiting for engineer Aultman to pick up his message packages. Like many Southern Pacific people, Toce devoted a major portion of her spare time to community service. Southern Pacific selected Toce over women employees in five divisions from Texas and Louisiana and officially bestowed upon her the title of Mrs. Southern Pacific. (Jeri Toce Dupuis.)

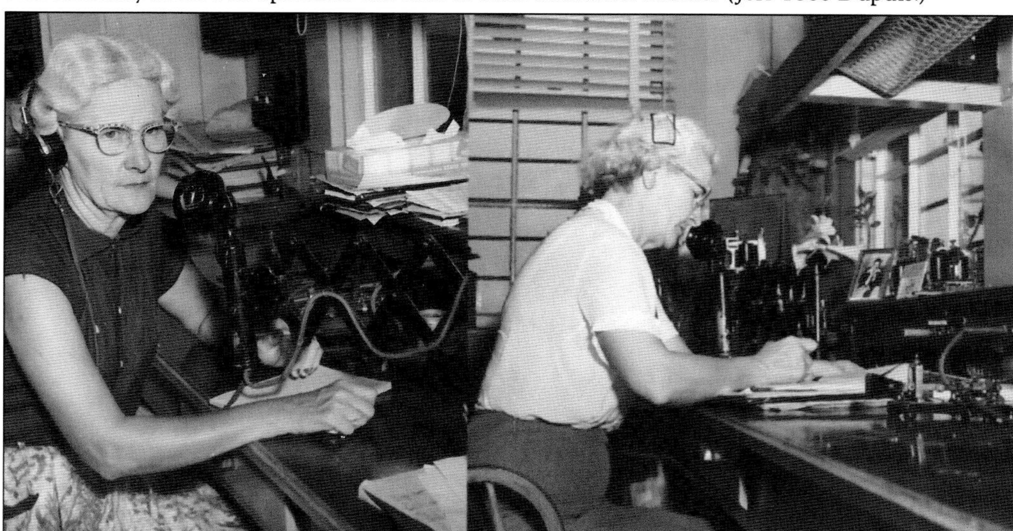

Thelma Toce, born in 1901 to Swedish parents, got her start as a telegrapher with Western Union in Houston, Texas, during World War I. After her training, Toce was assigned to Donna, Texas, for her first job. Shortly afterward, she was transferred to New Orleans and became the first and only wire chief for Western Union in the United States. In 1948, she regarded her biggest work opportunity as being appointed a full-time agent after working as a relief agent for the train office in Broussard, Louisiana. (Jeri Toce Dupuis.)

Two

Community Leaders in the Early 1800s

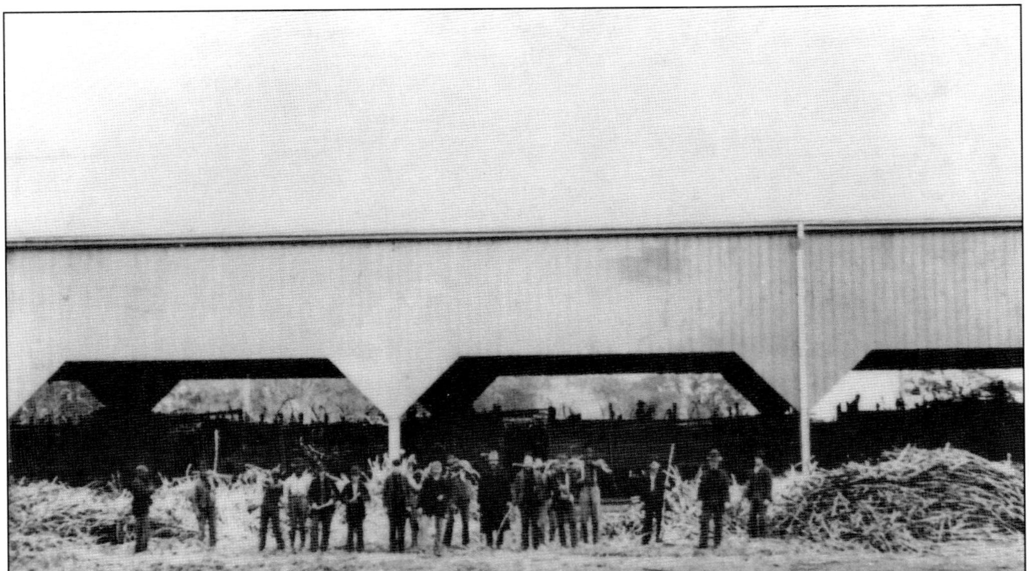

In 1889, Martial Billeaud, a prominent local sugarcane planter, converted his horse-powered syrup mill into a steam-powered sugar factory. Following World War II, the sugar industry experienced extremely difficult times. By 1943, the ownership of the Billeaud interests were restructured as stockholders contributed their agricultural lands to form a new corporation—Billeaud Planters, Inc., the parent company to the Billeaud Sugar Factory. (City of Broussard archives.)

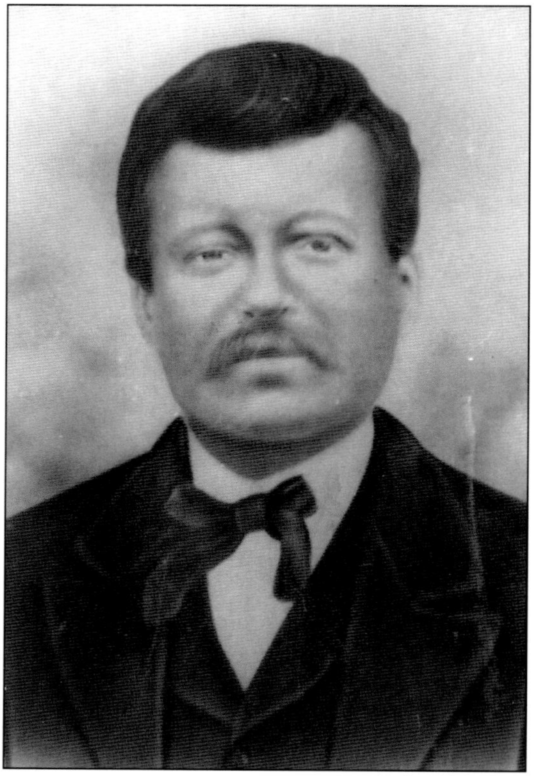

Pierre Jean Leon Billeaud, the progenitor of most of the Billaud, or Billeaud, families in Southwest Louisiana, was born in 1831 in Bourgneuf, France. He and his family arrived in Vermilionville in the 1840s. Billeaud became a prominent businessperson along with his brother Martial Billeaud Sr., owner of the Billeaud Sugar Factory. (Lafayette Parish Clerk of Court Louis J. Perret.)

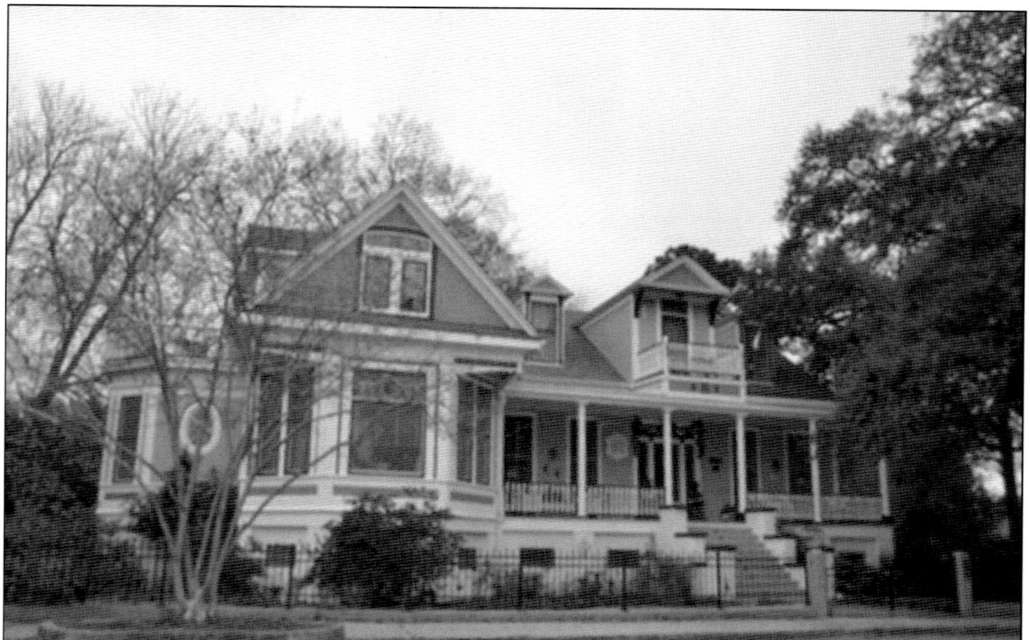

Martial Billeaud Jr. built this home in 1893 on Morgan Street. It was, however, either renovated or rebuilt according to an inscription on one of the front posts that indicates it was erected by Perrodin Brothers of Rayne, Louisiana, and with the date June 13, 1917. Martial Jr. was a son of the founder of the Billeaud Sugar Factory, Inc. (City of Broussard archives.)

Andre Billeaud was the son of Alexandre Billeaud, one of three remaining siblings from the 12 children of Jean Billeaud that lived to carry on the Billeaud name. Andre wed Marie Amelie Comeaux, the daughter of prominent businessman Alphonse Comeaux and Eulalie Billeaud Comeaux. Andre and Marie had one son, Lionel Billeaud, born in October 1900. (City of Broussard archives.)

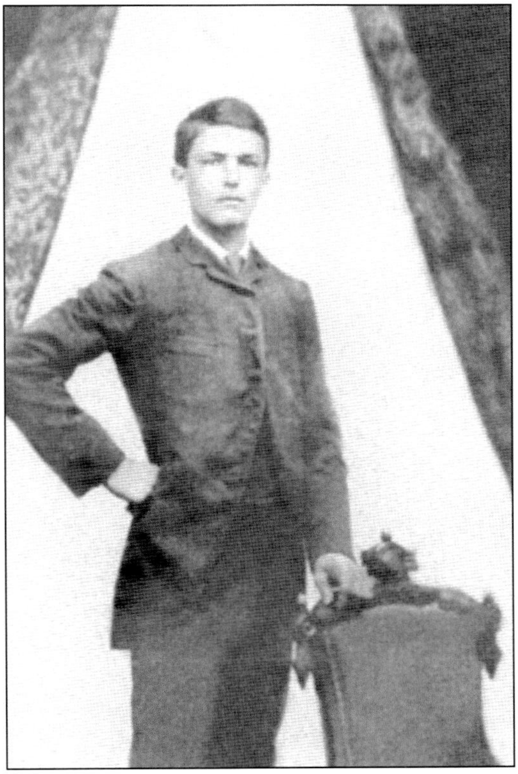

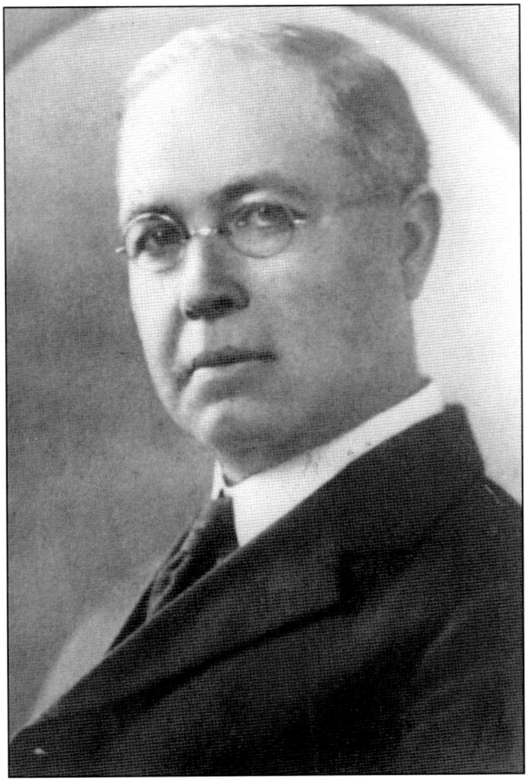

Broussard dates back to the 1870s, with its most conspicuous development taking place between approximately 1890 and 1910. Martial François Billeaud Jr., a well-respected landowner, born August 25, 1834, in Bourgneuf, France, arrived in the Unites States at the age of two. By age 16, he owned 1,300 acres of land and a large sugar mill. (City of Broussard archives.)

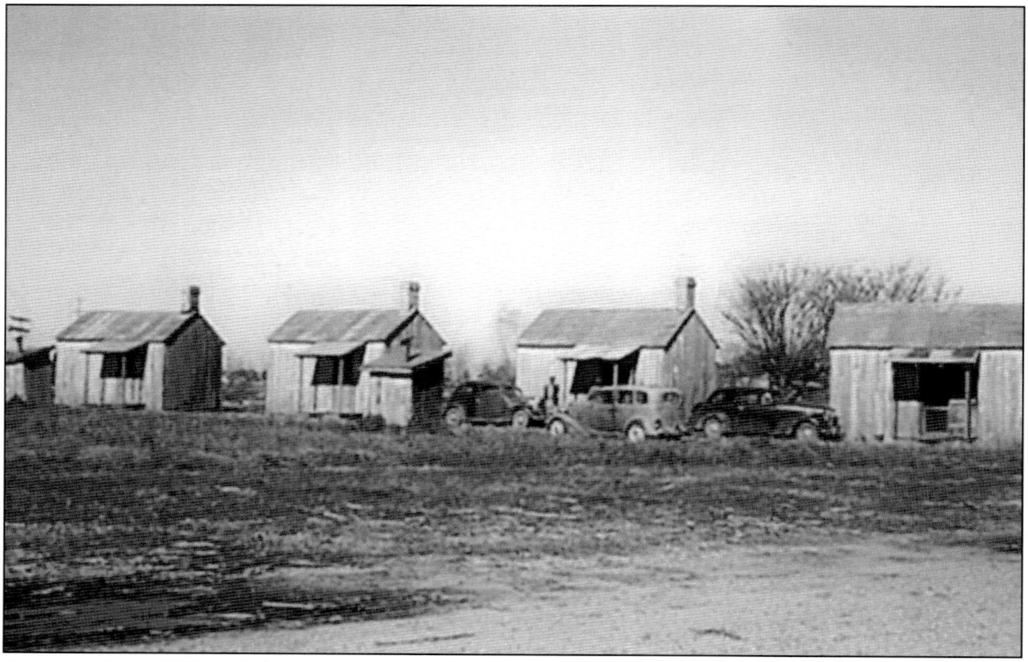

Several of the Billeaud Sugar Factory workers lived in small cabins. During the years following the Great Depression, sugarcane was rapidly gaining popularity over cotton, the main crop at that time, and many workers were needed for harvesting. (Author's collection.)

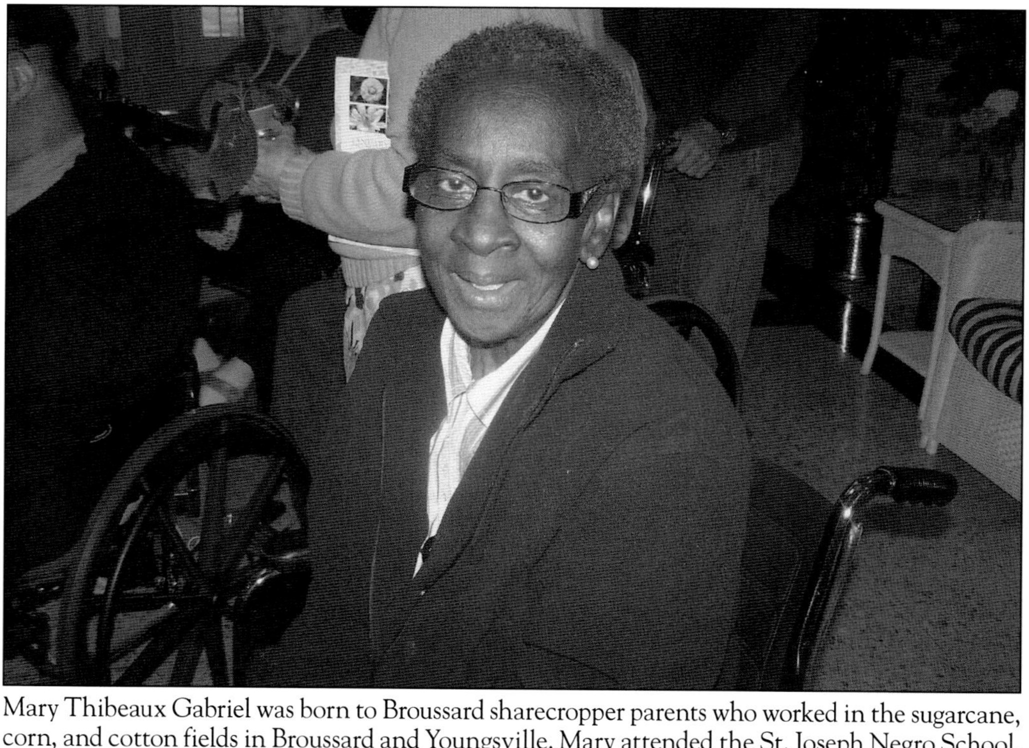

Mary Thibeaux Gabriel was born to Broussard sharecropper parents who worked in the sugarcane, corn, and cotton fields in Broussard and Youngsville. Mary attended the St. Joseph Negro School, which was built on the grounds of Sacred Heart parish. The school stood there until 1953, when it moved to donated property in St. Joseph parish. (Author's collection.)

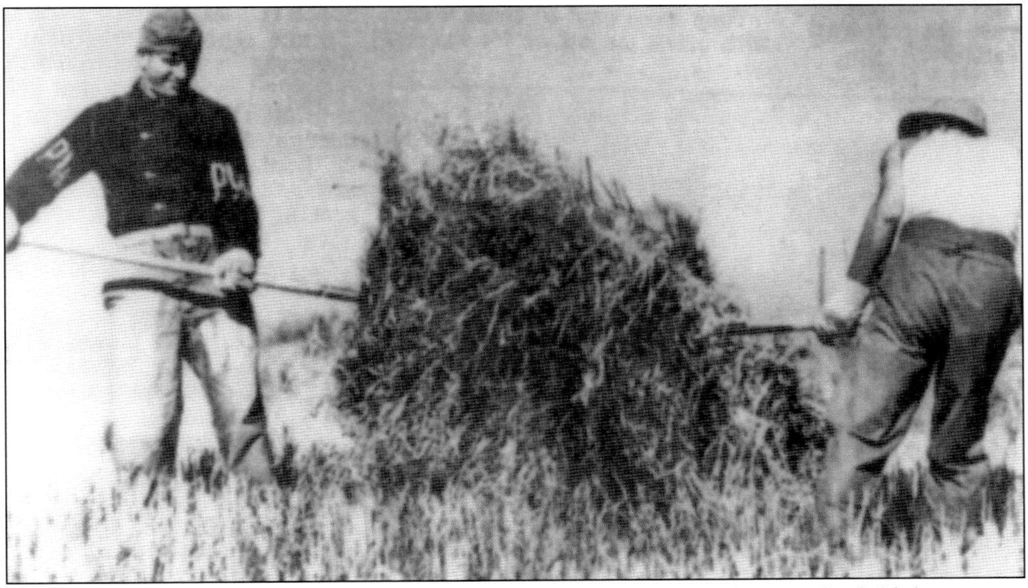

The Broussard and Youngsville area had German prisoners of war working in the fields harvesting cane and cotton and pitching hay, as evidenced by the man on the left with P-111 marking his status. (Lafayette Parish Clerk of Court Louis J. Perret.)

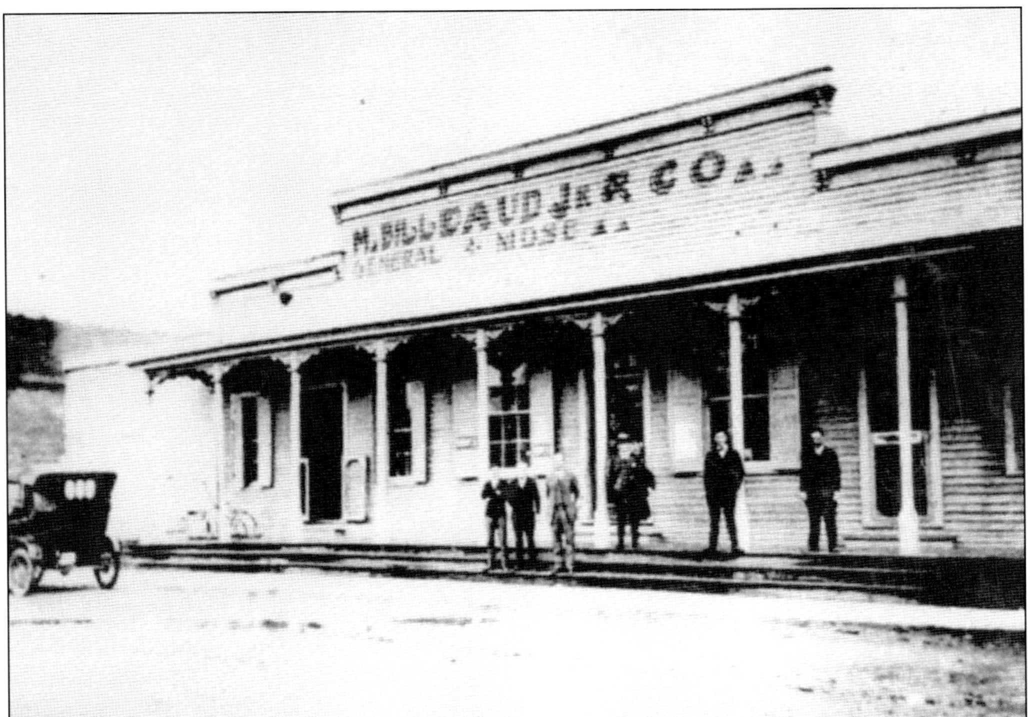

Martial Billeaud Jr. was the owner of Martial Billeaud Mercantile Store, one of five general stores supplying dry goods in the town square of Broussard during the late 1800s. It was a common sight to see townsfolk gathering to rehash politics of the day. (Billeaud Companies.)

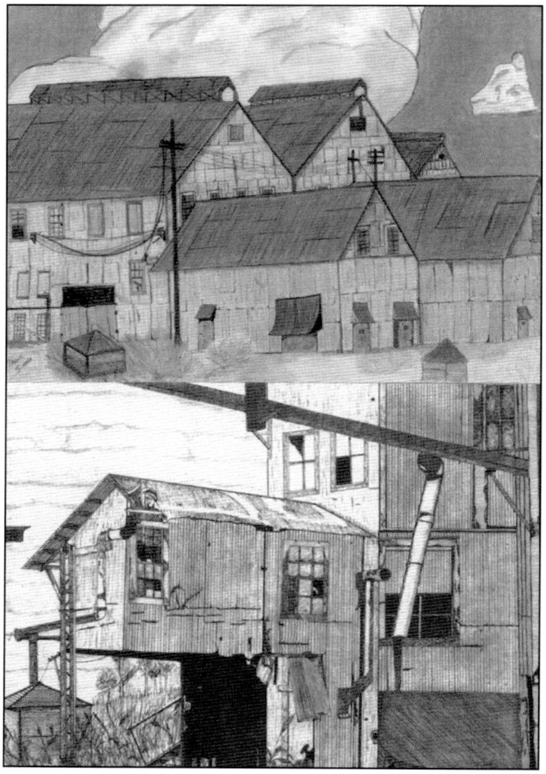

In the 1800s, a cotton-oil manufactory, a small sugar mill, and several syrup mills flourished in the Côte Gelée area along with five general merchandising stores, a bank, and two hotels. The Billeaud Sugar Mill operated from 1893 to 1903 and served as inspiration for many artists' works. Renowned pen-and-ink artist Frank T. Sierra, an adopted native of Southwest Louisiana, received numerous awards. Gov. David Treen recognized Sierra for his work on the Christopher Columbus quincentennial mural in St. Martinville in 1992. (Frank Sierra.)

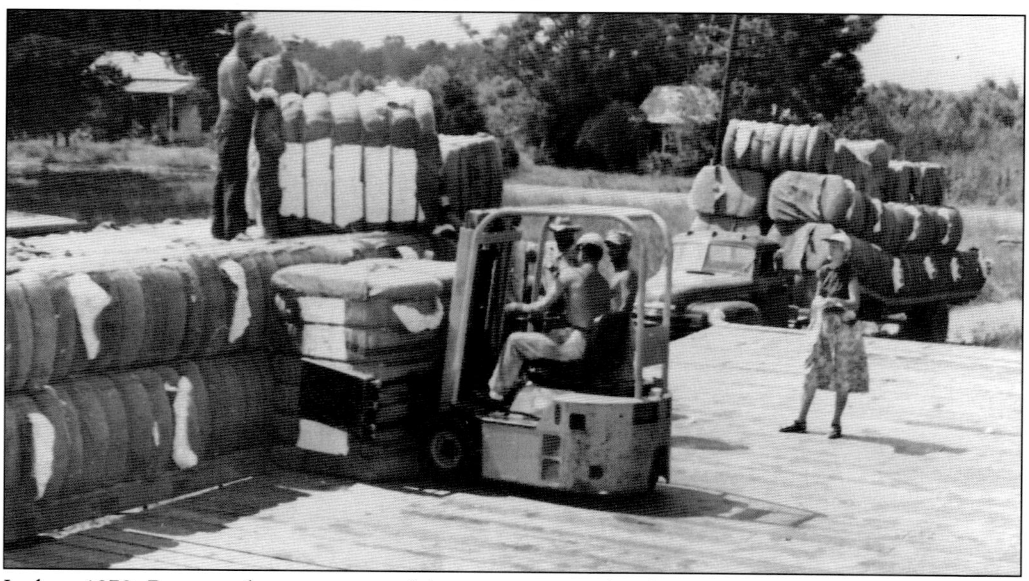

In late 1878, Broussard was a successful service center for the agricultural community, which had long depended on the cotton industry. Suddenly, the boll weevil brought great losses to the cotton crops, and the cotton-oil mill burned down, cotton gins were abandoned, and the people immediately turned to the sugarcane industry. The workers pictured here in the early 1960s are picking cotton by hand, but larger farms used machinery. Cottonseed was pressed for oil in use as salad oils, mixed with beef fat for cooking products such as lard, and also combined with alkalis in making laundry soap. (Liz Girard.)

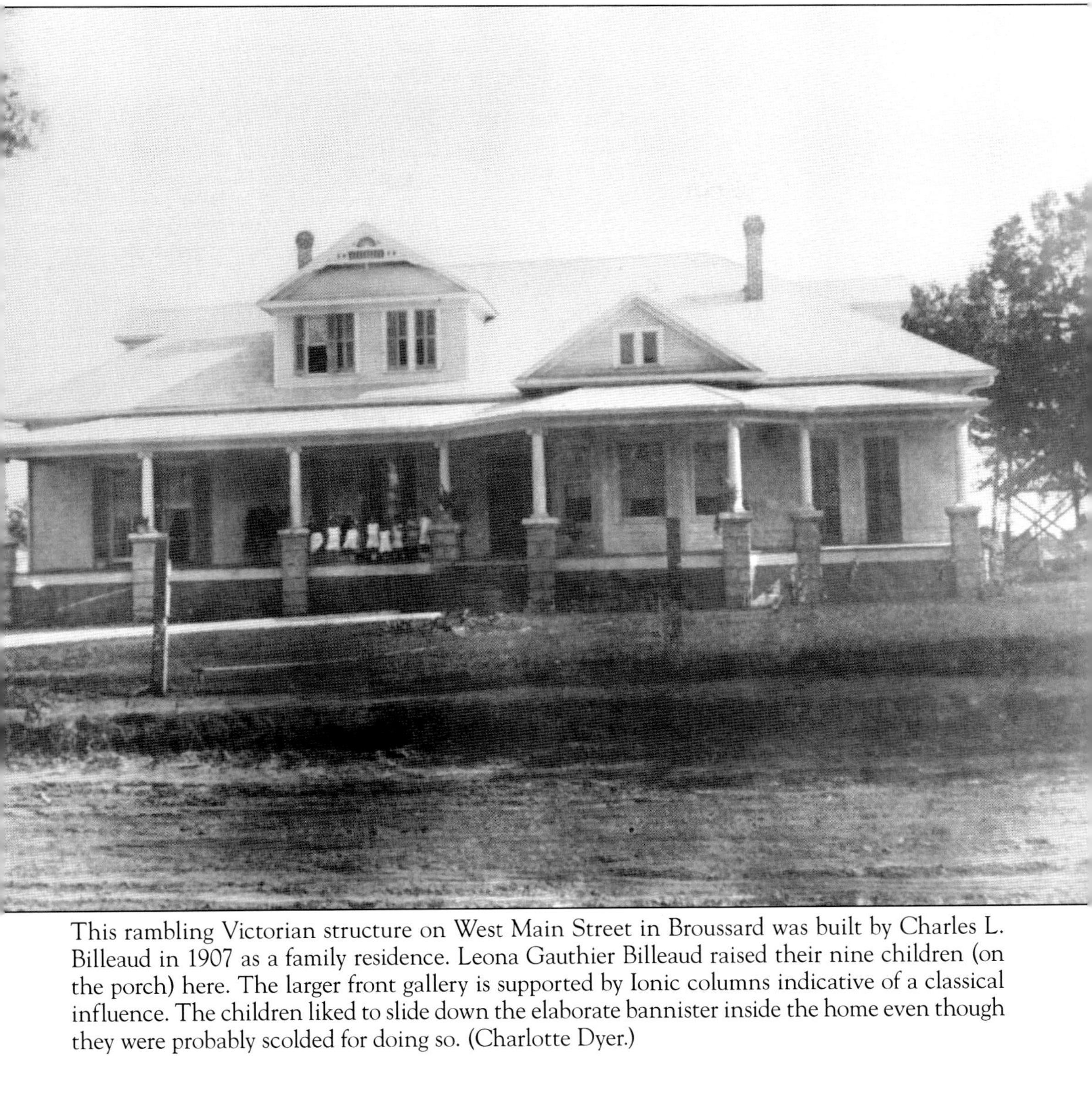

This rambling Victorian structure on West Main Street in Broussard was built by Charles L. Billeaud in 1907 as a family residence. Leona Gauthier Billeaud raised their nine children (on the porch) here. The larger front gallery is supported by Ionic columns indicative of a classical influence. The children liked to slide down the elaborate bannister inside the home even though they were probably scolded for doing so. (Charlotte Dyer.)

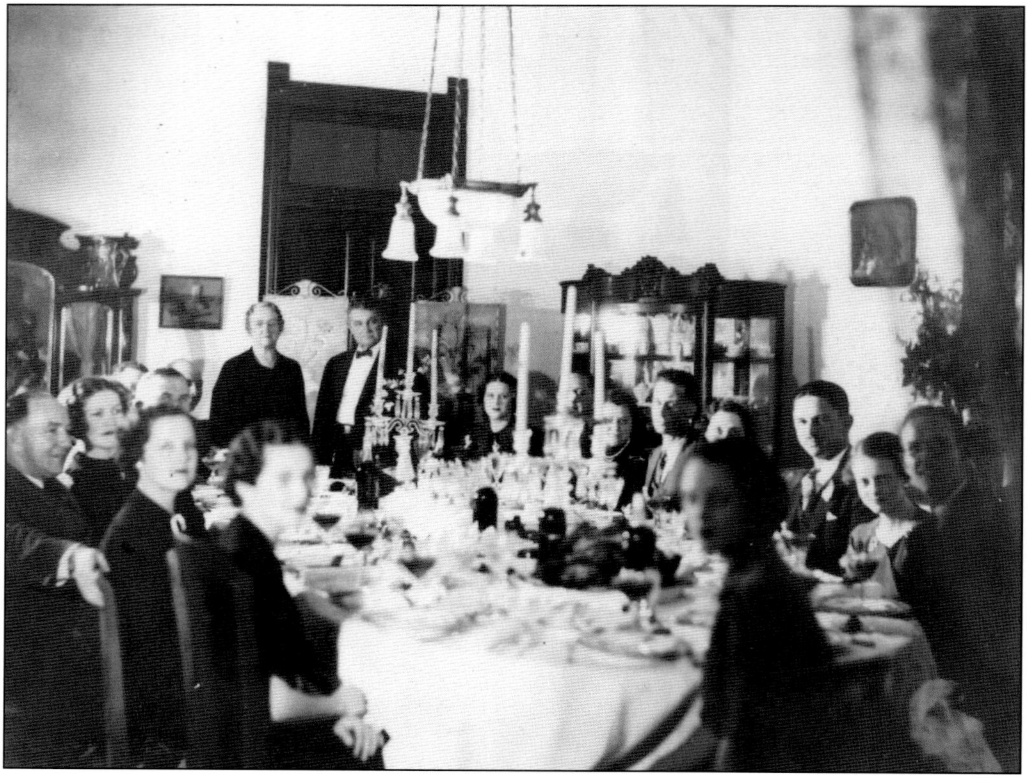

Pictured here is the Charles and Leona Gauthier Billeaud family hosting a formal Christmas dinner in 1940 surrounded by family and Sacred Heart Church's parish priest Fr. P.G. John Kemps. Charles served for 47 years as the manager of Billeaud Sugar Mill. (Charlotte Dyer.)

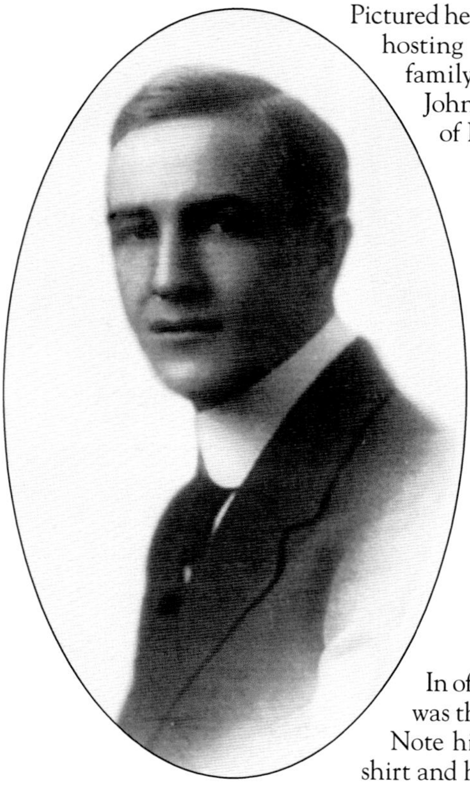

In office from 1926 to 1928, Dr. William Johnston Youngue was the fourth of 11 mayors to serve the town of Broussard. Note his classical style of dress for the period—a starched shirt and high, rounded collar. (City of Broussard archives.)

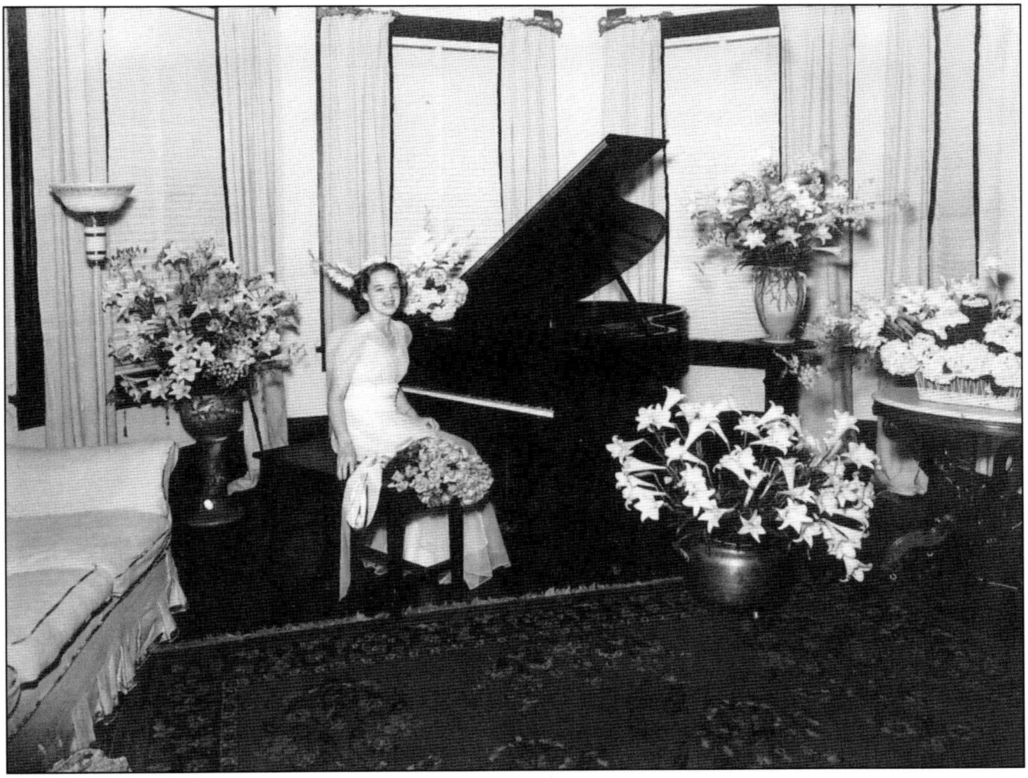

At age 16, Yvonne Youngue (1925–2010) was an accomplished pianist. She was the daughter of Dr. W.J. Youngue and Goldie Youngue. Yvonne is shown entertaining guests during a Christmas party at the family residence of Charles Billeaud. The Billeaud home was built in 1907 and once served as the convent for Sisters of Divine Providence that staffed St. Cecilia School until 1974. (Charlotte Dyer.)

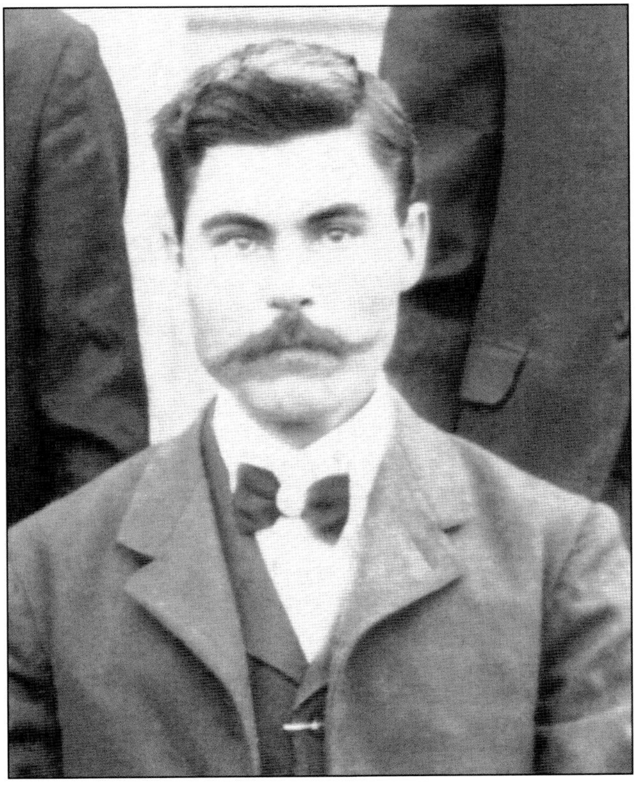

This unidentified young man is shown with a group of other elegantly dressed young professionals; a caption states he was a mayor, although nothing is known about the photograph's origin. (City of Broussard archives.)

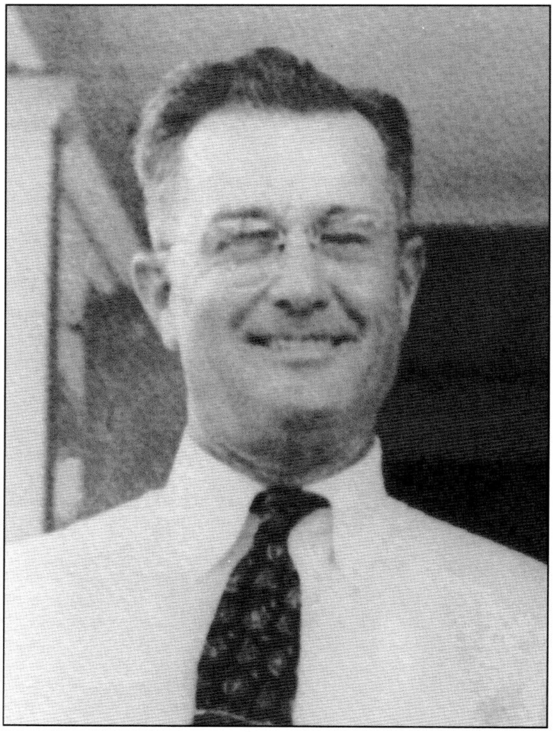

George E. Billeaud married Beatrice "Betsy" St. Julien Billeaud, one of J. Gustave St. Julien's daughters; they raised six sons and one daughter. All of their sons and one son-in-law served their country, variously during World War II, the Korean War, and peacetime. Additionally, George served as mayor of Broussard from 1939 to 1946. (City of Broussard archives.)

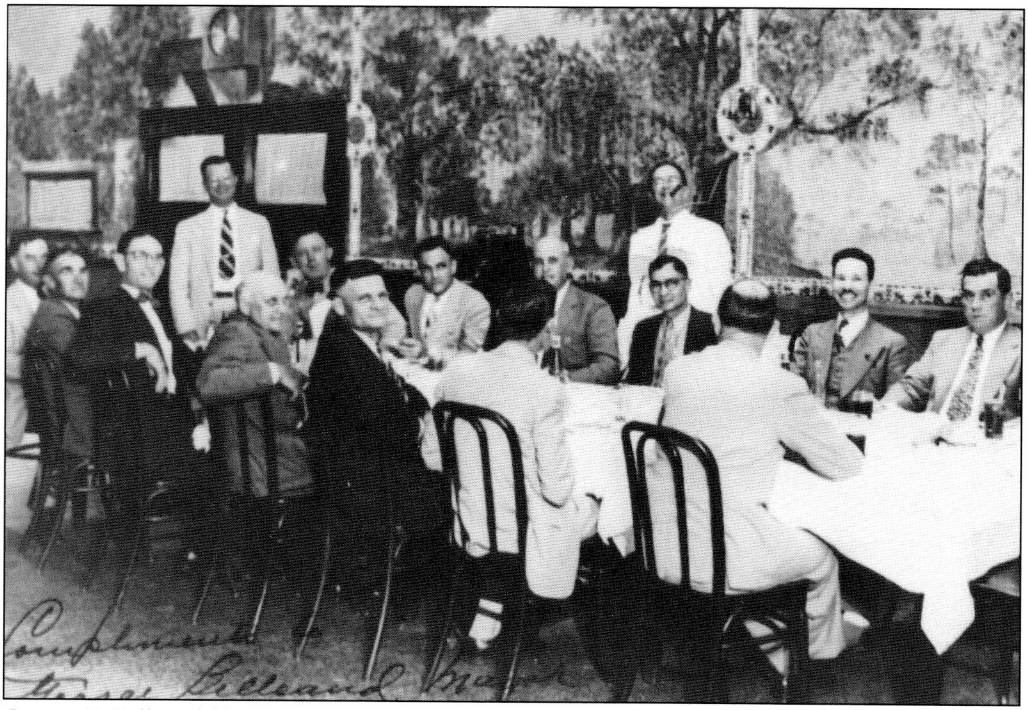

George E. Billeaud (front row, third from right) is attending a business luncheon during his later years with a group of petit jurors in Lafayette. George's grandfather Martial Billeaud owned several plantations near Broussard around the Bayou Tortue area and established the first sugar mill in 1872. (Lafayette Parish Clerk of Court Louis J. Perret.)

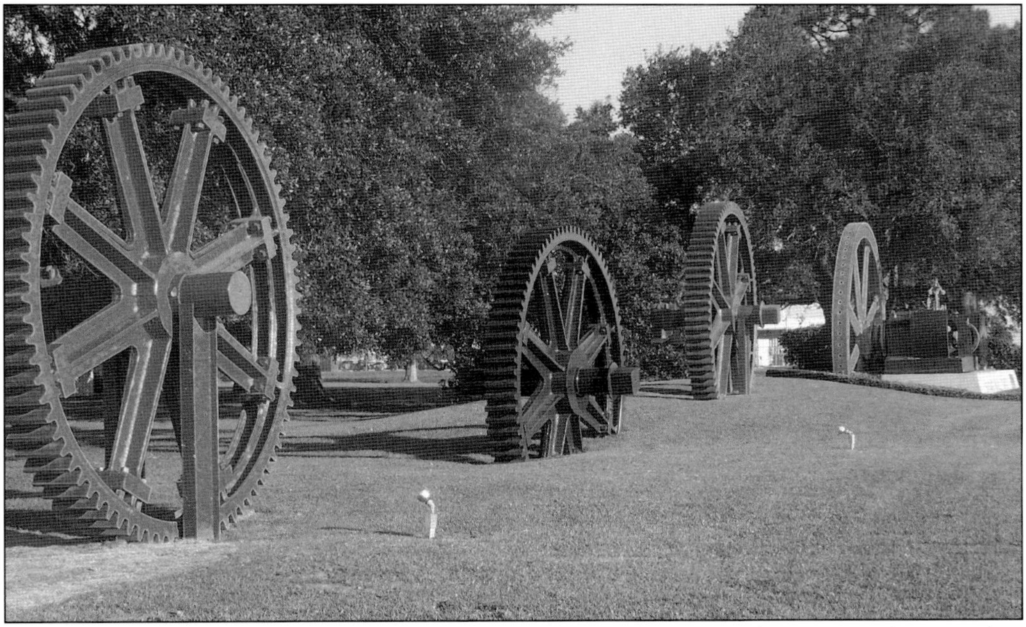

These four giant-sized gears painted red, blue, yellow, and green no longer turn but stand as testament at the corporate office, signaling to passerby on Highway 90 that it is a new day. Gone are the days of grinding cane to produce brown and white sugars and syrup. Billeaud Companies restructured following the mill closing and diversified into commercial real estate and land acquisitions. (Author's collection.)

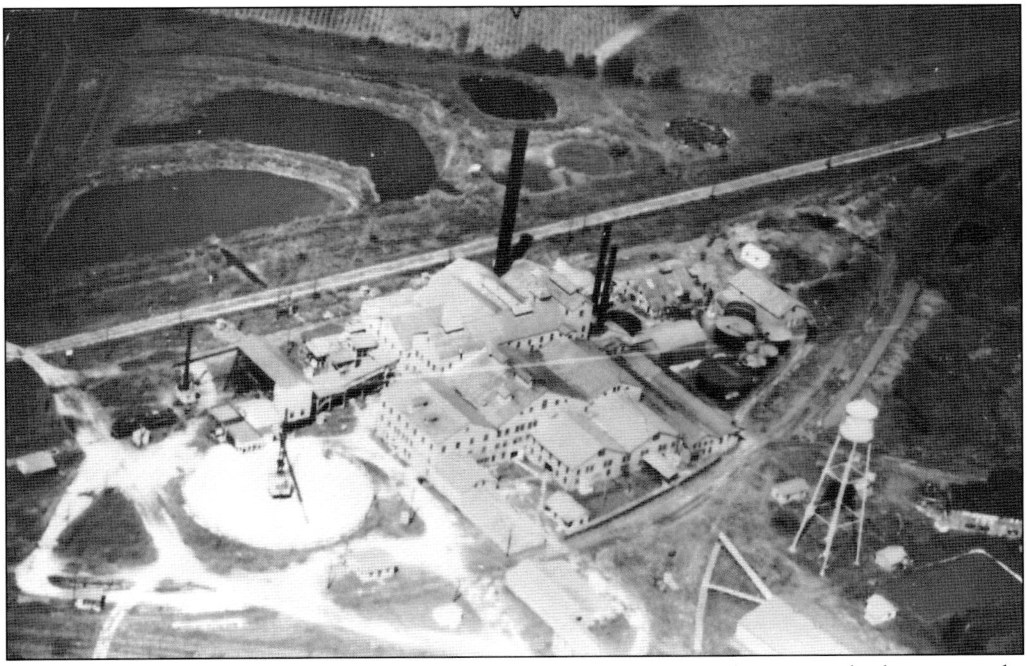

Billeaud Sugar Factory is seen in an aerial view looking down on Highway 90, which runs north-south through Broussard. The Billeauds were big contributors to the local economy, employing several hundred persons when the factory opened and affording farmers an avenue to market their crops. (Billeaud Companies.)

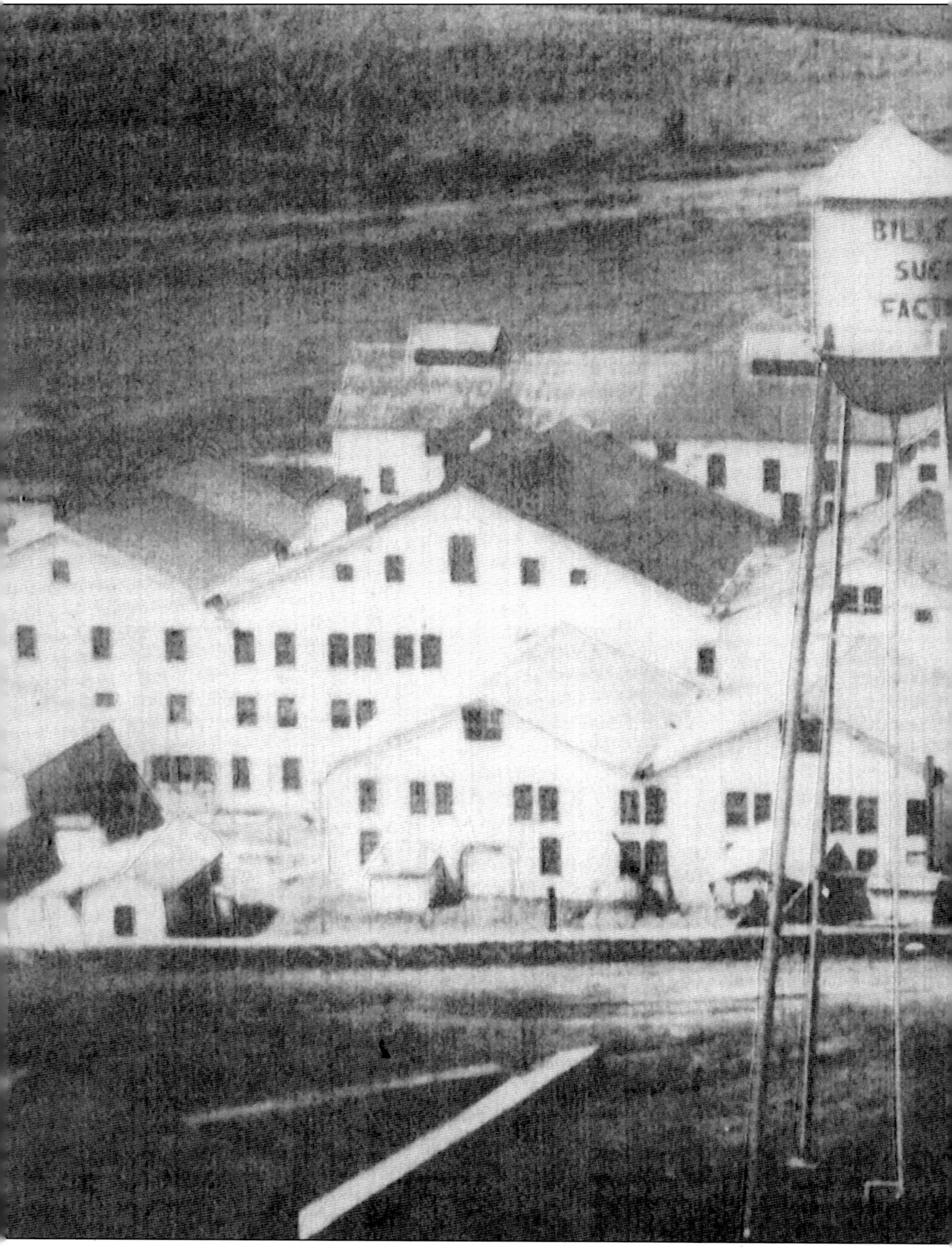

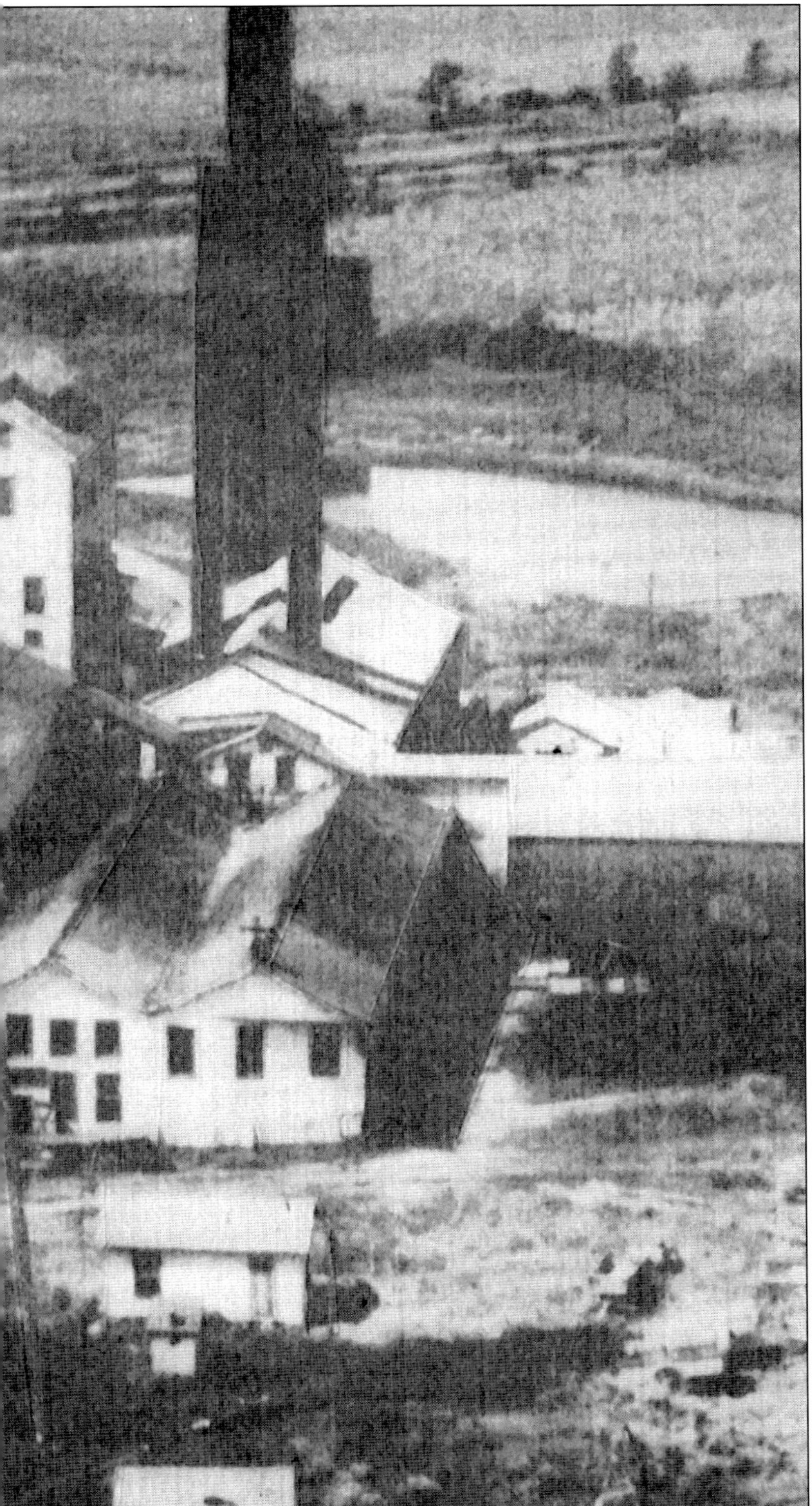

Following World War I, the sugar industry experienced difficult times. In 1943, the ownership of the Billeaud interests was again restructured as stockholders contributed their agricultural lands, forming a new corporation, Billeaud Planters, Inc., which later became the parent company of the Billeaud Sugar Factory. (City of Broussard archives.)

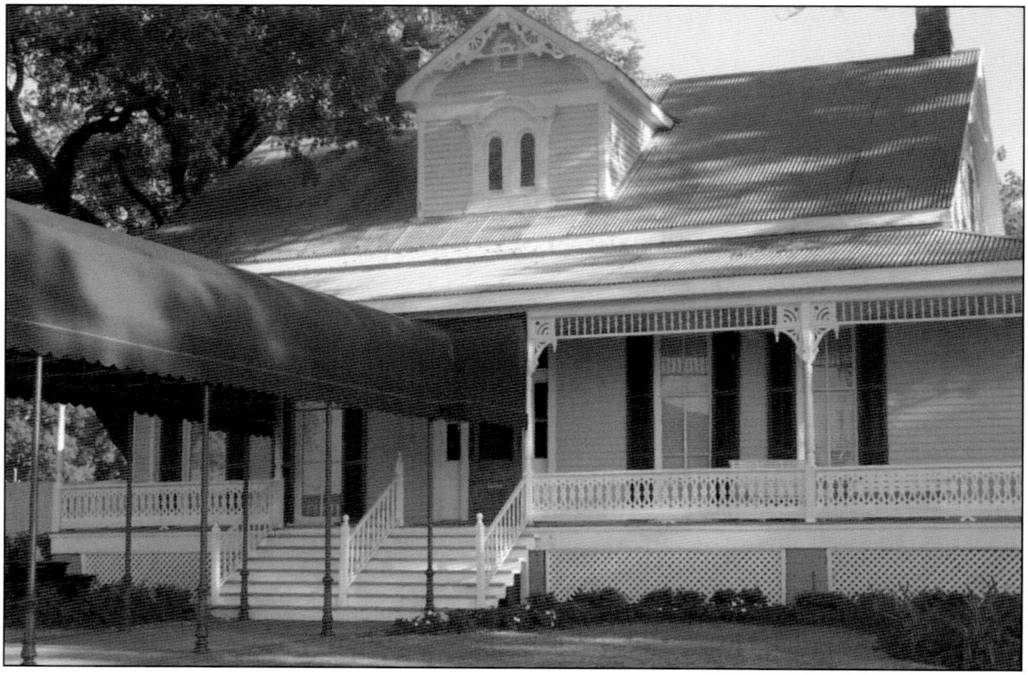

Paul Billeaud's original family residence built in 1880 on St. Nazaire Road is shaded by stately 100-year-old oak and pine trees. Since the 1970s, it has served as corporate headquarters for the Billeaud Companies real estate development and property management of one million square feet of retail and warehouse storage space in the Broussard and Lafayette markets. (Billeaud Companies archives.)

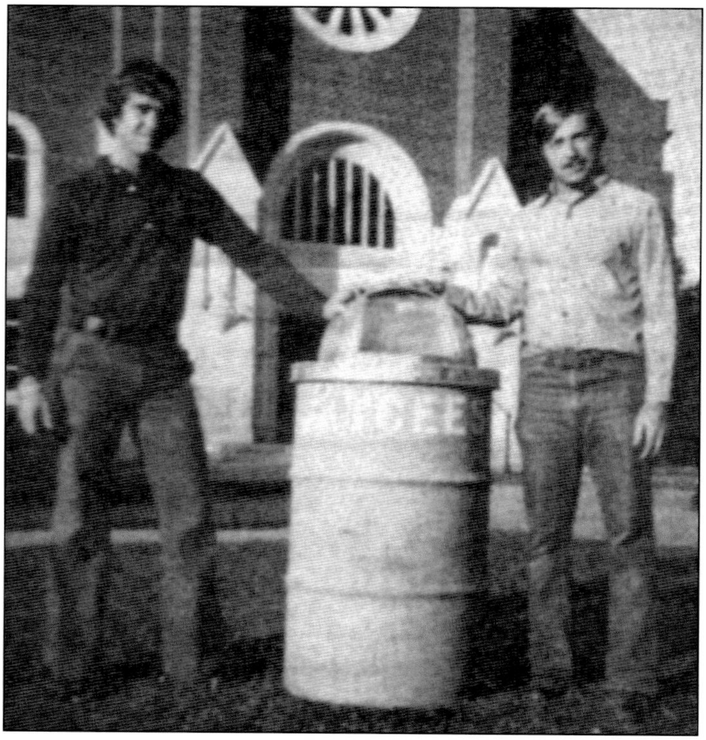

Cecil Chatman (left) and Charles "Chuck" Billeaud look at several trash cans donated to Sacred Heart Church by the Broussard Jaycees. This civic organization's goal was to help keep Broussard clean during the annual church fair that was held on the grounds of St. Cecilia School. A kick-off Poo-Yie party, school pageant, food, music, games, crafts, and raffles rounded out the typical Cajun good times. (Eula Bodin.)

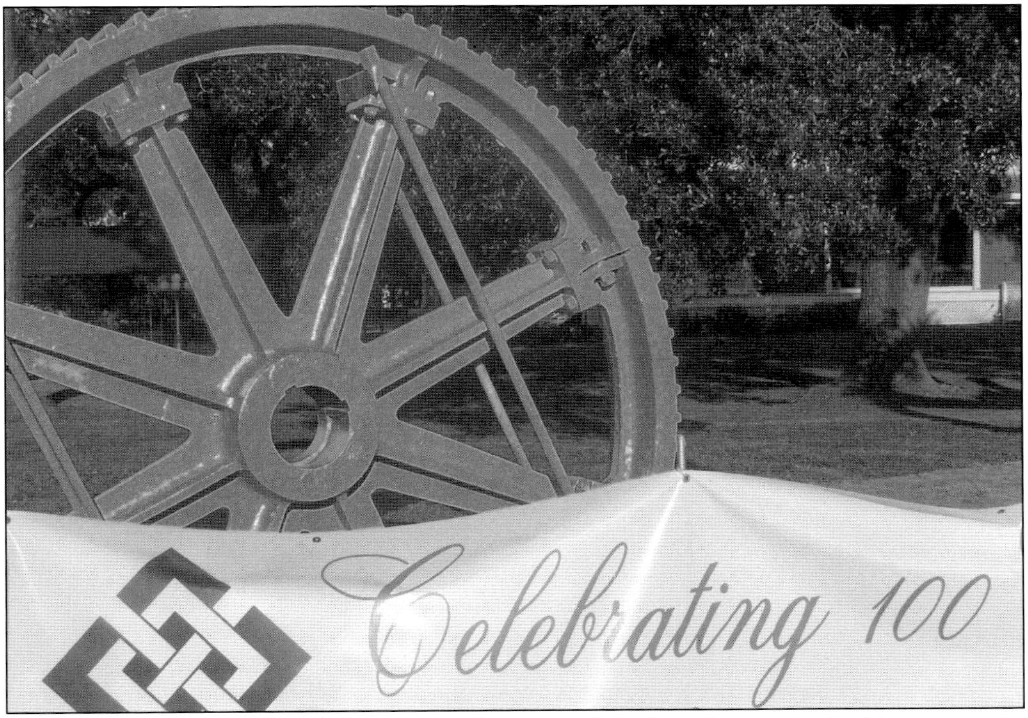

Chuck Billeaud, the Billeaud Company's chairman of the board, organized a big party at its corporate headquarters to celebrate the company's 100th anniversary on May 10, 2014. The banner advertising the celebration could be seen by passersby on Highway 90 tethered to a large yellow gear, a remnant from the old mill. (Author's collection.)

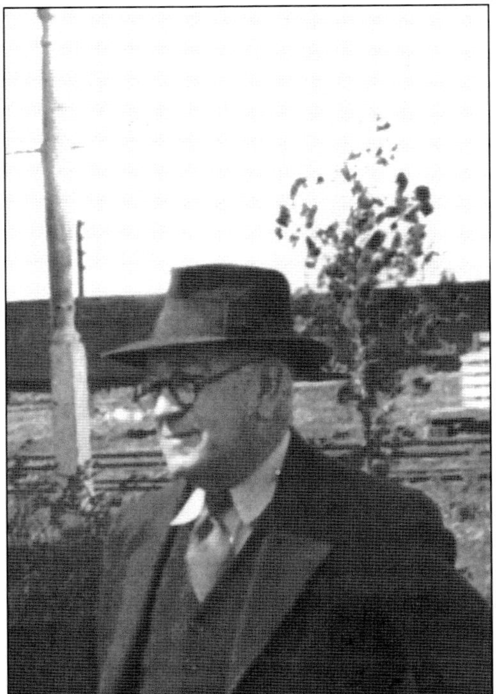

Herbert Billeaud served in the US Navy. He was noted for building the Alesia House in 1910 on North Morgan Avenue for his wife, Alice. The construction took five years to complete, as the cypress had to be cured in place while the home was being built. (City of Broussard archives.)

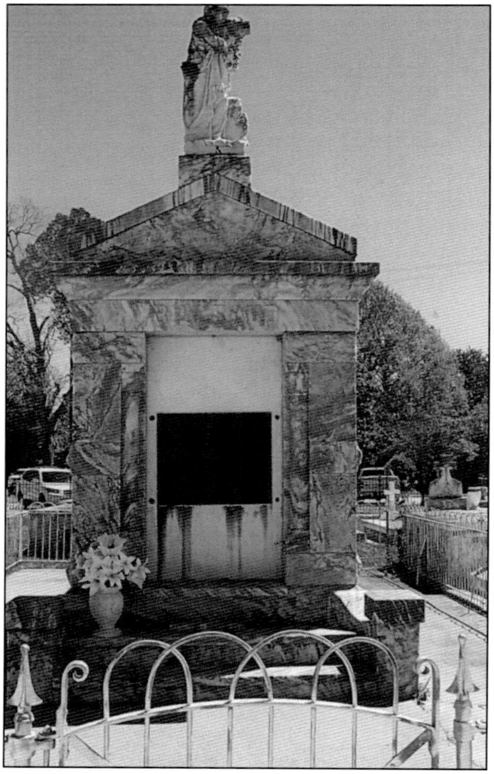

Generations of Billeaud/Billaud family members, who originated from Bourgneuf, France, are buried in this ornate tomb in the center of the Sacred Heart Church cemetery. A lovely angel stands atop the tomb, with its facade of multihued marble, surrounded by an iron fence painted silver. (Author's collection.)

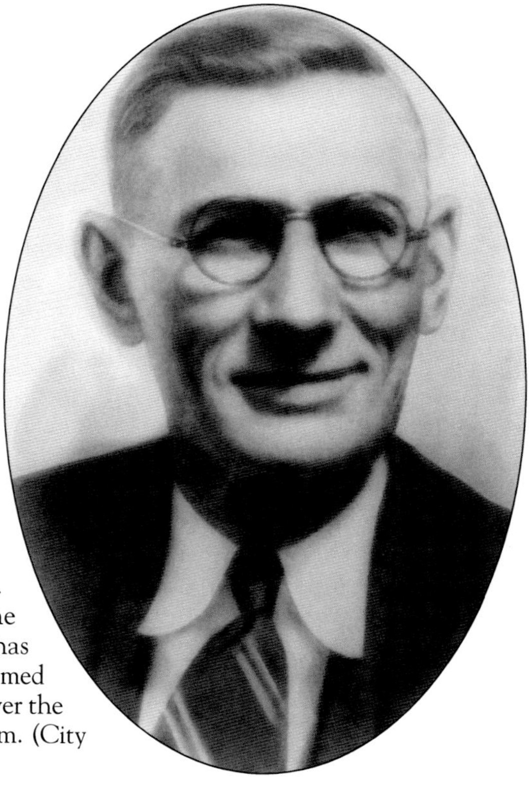

Eugene Soulier purchased the Alesia House, located at 110 North Morgan Avenue, during the 1940s and lived there until 1959. The home was built by Herbert Billeaud for his wife, Alice, (for whom it was named) during the early 1900s. Attorney Walter J. Rippas's law office is the present-day occupant of the structure, which has a reputation for being haunted. A specter nicknamed "Mr. Water" has been known to splash water over the lavatory and mirror in a seldom-used bathroom. (City of Broussard archives.)

Three

Two Church Parishes for the Community

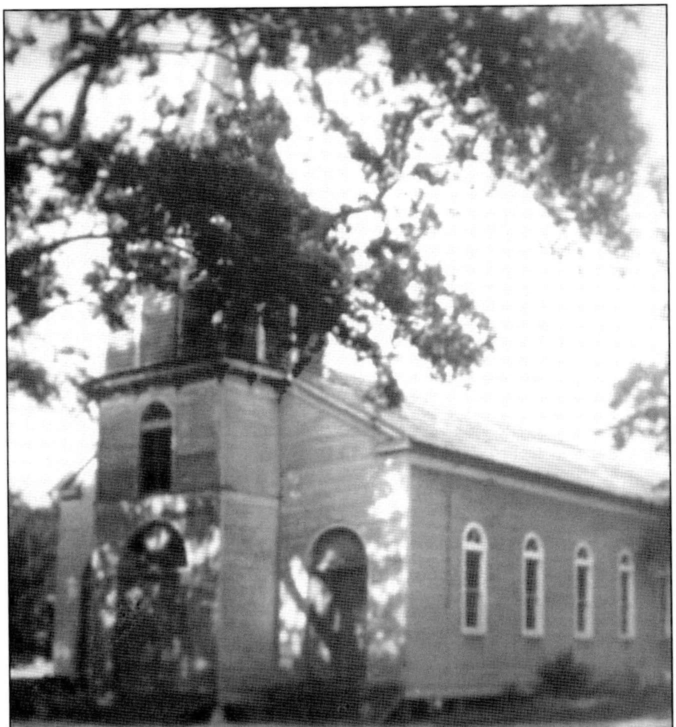

A Youngsville traveling priest celebrated Mass in Valsin Broussard's general store until the official organization of Sacred Heart parish in 1883. Broussard's original wooden Sacred Heart Church was nestled between the current Broussard Public Library and B.J.'s Sandwich Shoppe. The first church had two pews for African American parishioners, who paid 10¢ per seat and were seated separately from their white counterparts. The church and presbytery burned down on November 17, 1886, and Fr. Christopher Cuny, an unpopular priest, was escorted out of town. (Phyliss Boumans.)

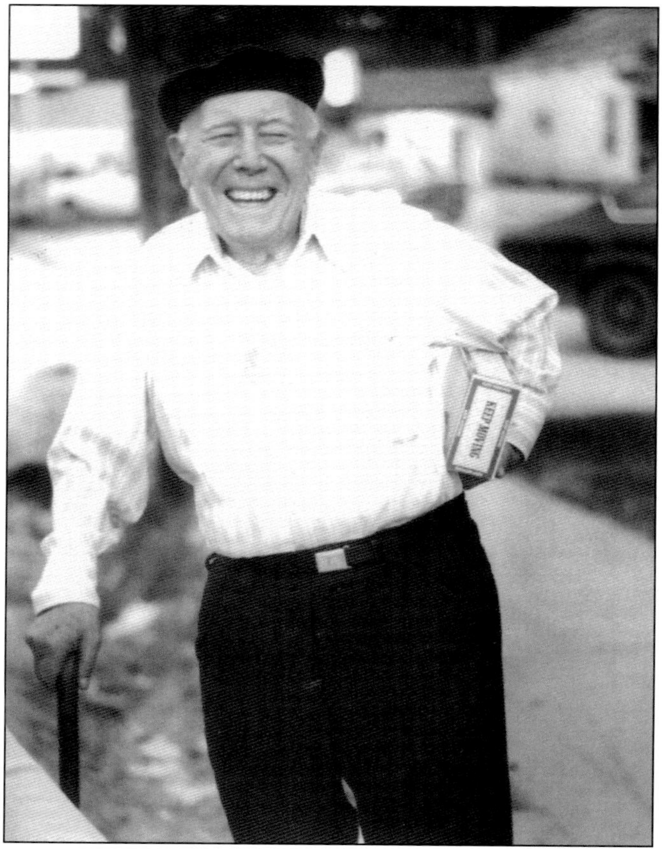

The man many consider Sacred Heart Church's most lovable priest, Fr. P.G. John Kemps, a Dutchman from Venroy, the Netherlands, served the parish for 41 years. Father Kemps received his papal honors as monsignor in July 1966 from Bishop Maurice M. Schexnayder. Broussard's older folks' childhood memories are of Father Kemps playing Halloween pranks, smoking cigars, and—best of all—reestablishing the annual community church fair in 1933. Most noteworthy is the construction of a new church building during his tenure. (Eula Bodin and Sacred Heart Church.)

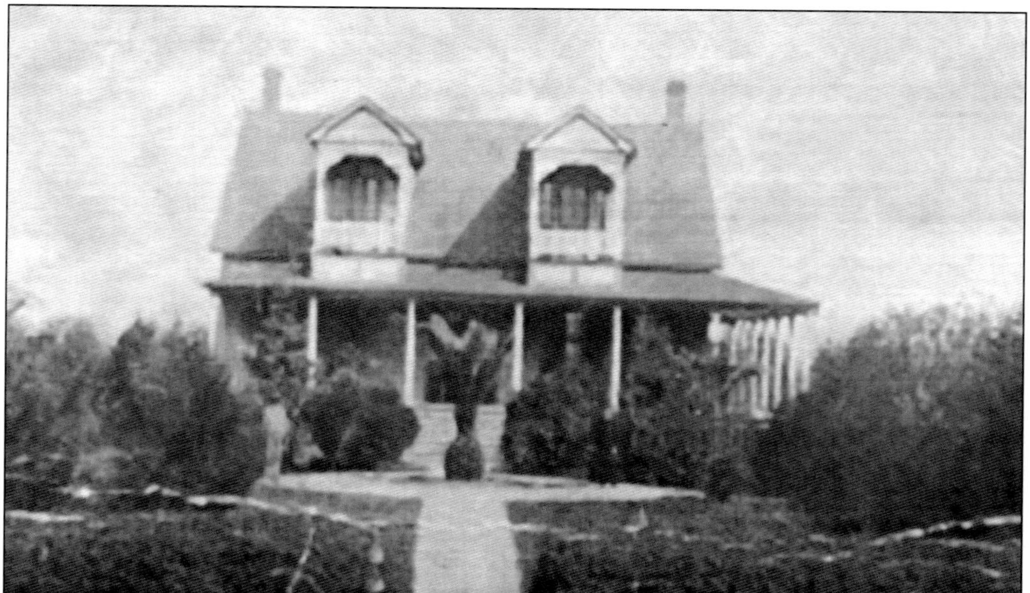

A new presbytery was built for Sacred Heart Church parish in the early part of 1960, during Fr. P.G. John Kemps's long tenure in the community—from 1933 until his retirement in 1976. (Sacred Heart Church archives.)

A new church bell donated by Della Bellard is hoisted to the tower of Sacred Heart Church by a construction crew in 1954. A second parish for black residents was realized in 1953 through an acre of land willed by Louis "Loul" Billeaud for the establishment of St. Joseph parish. (Sacred Heart Church archives.)

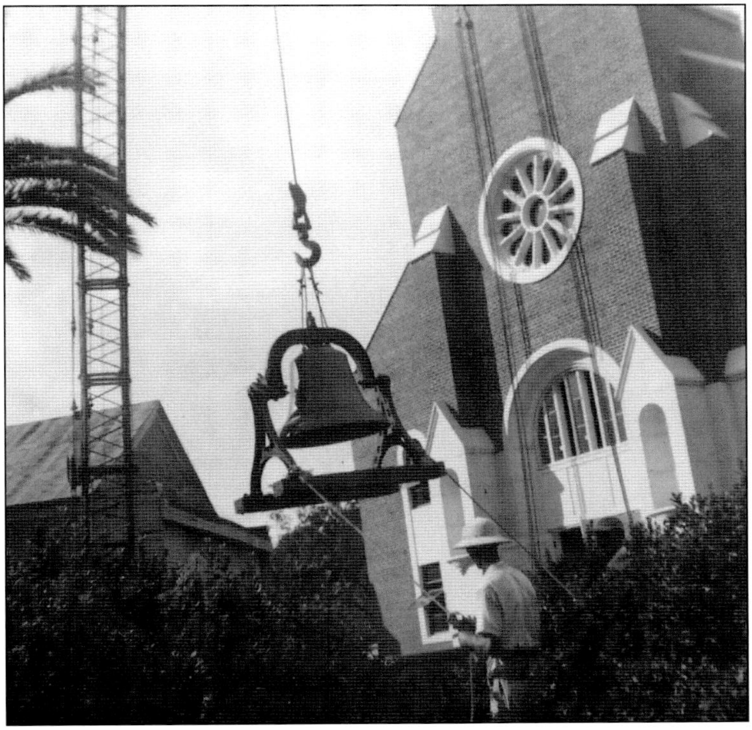

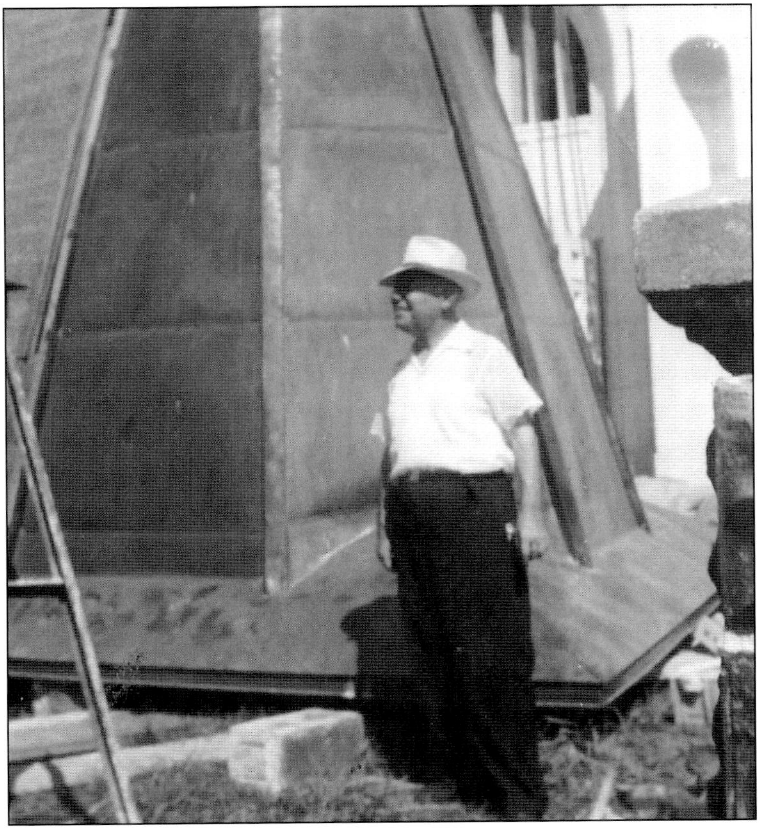

Fr. P.G. John Kemps, the lovable Dutch priest, seems a bit dwarfed by the huge steeple being erected atop the new Sacred Heart Catholic Church around 1954. The community was elated to have a new church building. (Sacred Heart Church archives.)

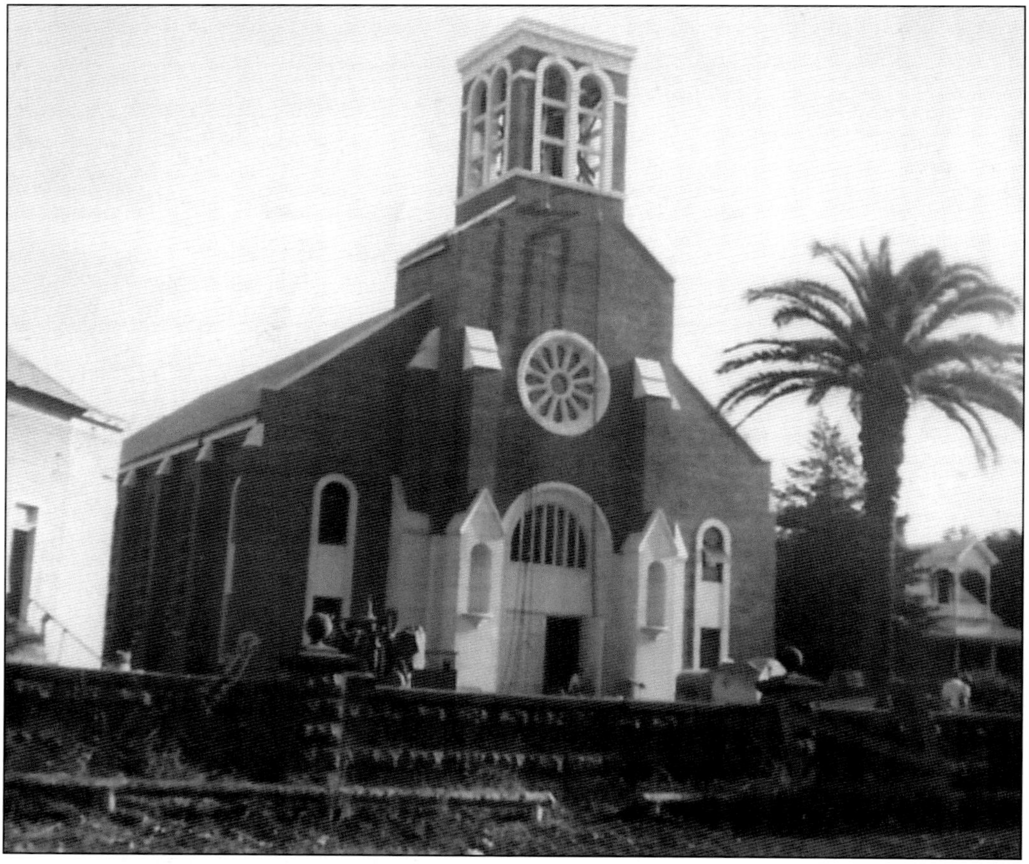

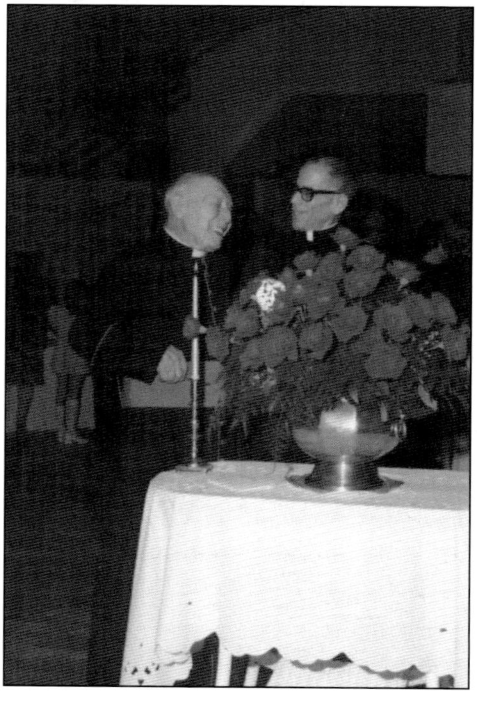

Prior to a major 2006 renovation, Sacred Heart Church and its cemetery grounds were surrounded by a short stone wall. People can be seen walking near the presbytery in the background; both structures were rebuilt after the fire of 1886, from which several legends stem about Rev. Christopher Cuny's actions. (Phyliss Boumans.)

Fr. P.G. Johns Kemps (left) is pictured here during a lighthearted moment with Fr. Daniel Bernard, a former pastor who was born in Broussard, serving at St. Theresa of the Little Flower Church in Arnaudville. Both priests seem to be enjoying the reception following the dedication of Sacred Heart Church in 1954. (Sacred Heart Church archives,)

Claire Bernard Bonin (right) and an unidentified woman, members of the Ladies Altar Society, assist Fr. P.G. John Kemps at the refreshment table during the 1954 dedication for the parish's new Sacred Heart Church. Claire Bernard Bonin's brother is Fr. Daniel Bernard. (Eula Bodin and Sacred Heart Church.)

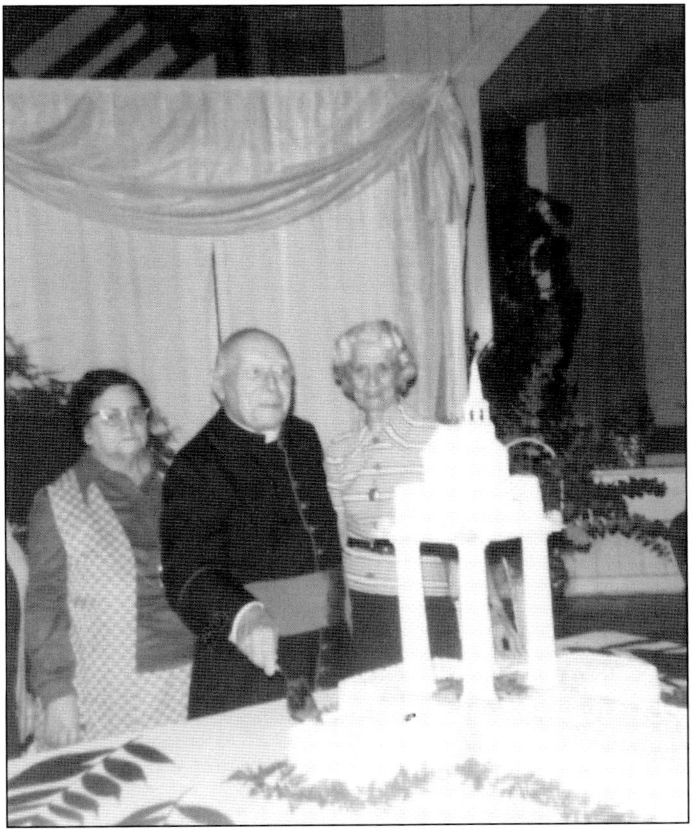

Fr. P.G. John Kemps cuts the cake during the celebration of the new Sacred Heart Church. Behind Father Kemps is a group of Ladies Altar Society workers. Claire Bernard Bonin (left) served in many roles at the church and St. Cecilia School until she was well into her 90s. (Eula Bodin and Sacred Heart Church.)

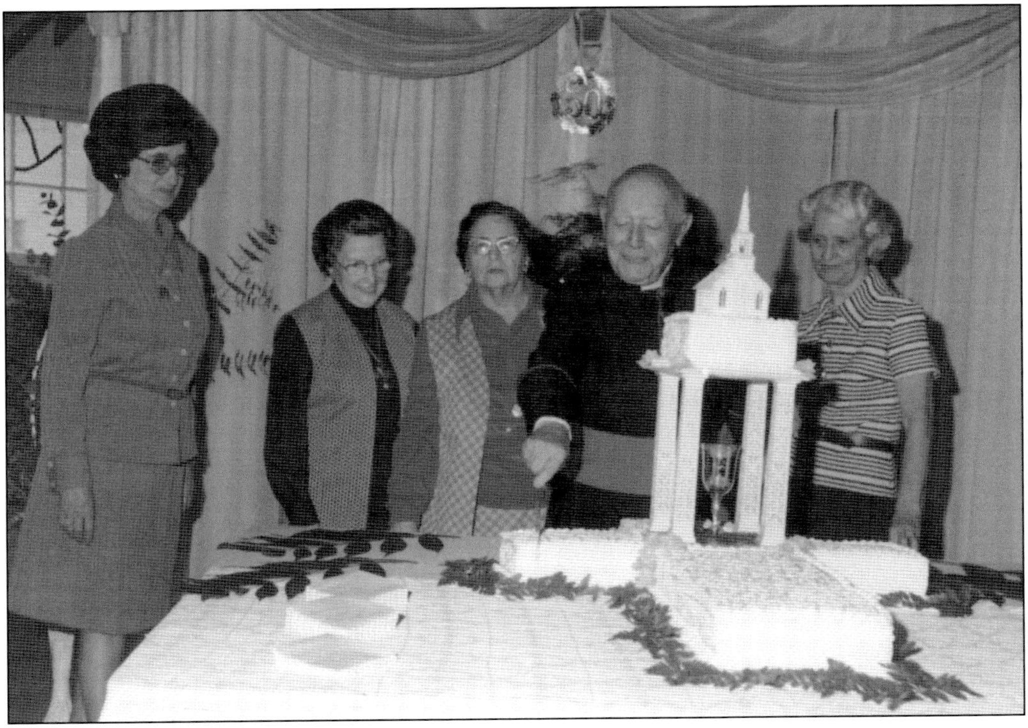

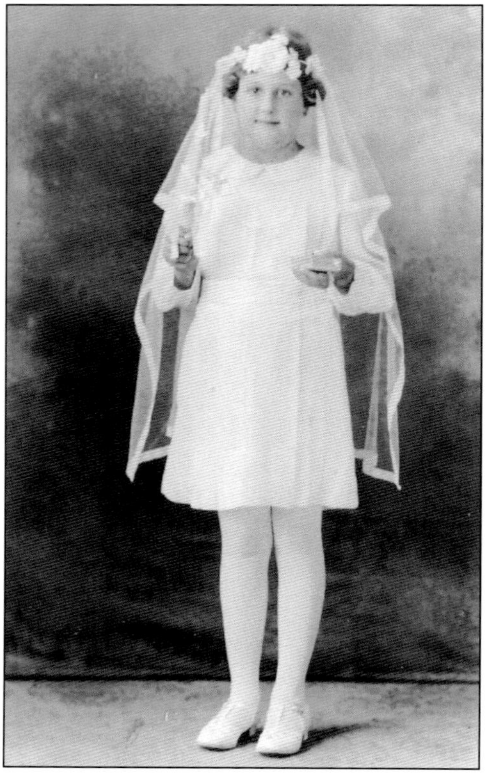

Doris Langlinais is pictured here in the 1930s taking her First Communion at Sacred Heart Church. Langlinais, now nearing her 90th birthday, has fond memories of her school years. (Doris Langlinais Larriviere.)

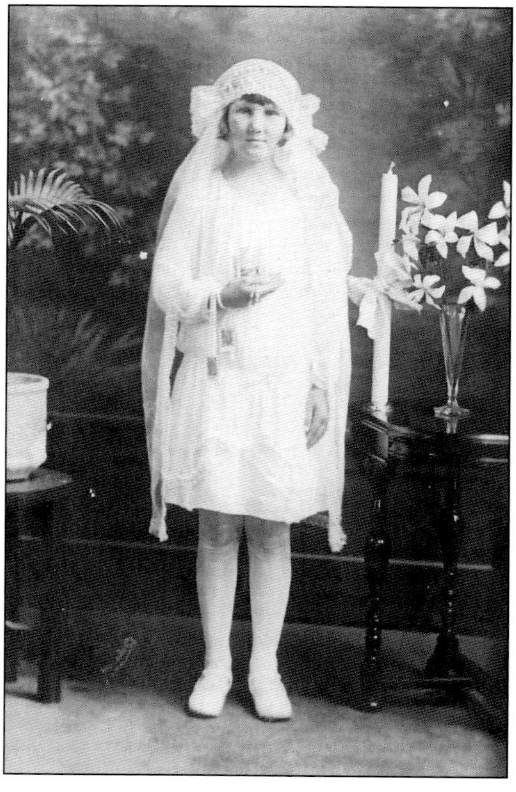

Hazel Mouton is a participant in the sacrament of First Communion at Sacred Heart Church in Broussard. She is garbed in a traditional First Communion/ Confirmation dress and veil sometime in the 1930s. (City of Broussard archives.)

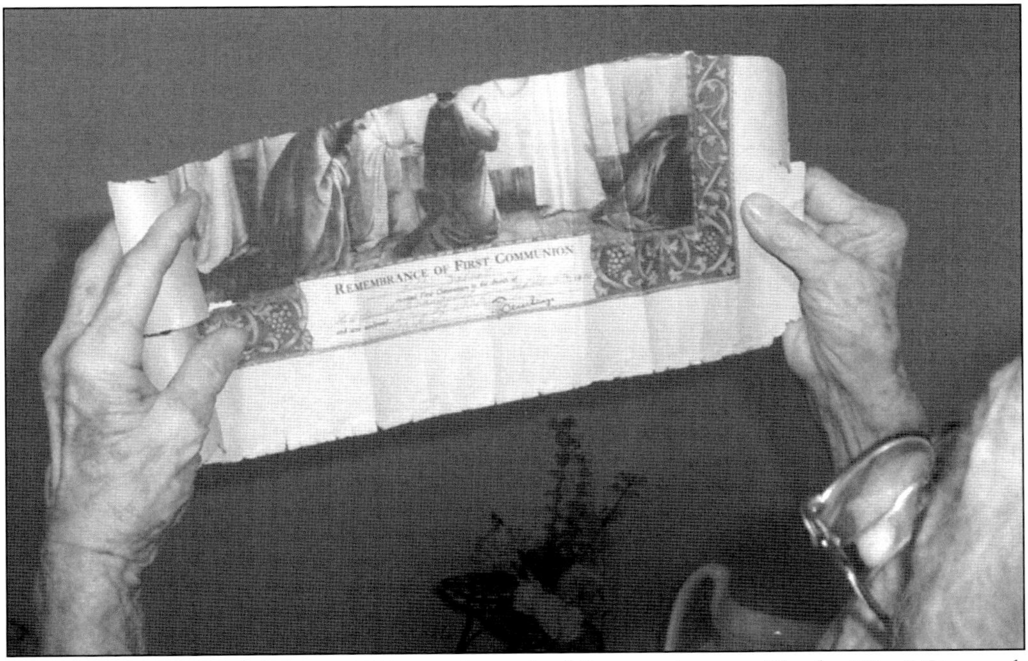

Attie Talbot Girouard, born in 1914, was the wife of Broussard mayor Charles "Boy" Girouard. Attie had her First Communion at St. John the Evangelist Church in Lafayette. The certificate in her hands is dated June 4, 1916, and bears the signature of Fr. William J. Teurlings, a Dutch priest. (Author's collection.)

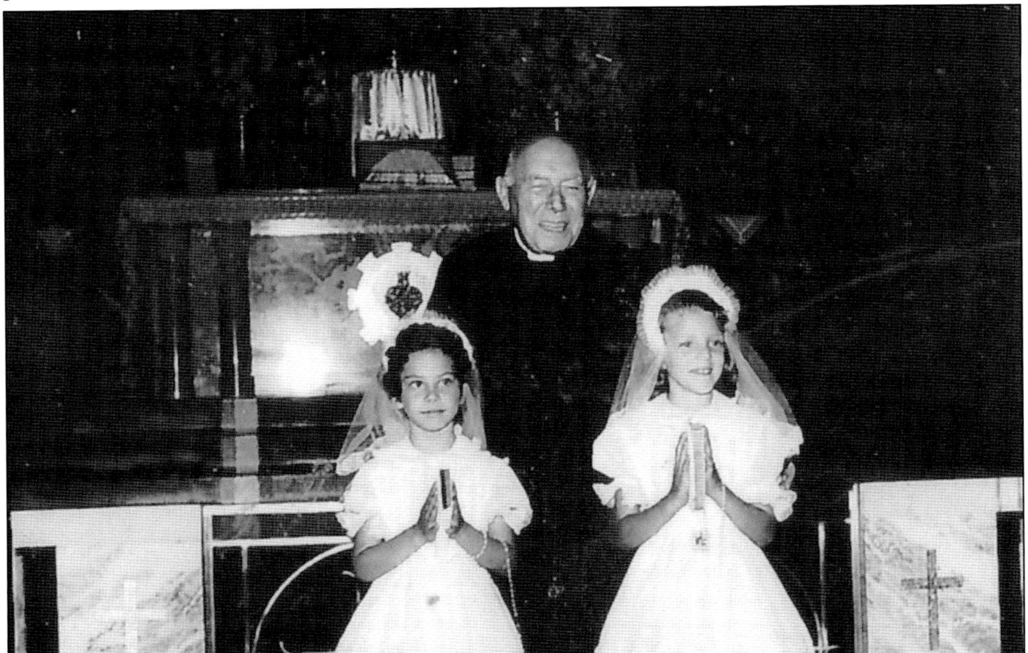

Two angelic young girls receive the sacrament of First Communion. Fr. P.G. John Kemps presided over many such religious ceremonies during his long and memorable tenure at Sacred Heart Church in Broussard. (Eula Bodin.)

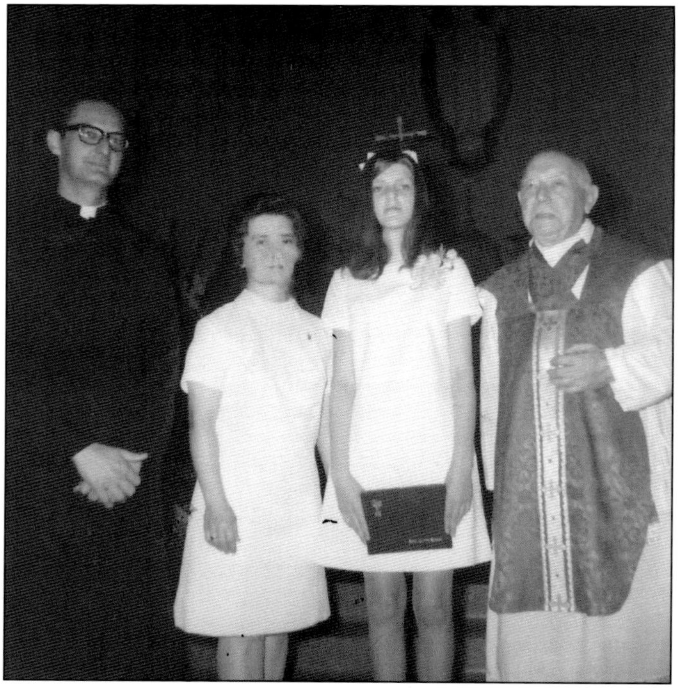

Fr. Martin "Marty" Leonard (left); Sr. Rose Corine, Order of Sisters of Divine Providence; and Fr. P.G. John Kemps present elementary student Kathy Bonin with a certificate during eighth-grade commencement at St. Cecilia School. (Eula Bodin.)

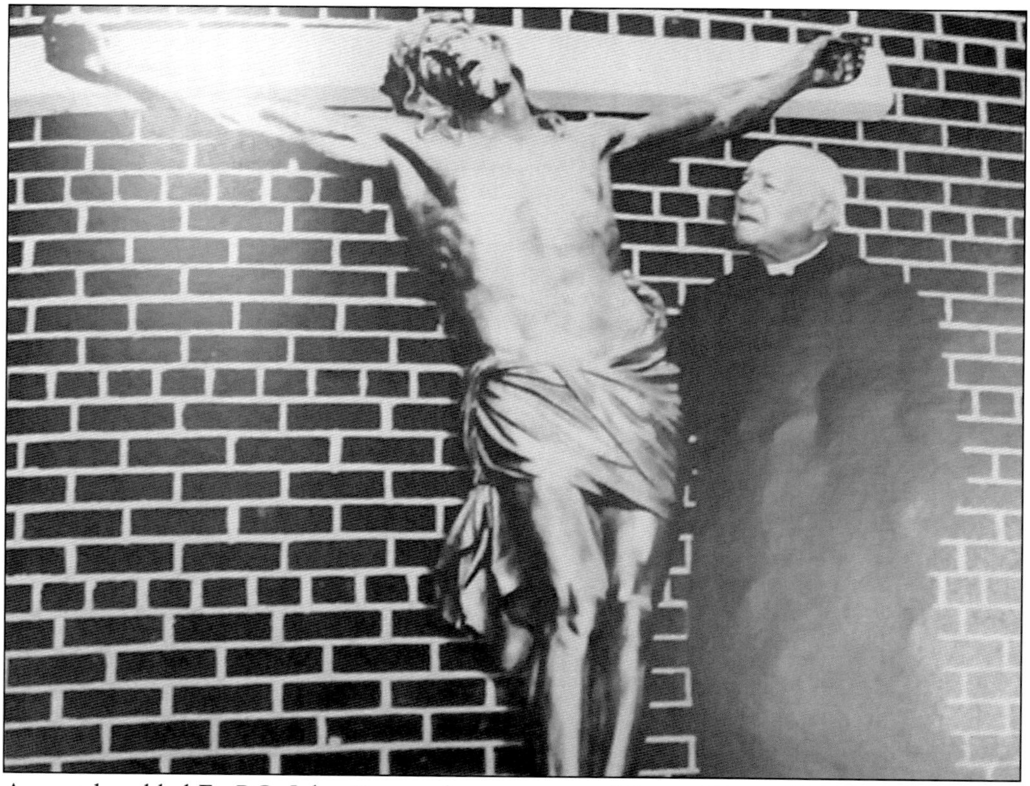

A most humbled Fr. P.G. John Kemps, former pastor of Sacred Heart Church in Broussard, touches the side of a statue of Jesus crucified. This photograph epitomizes the Christian belief in the Resurrection. (Eula Bodin.)

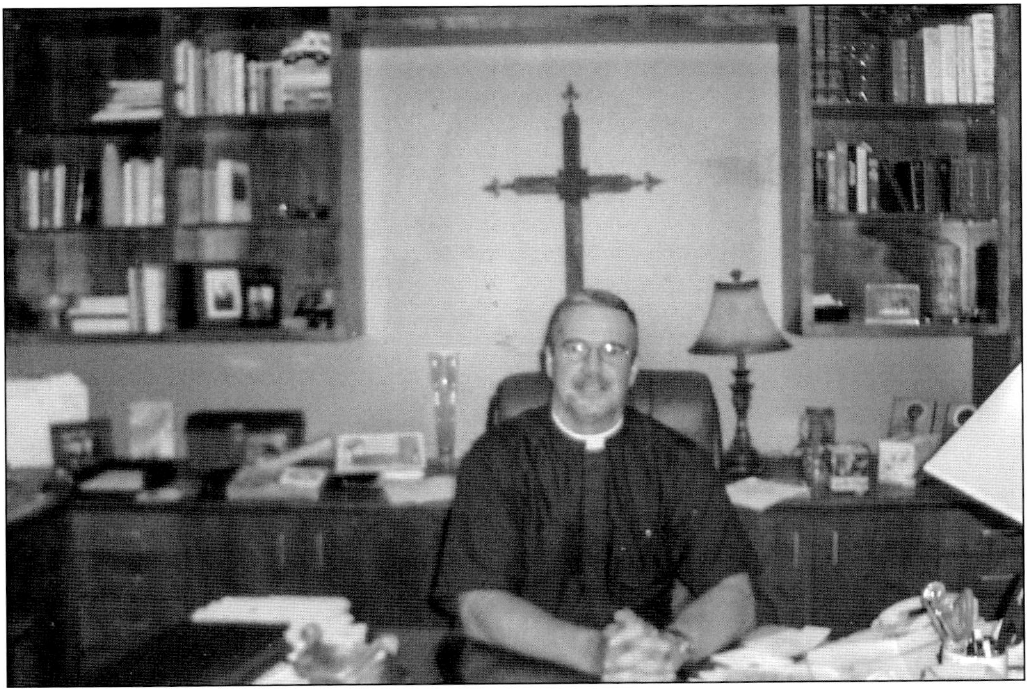

During Fr. Louis Richard's tenure at Sacred Heart, from October 2002 to July 2014, the church started a historic ground breaking for a major renovation program. In 2013, Father "Louie," as the parishioners affectionately addressed him, won a local Jefferson Award. The prize is part of a program started by Jacqueline Kennedy Onassis, Sen. Robert Taft Jr., and Sam Beard that recognizes ordinary persons making a difference in their local communities through volunteerism and community service. (Author's collection.)

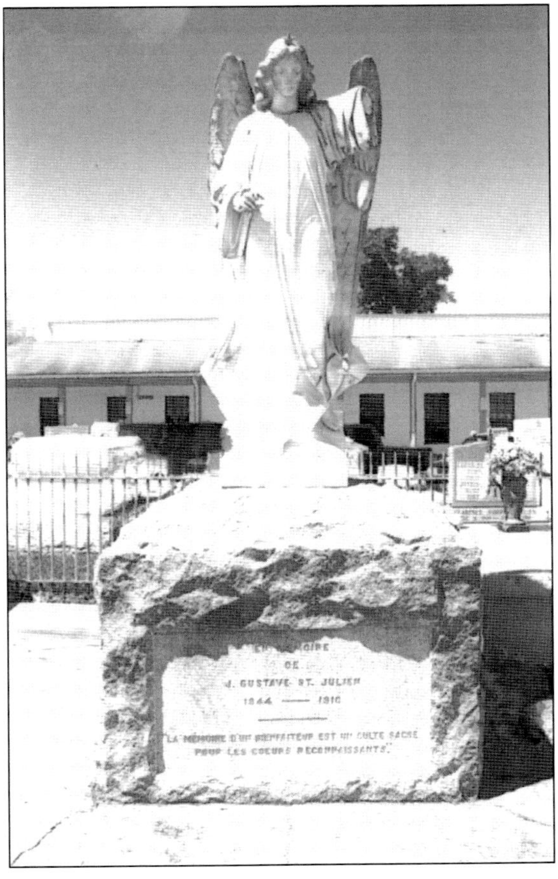

An archangel guards the tomb of J. Gustave St. Julien, father of Aurelien St. Julien, head of the vigilance committee in 1850. J. Gustave was known as the builder of the former drugstore on Morgan Street now housing B.J.'s Sandwich Shoppe. Behind the tomb is St. Cecilia School's Bishop Jarrell Hall, which was constructed in 1982 and named in his honor, as he was the pastor at the time of construction. (Author's collection.)

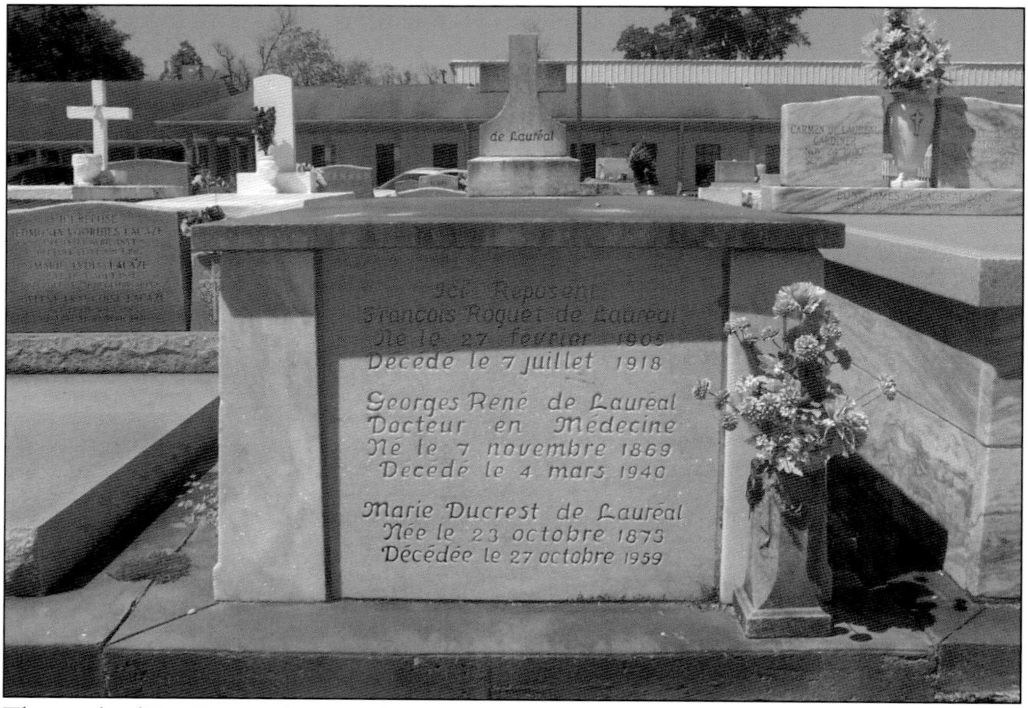

The tomb of Dr. George de Laureal in Sacred Heart Church cemetery is one of several graves that are inscribed in French. Also buried here are his wife, Marie Ducrest de Laureal, and son François Roguet de Laureal. (Author's collection.)

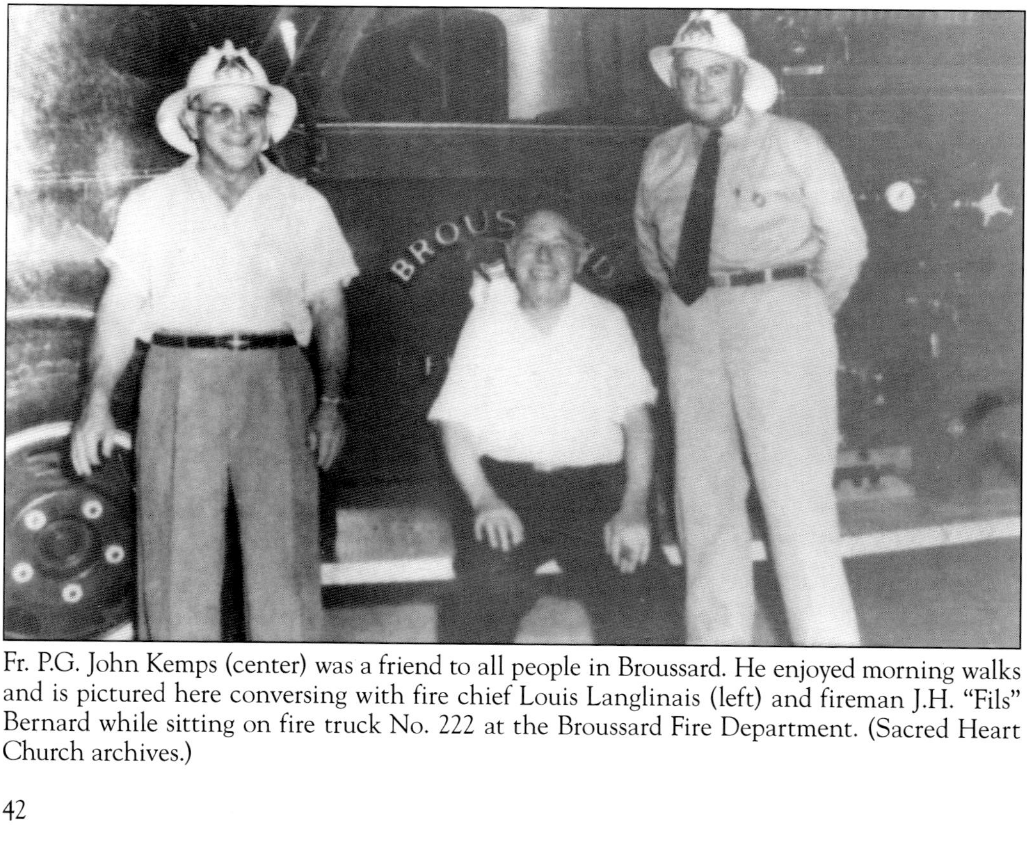

Fr. P.G. John Kemps (center) was a friend to all people in Broussard. He enjoyed morning walks and is pictured here conversing with fire chief Louis Langlinais (left) and fireman J.H. "Fils" Bernard while sitting on fire truck No. 222 at the Broussard Fire Department. (Sacred Heart Church archives.)

This beautiful crucifix once graced the front of Sacred Heart Church. It was relocated near the mausoleum area in the church cemetery during a major renovation project in 2004. A stone wall that circumnavigated the property was also removed to create a more open and welcoming entrance during that project, which was completed in 2006. (Emma Hollier.)

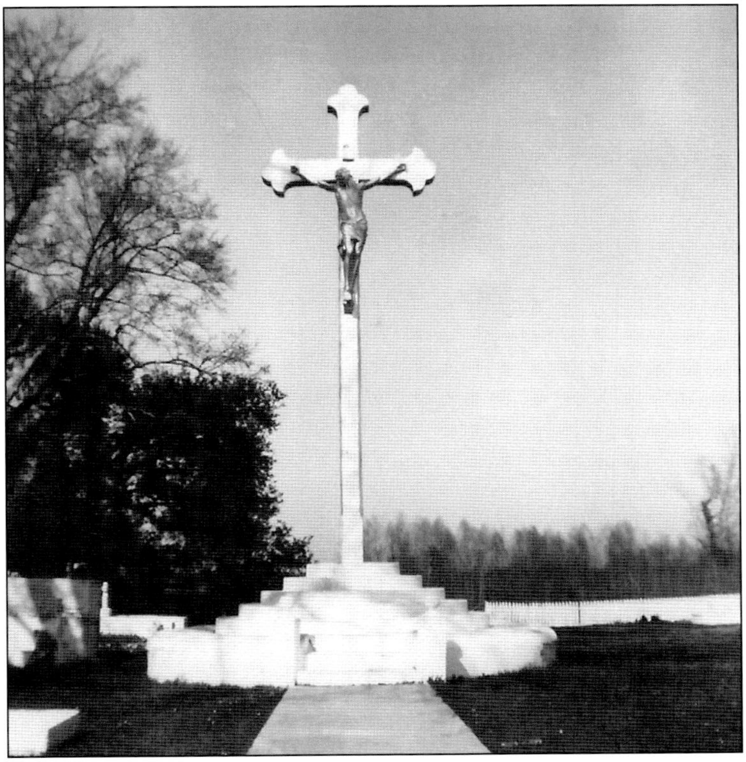

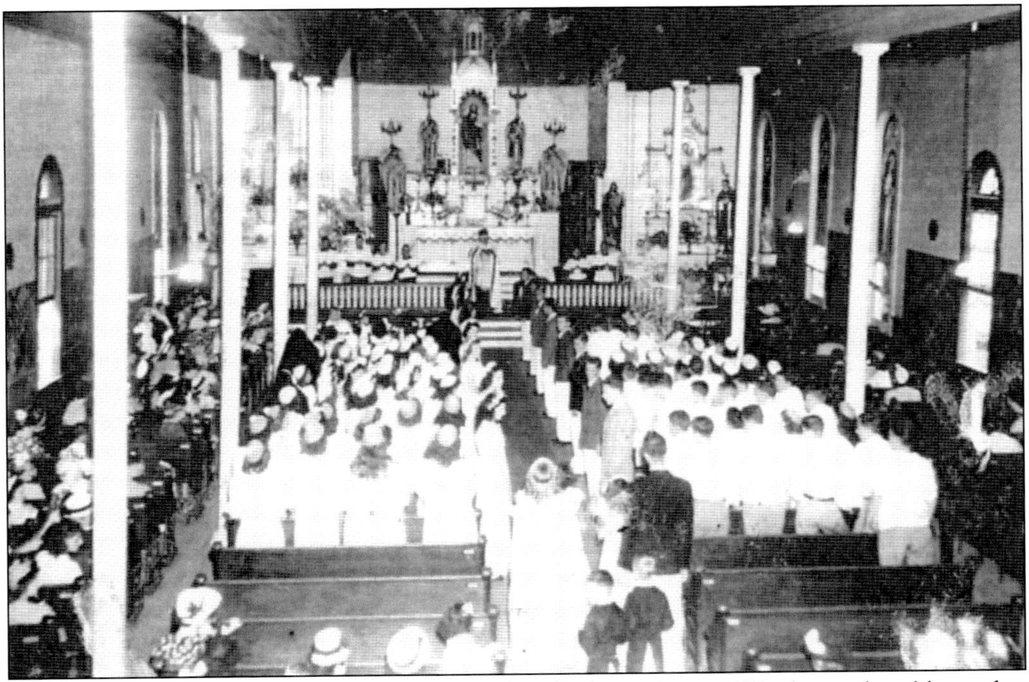

This wedding photograph at Sacred Heart Church, from about 1954, shows the old wooden church with its gleaming hand-carved pews, benches, and columns, ornate stained-glass windows, stations of the cross on opposite walls, and a railing that separated the altar from the sanctuary. (Eula Bodin.)

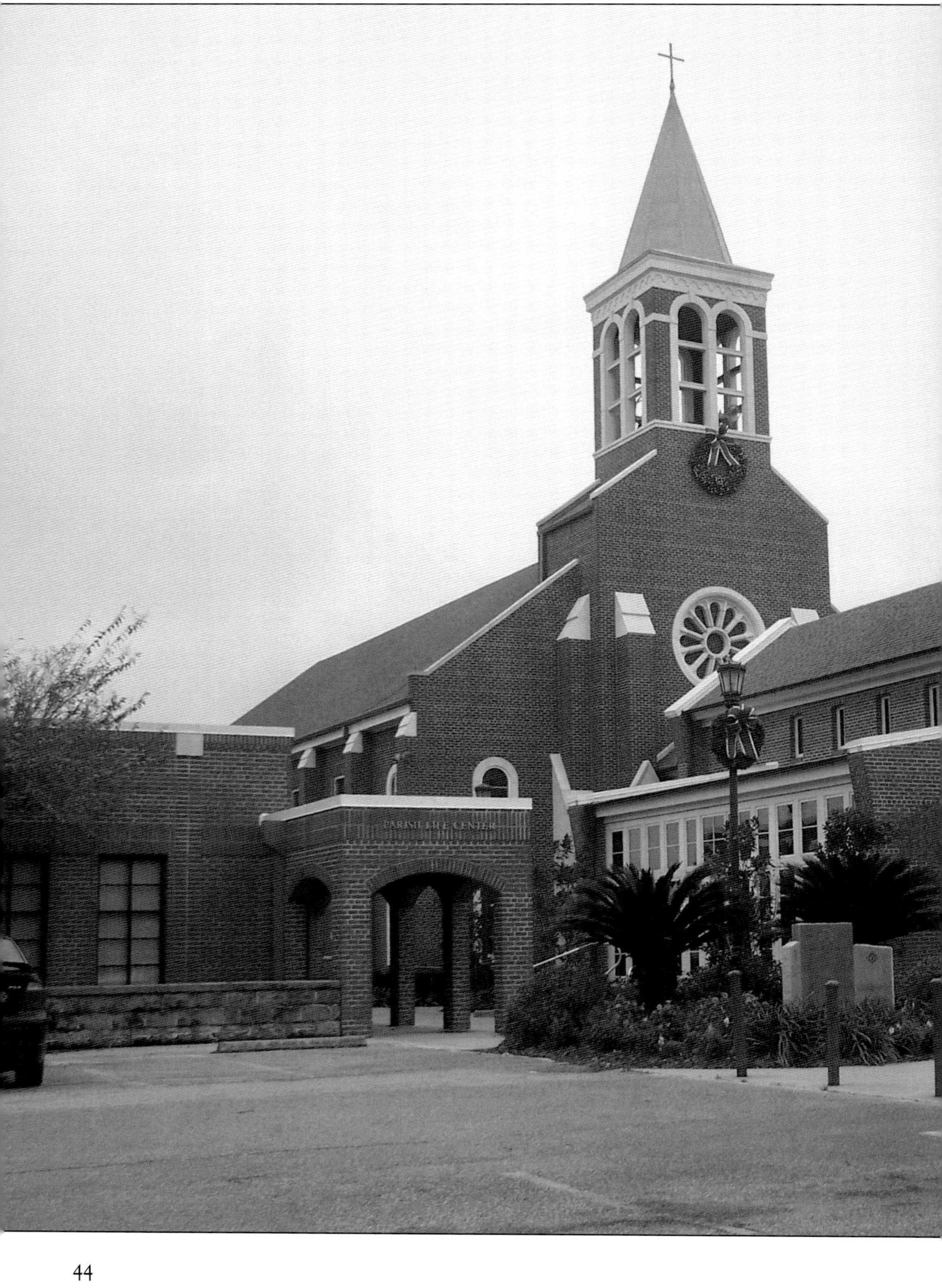
PARISH LIFE CENTER

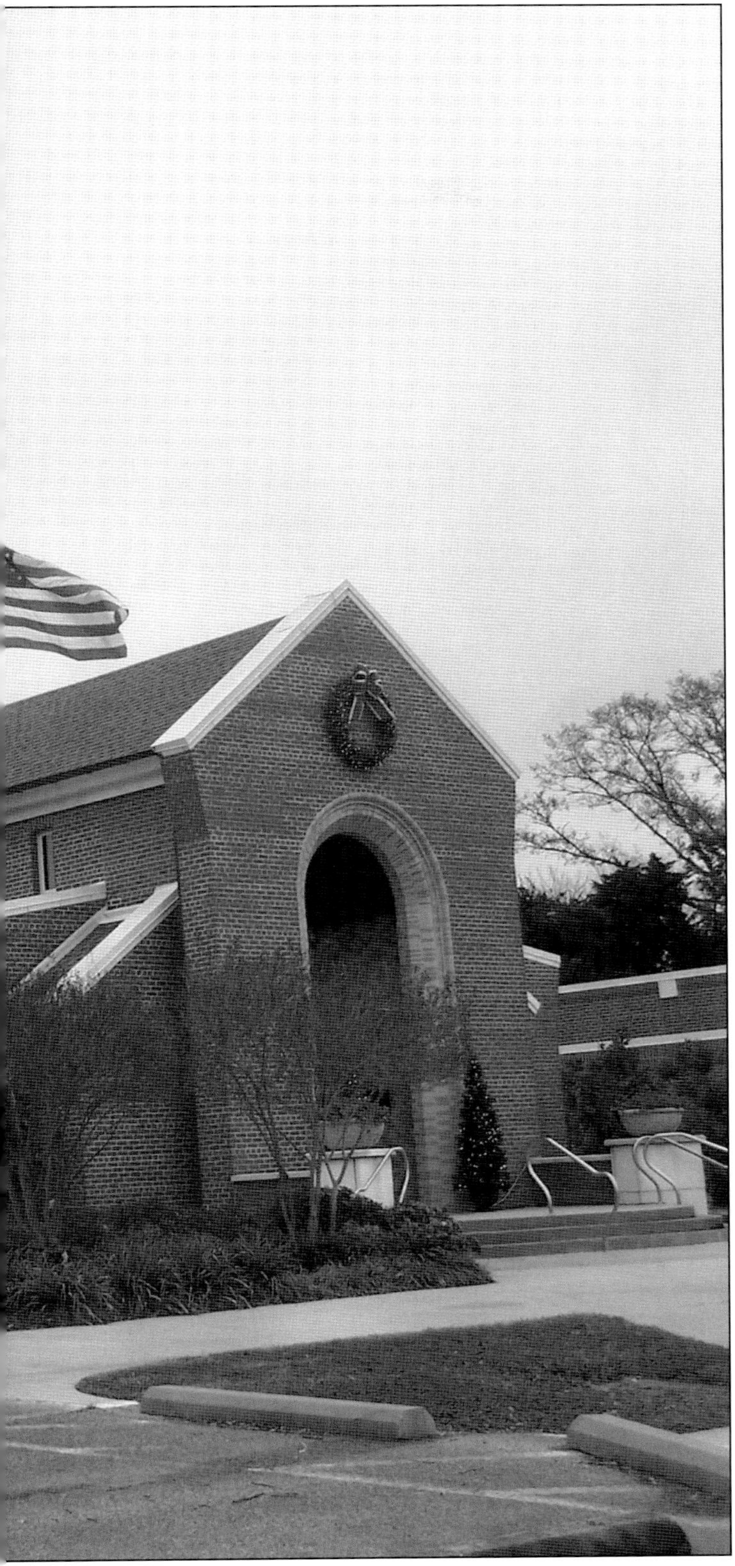

Sacred Heart Church began a two-year major renovation parish program in 2004, five decades after construction of the older Sacred Heart Church. The project was completed in 2006 with the addition of an administrative building, parish-life building, and a narthex—gathering spaces that brought the facility into the 21st century. (Author's collection.)

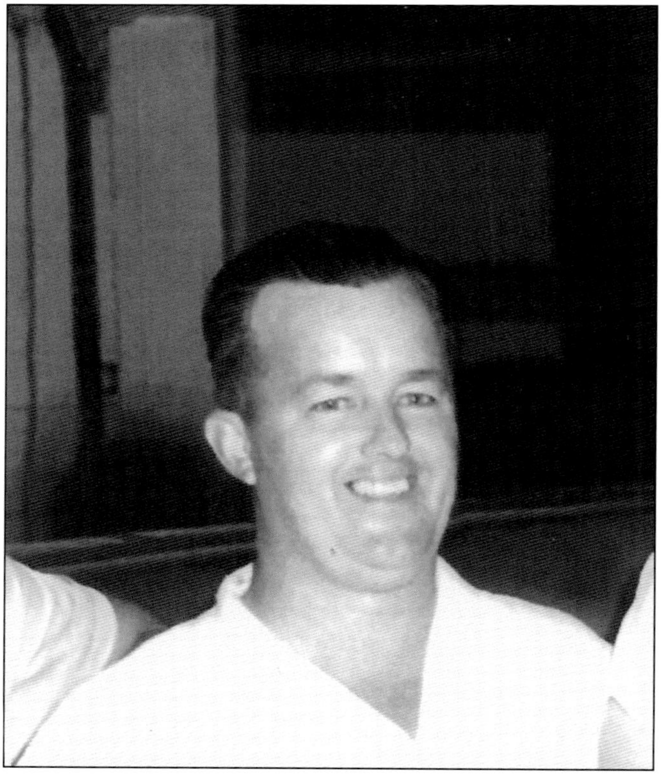

Blaise Donald Malagarie (September 16, 1919–May 9, 2008) was the great-grandson of Jean Baptiste Malagarie, the first postmaster of Broussard, and also the first child baptized at Sacred Heart Church. He served as the "oldest altar boy" until his death. Blaise was a veteran of World War II, serving with the 156th Infantry Division (31st) and receiving the Purple Heart and Silver Star medals. Blaise served on the Broussard Town Council from 1955 to 1967, with eight of his twelve years as mayor pro tem. He and his wife, Lucille "Cheney" Malagarie, were the first king and queen of a Broussard Mardi Gras parade. (Author's collection.)

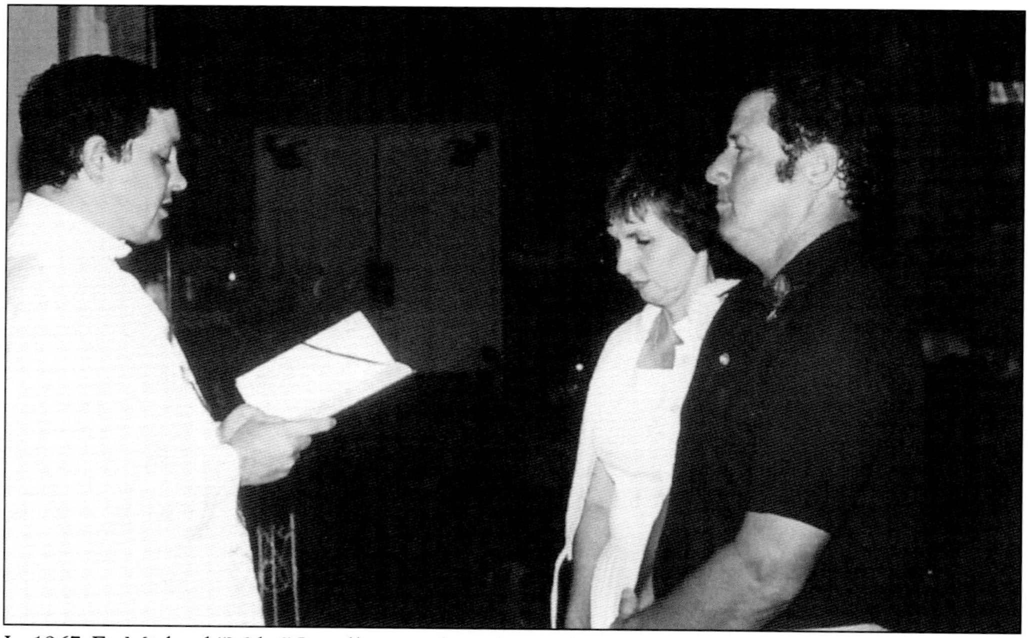

In 1967, Fr. Michael "Mike" Jarrell was ordained into the priesthood, later rising to rank of bishop of Lafayette. Father Jarrell served as Sacred Heart Church's pastor from 1976 until his transfer in early 1984 to Ville Platte, Louisiana. James and Judy Billeaud have wonderful memories of Father Jarrell officiating as they renewed their 25th wedding anniversary vows, as seen here. (Eula Bodin.)

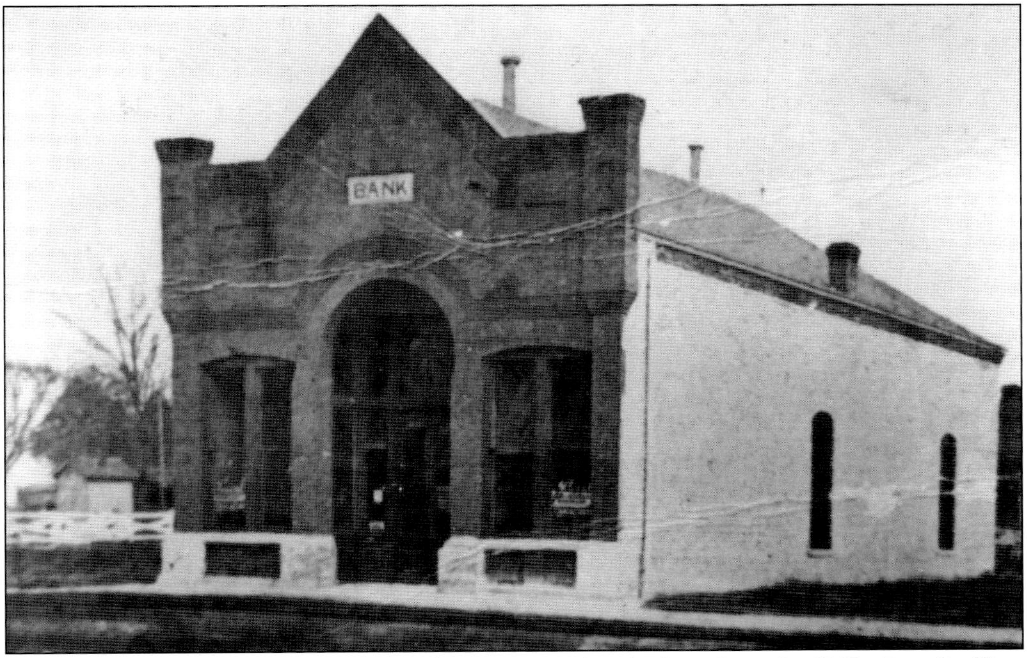

First Baptist Church of Broussard, a Southern Baptist church, dates from the 1950s. Rev. St. Clair Bower, pastor of Northside Baptist, felt the need to establish an area mission. The church was able to rent the old Broussard Bank, and the structure served as a meeting place for the mission. (First Baptist Church of Broussard.)

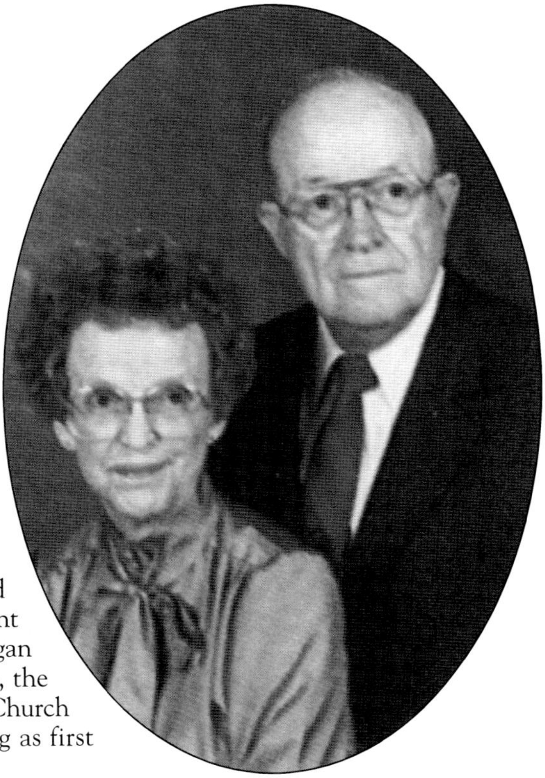

Rev. St. Clair Bower, pastor of Northside Baptist, and his wife, Annie Bowers, are pictured here. A survey was conducted to assess the potential for a church in Broussard in 1955. Back then, Baptists were holding tent revivals in the old bank on the corner of Morgan and Monroe Streets. By September 21, 1958, the mission was organized as the First Baptist Church of Broussard, with Rev. Elroy Jones serving as first minister. (Northside Baptist Church.)

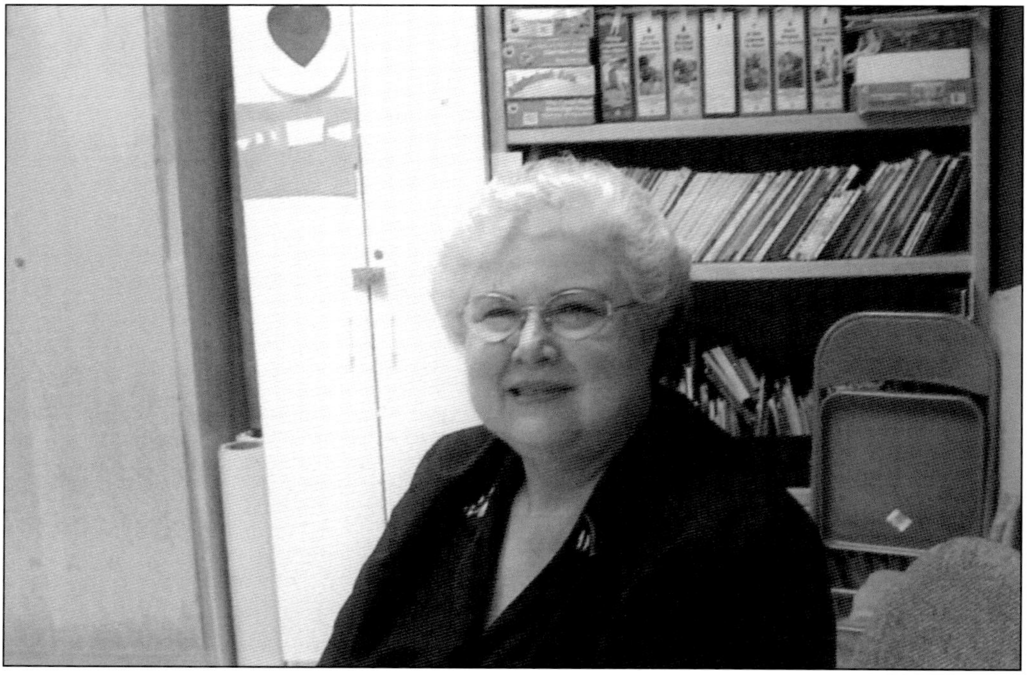

Over the years, 13 men have served as pastors of First Baptist Church of Broussard. Sister Judy Lord and her husband, pastor L.C. Lord, served from 2003 to 2006. The church grew from one lot in 1958 to several buildings on seven lots in 1984. (Author's collection.)

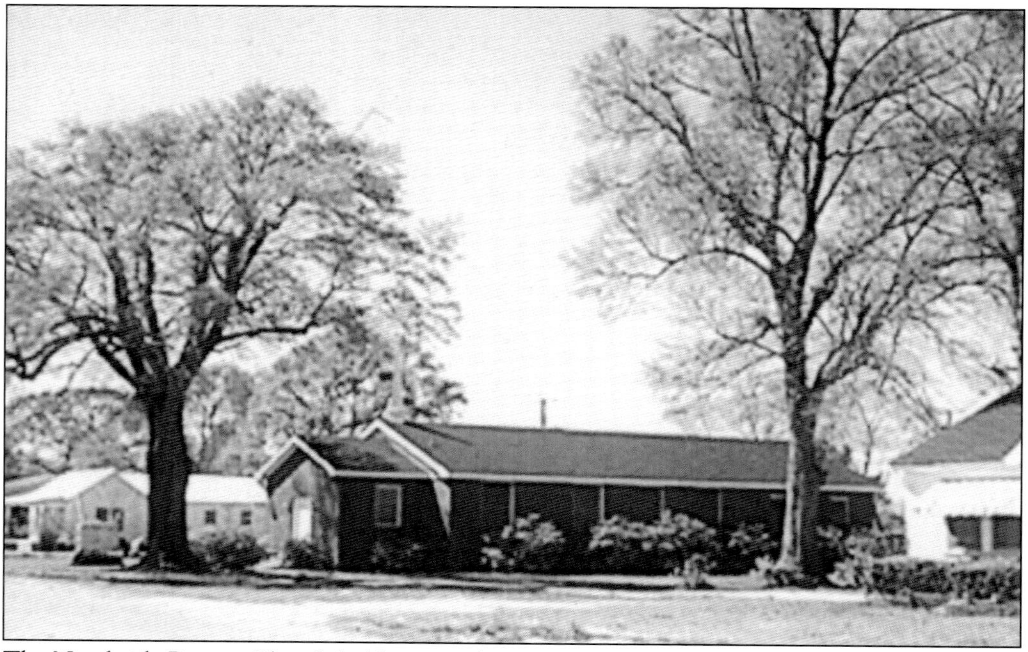

The Northside Baptist Church held a revival in Broussard in the early 1950s and rented the old Broussard Bank to hold revivals in an attempt to establish a mission church. In 1956, construction began on a church building on Morgan Street. The First Baptist Church of Broussard opened its doors on September 21, 1958. Rev. Elroy Jones, a contractor, built the church and was called as its first pastor. (First Baptist Church of Broussard.)

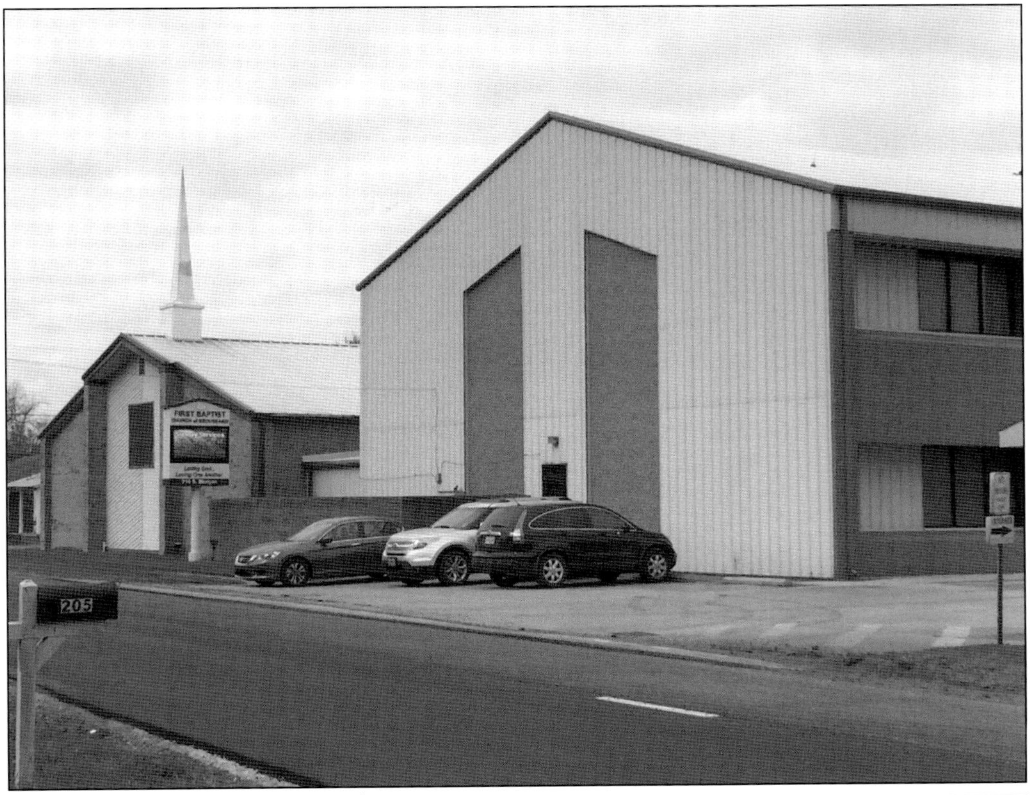

First Baptist Church of Broussard's congregation has grown significantly since the days of tent revival meetings in 1955 and 1956. In those days, Rev. Amadie Janice, a French-speaking pastor, teamed with Rev. St. Clair Bower, pastor of Northside Baptist Church, to get sermons across to the congregation. (Lisa Ledet.)

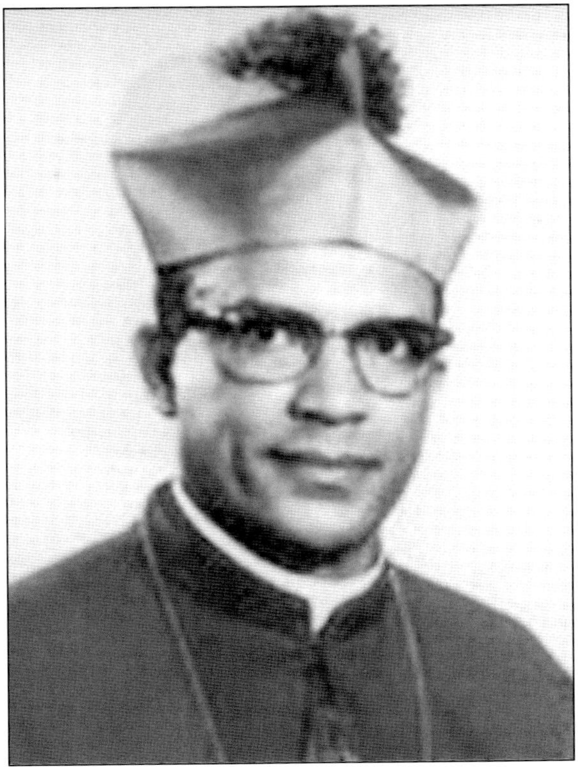

Rev. Harold Perry was appointed by Bishop Jules Jeanmard of the Diocese of Lafayette to St. Joseph Mission in Broussard, with the need for another parish recognized in 1952. Religious classes for adults and children were initiated at the school. (St. Joseph Catholic Church archives.)

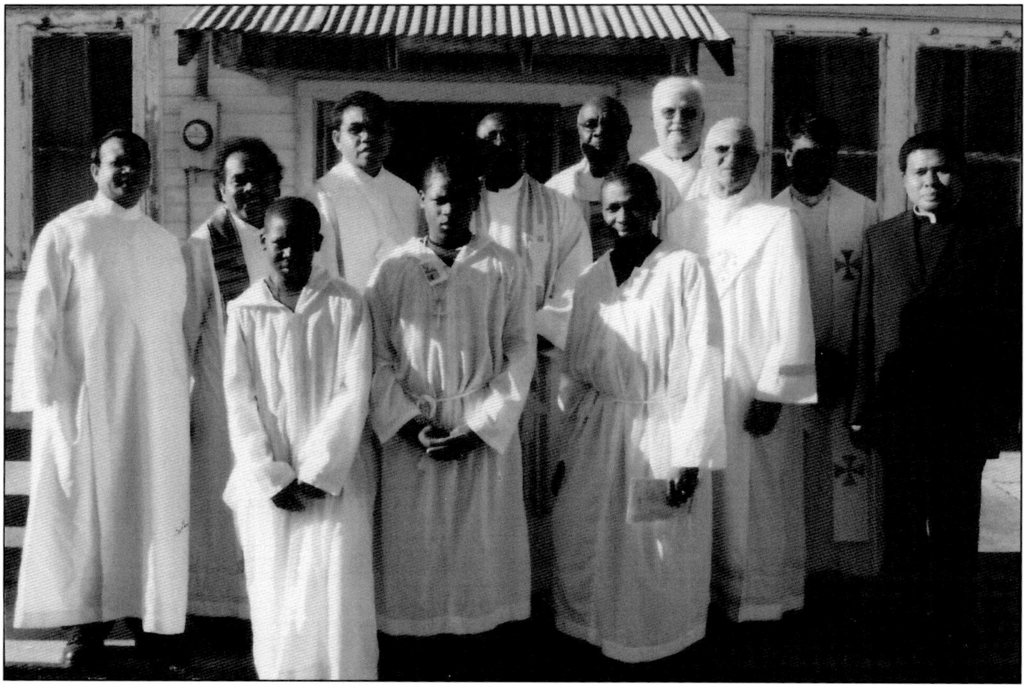

Past priests who served at St. Joseph Church and three altar servers were present at St. Anthony Church in Cade, Louisiana, to assist with the 50th anniversary of the mission church that began in 1952. (Fr. Arockiam Arockiam, SVD.)

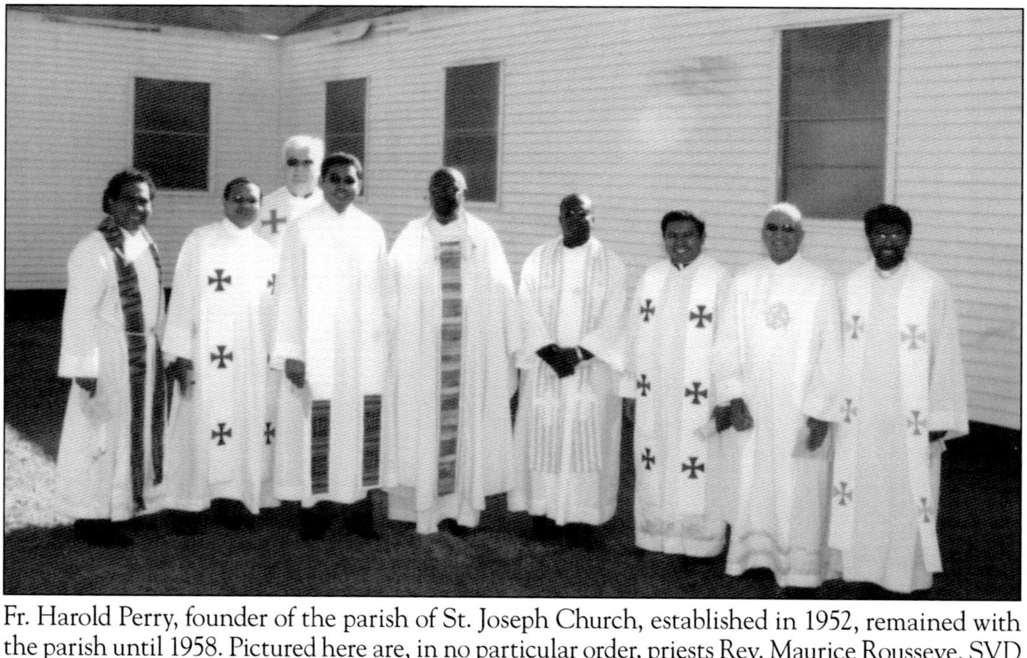

Fr. Harold Perry, founder of the parish of St. Joseph Church, established in 1952, remained with the parish until 1958. Pictured here are, in no particular order, priests Rev. Maurice Rousseve, SVD (1959–1966), Rev. Mark Figaro, SVD (1966–1969), John W. Dauphine, SVD (1969–1978), Francis Dixon, SVD (1978–1984), Rev. W. Olivier, SVD (1984–1988), Lewis Gerald, SVD (1988–1991), Rev. Brendan Murphy (1991–1999), Michael Sucharski (1999–2000), and Rev. Lambert Lien (2003–2010). (Fr. Arockiam Arockiam, SVD.)

Four

Public and Private Schools Emerge

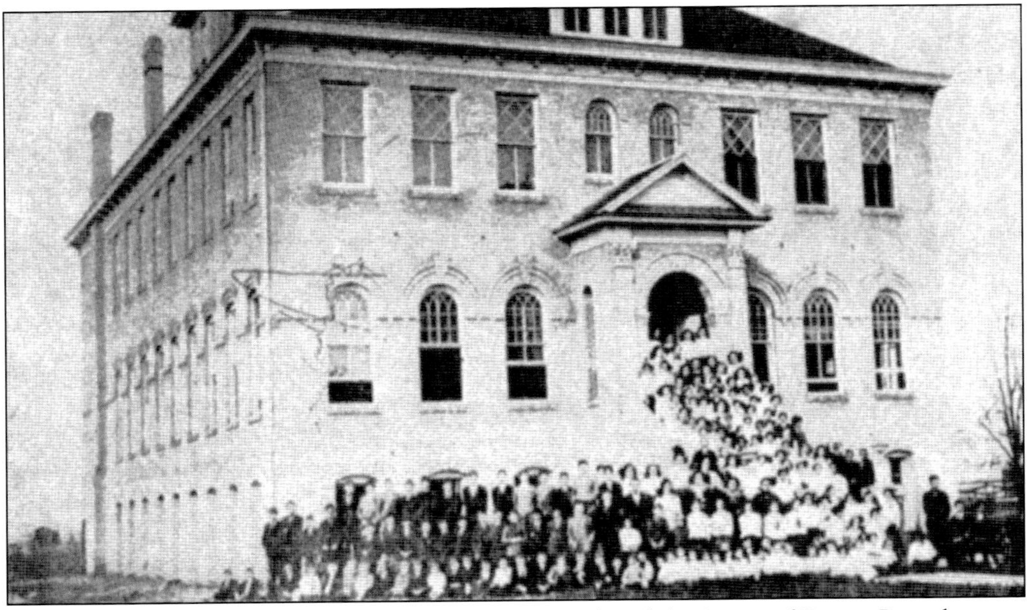

Begun in 1909, the St. Cecilia School in Broussard employed the Sisters of Divine Providence to educate students, and the sisters did so until 1974. At that time, the bishop of Lafayette made an initiative to consolidate all Catholic high schools. Since then, the faculty consists of lay teachers. (Lafayette Parish clerk of court Louis J. Perret.)

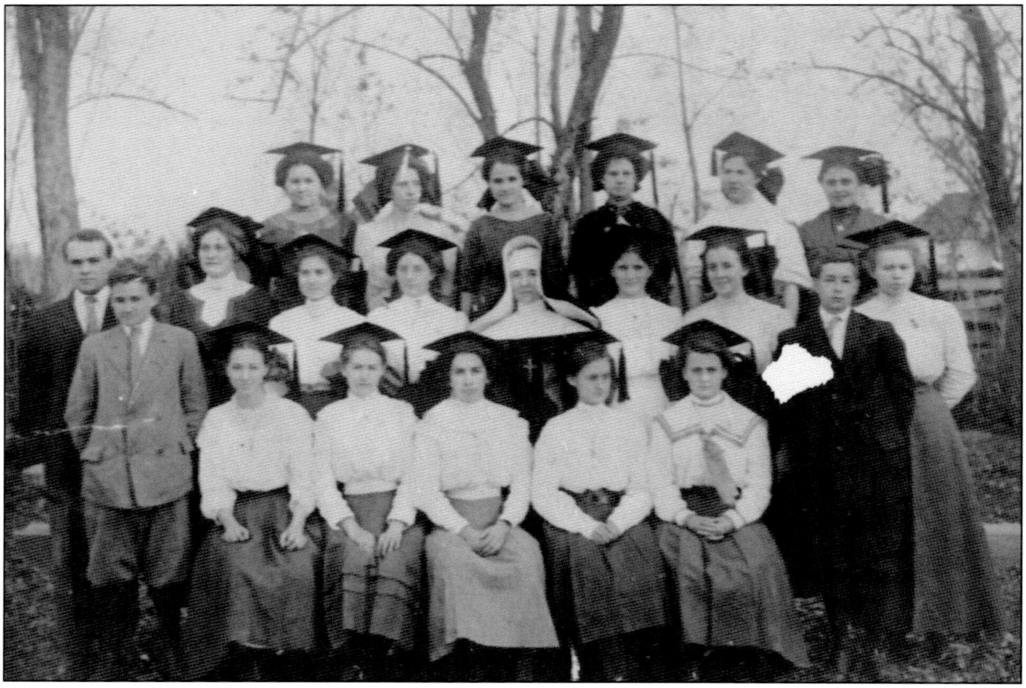

Pictured here are the St. Cecilia High School seniors in 1911 along with faculty. Writing on the back of the photograph indicates that Fabiola Belle Bourque Chastant is "on left." St. Cecilia School has always offered a religious education for both public and parochial schoolchildren. (Lafayette Parish Clerk of Court Louis J. Perret.)

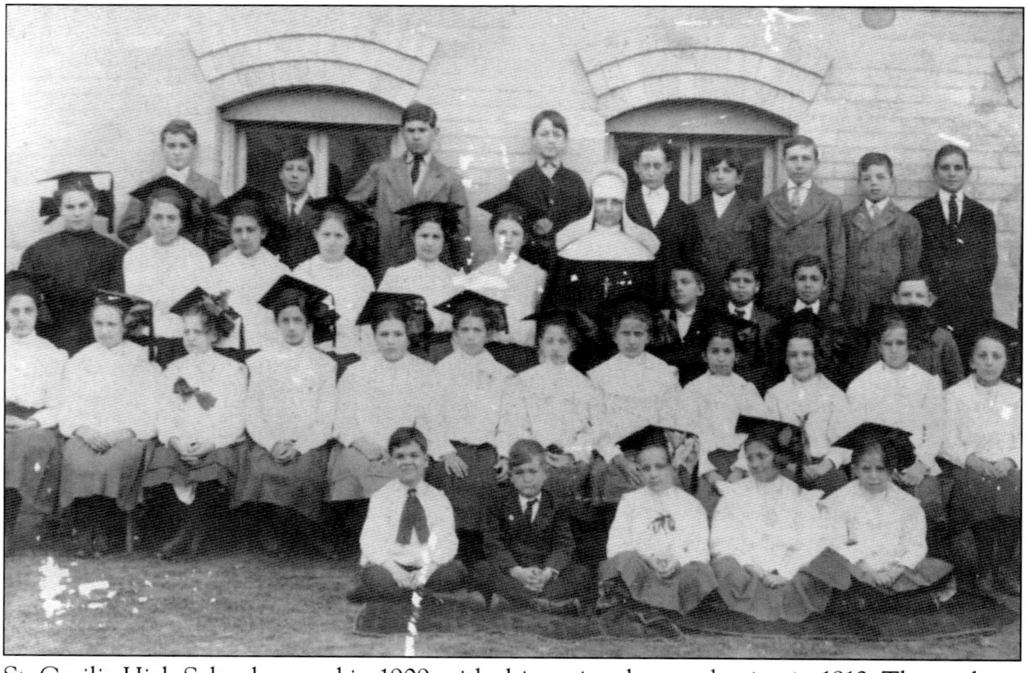

St. Cecilia High School opened in 1909, with this senior class graduating in 1912. The students are pictured with their teacher, a nun from the order of Sisters of Divine Providence (CDP). (Lafayette Parish Clerk of Court Louis J. Perret.)

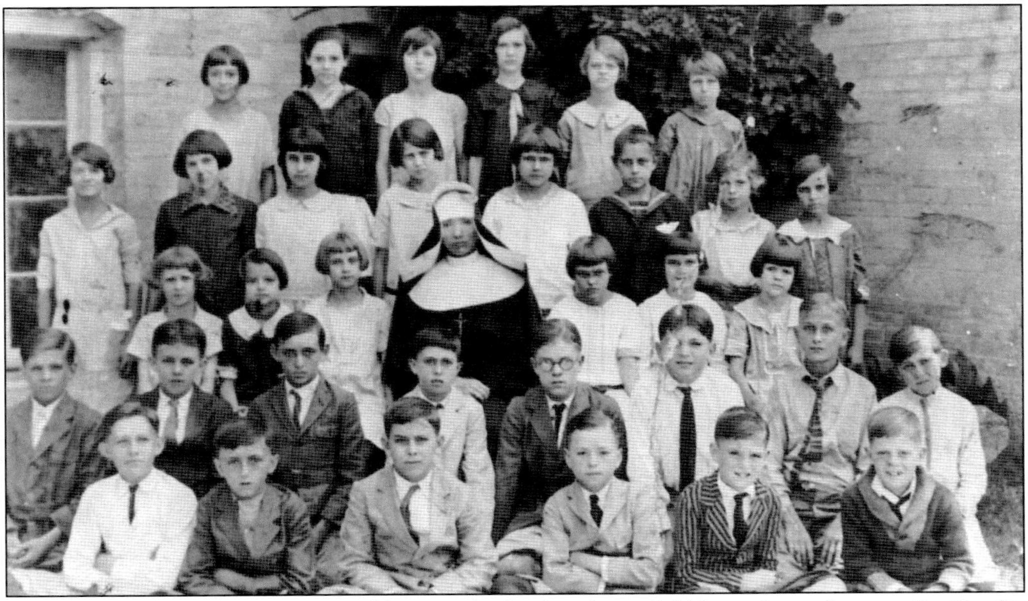

Sister Emmanuel, CDP, is pictured here with the fourth- and fifth-grade students at St. Cecilia School in 1925. The nuns came from San Antonio, Texas, and were not accustomed to the Acadiana French culture. (Lafayette Parish Clerk of Court Louis J. Perret.)

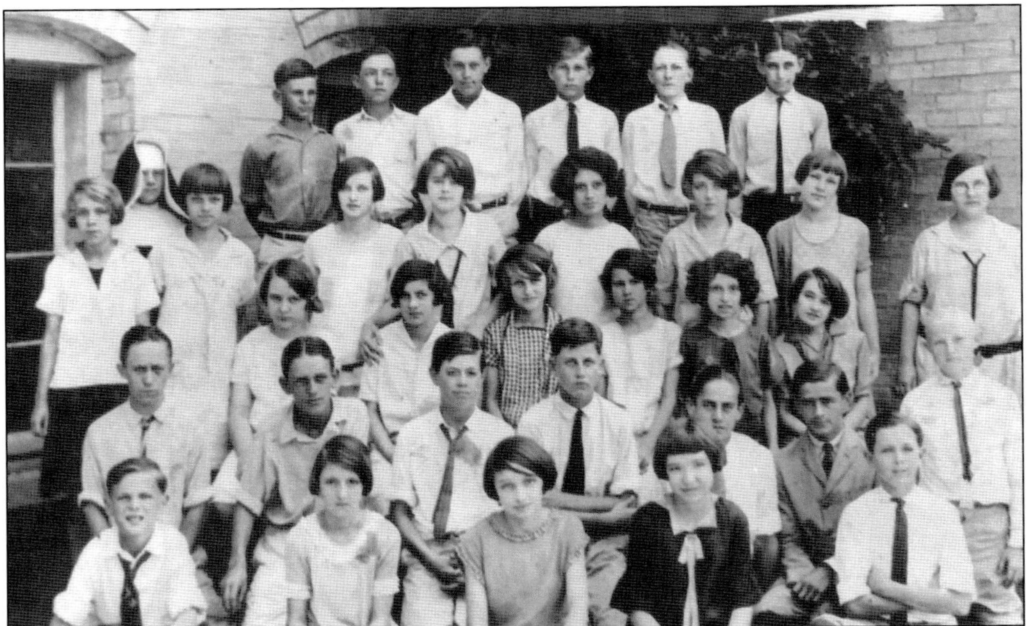

Sister Alberta, CDP, is shown here with the sixth- and seventh-grade classes in 1925. Pictured, in no particular order, are George Malagarie, Robert Comeaux, John Reaux, H. Comeaux, P. Bernard, Kermit Girouard, Sister Alberta, Marcelle Ducrest, C. LeBlanc, Lola Bernard, Belle Broussard, Pauline St. Julien, Lucy Soulier, Flossie Landry, Tootsie Broussard, Sophie Bernard, Cecile Dumisnel, Hilda Broussard, Vivian Labbe, Germaine St. Julien, Maude Boulet, Paul Bernard, Rene Theriot, Autoway Gonzales, C.K. Langlinais, Clagg Verret, Willis Malagarie, Wilton Bud Labbe, David De Laurel, Anna Belle Duhon, Bee Peck, Beatrice Girouard, and Ned Labbe. (Lafayette Parish Clerk of Court Louis J. Perret.)

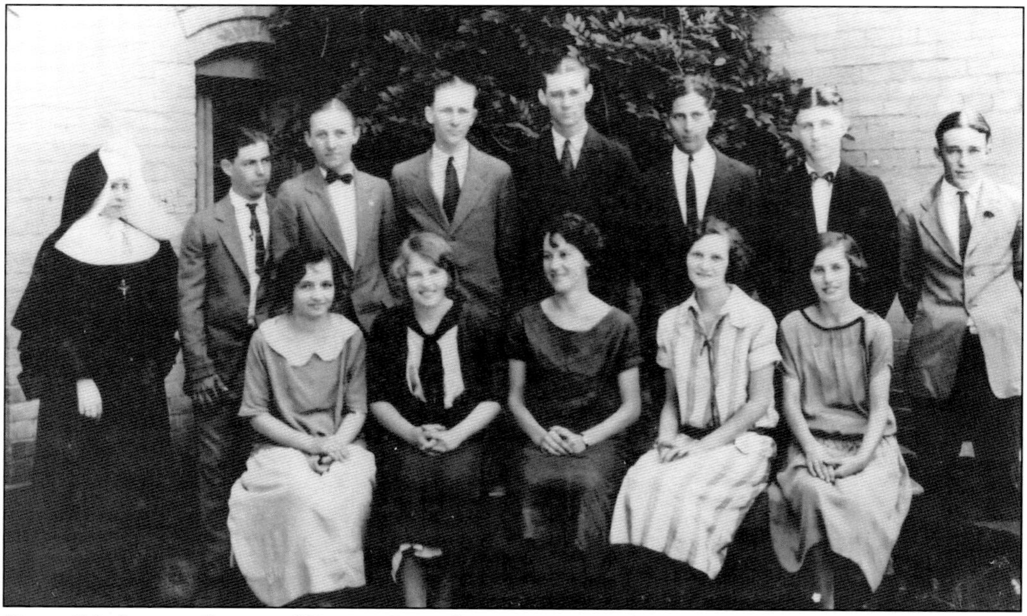

Sister Ildiphonse, Sisters of Divine Providence, is pictured with the St. Cecilia senior class of 1925. They are, from left to right, (first row) Lucille Corne, Jeanne Labbe, Agnes Reaux, Cecile Melancon and Eunice Bernard; (second row) Louis St. Julien, Irvin Verret, Robley Duhon, Roy Gonzales, Gaston Labbe, Eugene St. Julien, and Arthur Boulet. (Lafayette Parish Clerk of Court Louis J. Perret.)

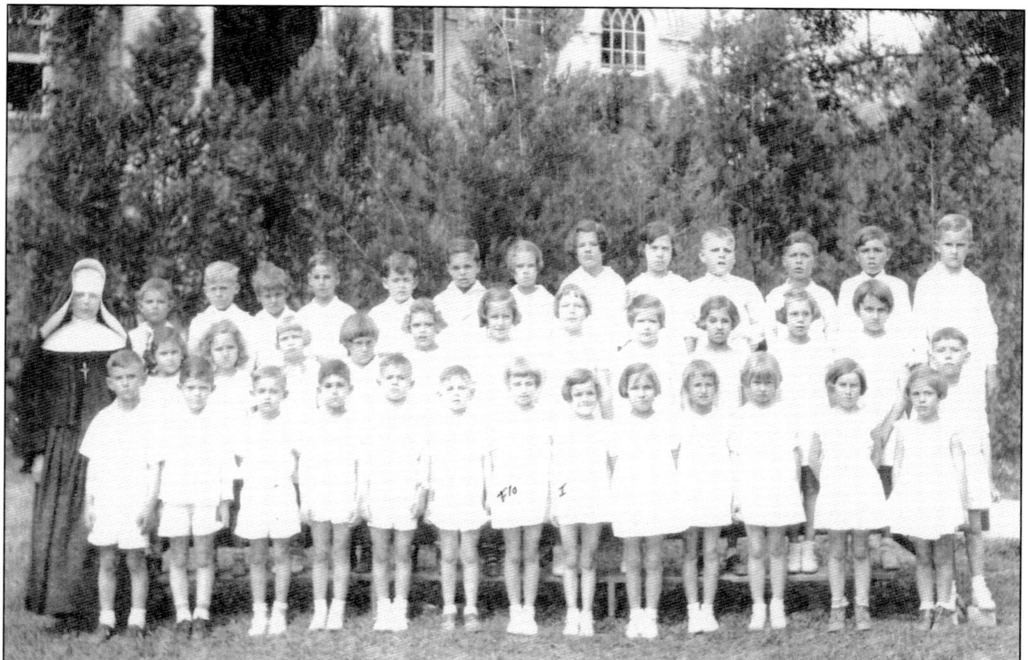

Pictured here are the primer and first-grade classes of 1936–1937. Ida Belle Girouard (Pesson), front row, eighth from left, is the daughter of Frank Girouard Sr. and Olphida Comeaux and granddaughter of Joseph Oscar Girouard, an influential planter considered to be a leader among his people in the late 1800s. (Ida Belle Girouard Pesson.)

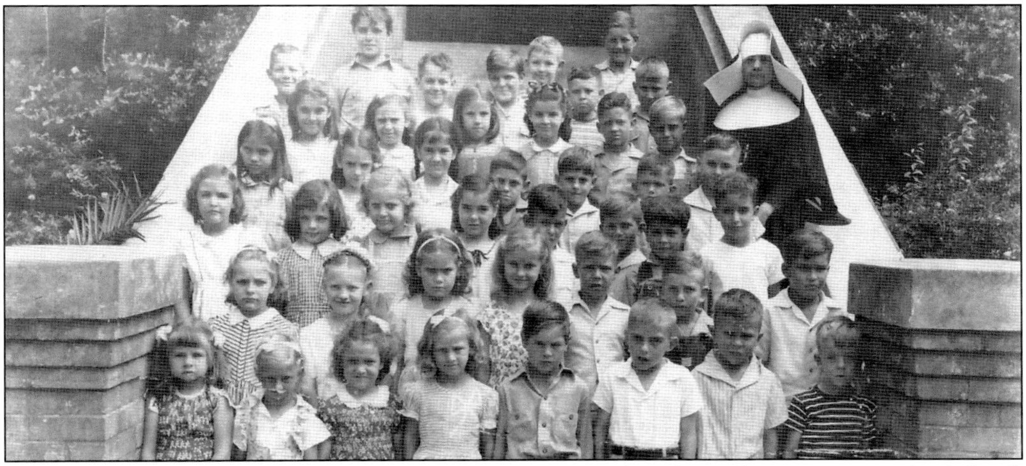

Pictured here are the 1945–1946 classes of first and second grade students at St. Cecilia School. Cecile Pineal (not pictured) served as St. Cecilia's principal at that time. (Courtesy Lafayette Parish Clerk of Court Louis J. Perret.)

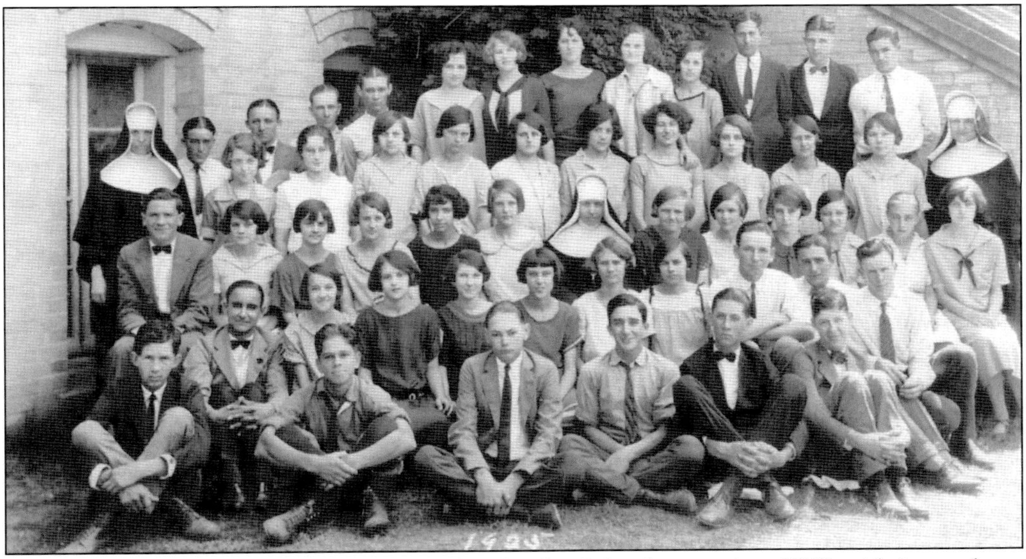

During Rev. Arthur Drossaerts's tenure, St. Cecilia School opened in 1909 with its students under the guidance of the Sisters of Divine Providence from San Antonio, Texas. In 1974, the bishop of Lafayette, in an effort to consolidate all parish Catholic schools, closed the high school department. Pictured here in 1925 are, from left to right, (first row) Maurice St. Julien, Roy Ducrest, Dennis Monte, Charles Boulet, Earl Gonzales, and Clarence St. Julien; (second row) Elton "T Gris" Girouard, Marie Boulet, Adele Bernard, Mae Goldrich Duhon, Jeanne Billeaud, Solange Monte, Claire Bernard, Wallace Duhon, Charlie Bernard, and Mayeau Duhon; (third row) Hugh DeLaureal, Mae Broussard, Hazel Gautreaux, Claudia Broussard, Theresa Bernard, Sylvia LeBlanc, Sister Ildaphonse, Rhena Duhon, Martha Girouard, Hazel Girouard, Theresa Bower, Corinne Bernard, and Jeanne Langlinais; (fourth row) Sister Generosa, Mable Billeaud, Jeanne Malagarie, Aline Dumesnil, Marie Louise Broussard, Henrietta Dumesnil, Alice Ste. Marie, Isabelle St. Julien, Leona Billeaud, Isabelle Labbe, Rhena Romero, and Sister Alma; (fifth row) Arthur Boulet, Irvin Verret, Robley Duhon, Roy Gonzales, Lucille Corne, Jeanne Labbe, Agnes Labbe, Cecile Melancon, Eunice Bernard, Gaston Labbe, Eugene St. Julien, and Louis St. Julien. (Lafayette Parish Clerk of Court Louis J. Perret.)

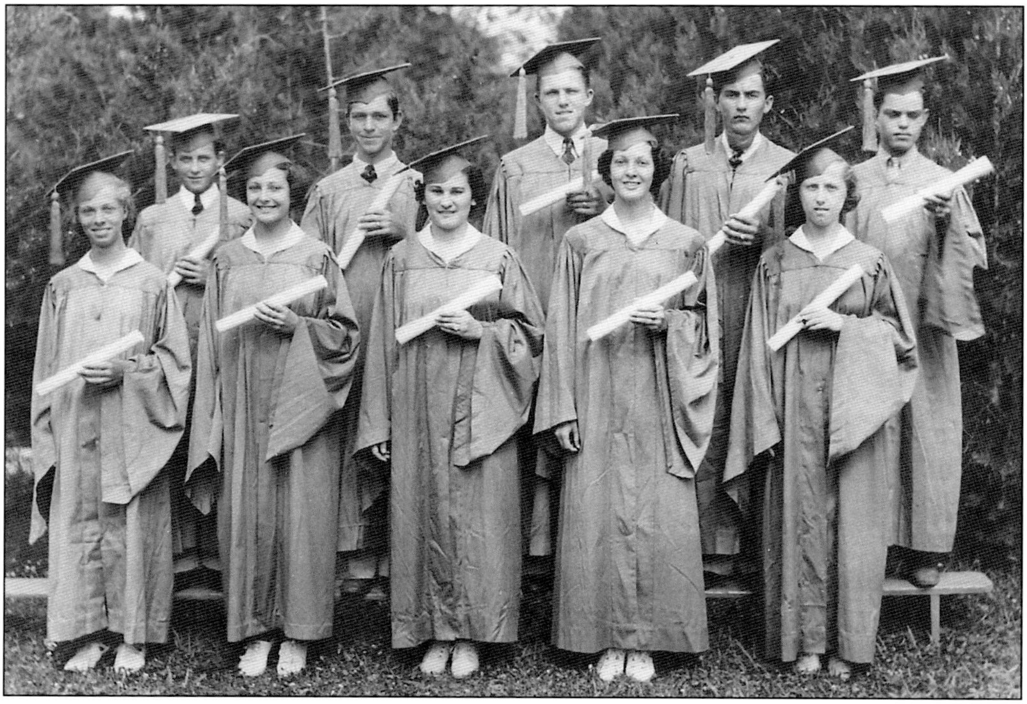

Pictured here are members of the class of 1937. They are, from left to right, (first row) Verna Ducrest, Corita Stromer, Euna Bernard, Lucille Beaulieu and Jeanette Comeaux; (second row) Willis Broussard, Felix Ducrest, George Billeaud Jr., Patrick Bernard, and Martial Billeaud. (Lafayette Parish Clerk of Court Louis J. Perret.)

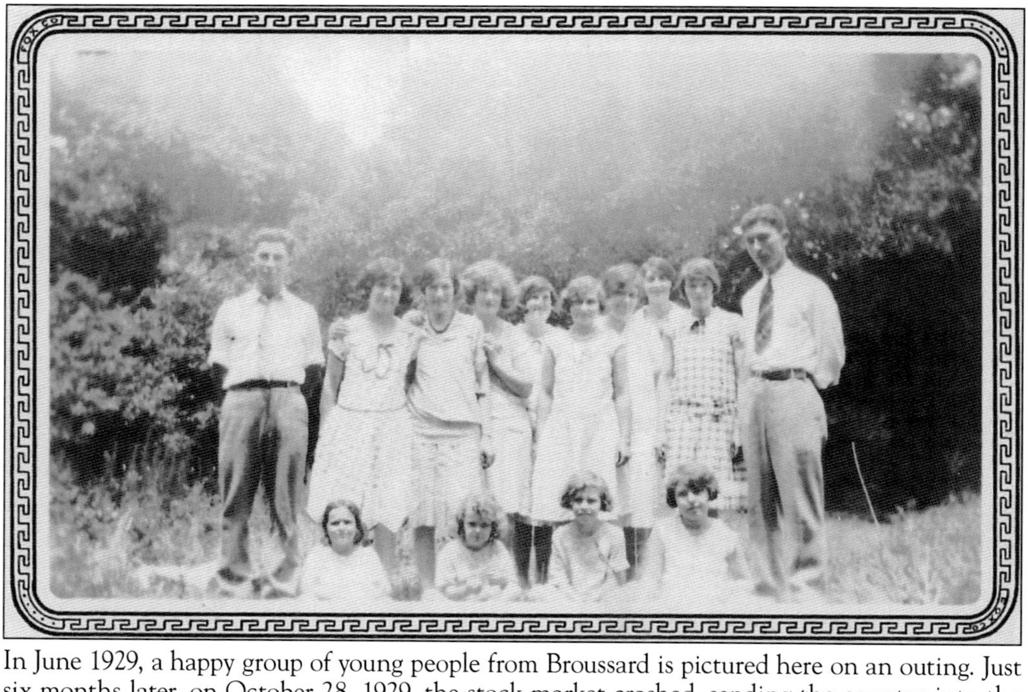

In June 1929, a happy group of young people from Broussard is pictured here on an outing. Just six months later, on October 28, 1929, the stock market crashed, sending the country into the Great Depression. (Lafayette Parish Clerk of Court Louis J. Perret.)

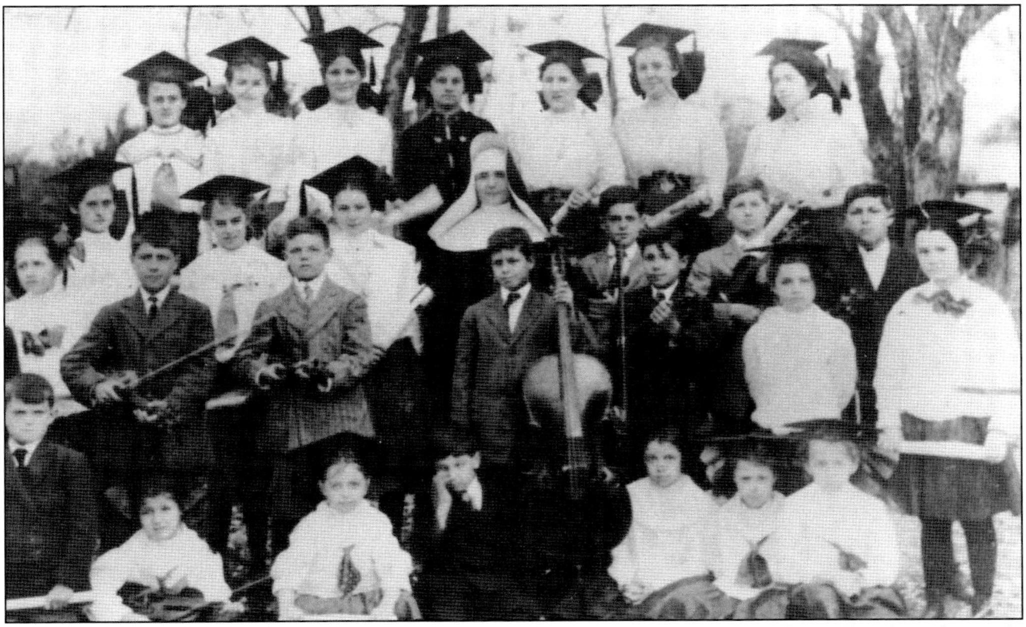

This class of budding orchestra musicians attended band class at St. Cecilia School in the early 1900s. This group includes, in no particular order, Jeanne Bernard, Stella Labbe, Beulah Girouard, Nettie Malagarie, Rita Melancon, Eva Girouard, Nellie Bernard, Louisa Bernard, Stella Girouard, George DeLaureal (who became a doctor and married Marie Ducresy), George, Curley, Allen, Roy, Lionel, Willie, Manning and Marie Louise Billeaud, Carmen and Todd DeLaureal, Hugh Billeaud, Hilda Billeaud, Walter Comeaux Sr., Veda and Louise Billeaud, and Bernice Stromer. (Courtesy Lafayette Parish Clerk of Court Louis J. Perret.)

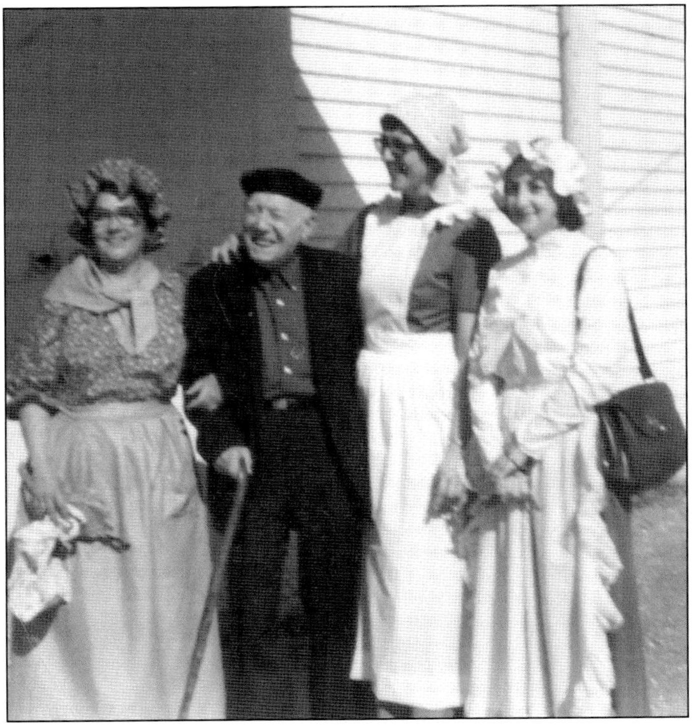

Sacred Heart Church pastor Fr. P.G. John Kemps is pictured here in the company of Polly Billeaud Garber (left), Clarisse Vollenweider (third from left), and ? DeLaureal, in costumes at the annual community fair. In the background is the old gym at St. Cecilia School that was constructed in 1935 and burned on the night of October 8, 1981. Shortly thereafter, Sacred Heart parish began a restoration campaign that included a new air-conditioned facility and gymnasium. (Ida Belle Girouard Pesson.)

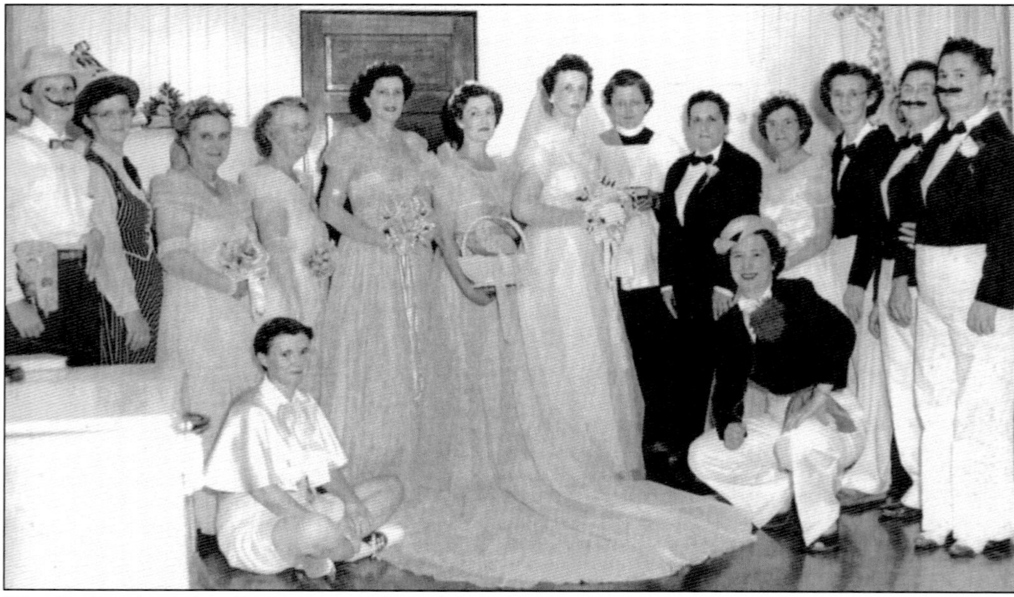

The St. Cecilia School's Parent Teacher Club held a fundraiser in 1952, putting on an "All Woman Shotgun Wedding." Pictured are, from left to right, Carmen Comeaux (sheriff), Della Landry Prejean, Amanda Girouard, Mrs. Willie Garber, Lola Girouard, and Florence Bonin (bridesmaids), Vida B. Girouard (bride), Estelle Morvant (priest), Pauline Langlinais (groom), Bella LeBlanc, Jeanette Girouard, Delussia Duhon, and Henrietta Heber. In the front are Martha Langlinais (left) and Irma Mullins. (Velma L. Reaux.)

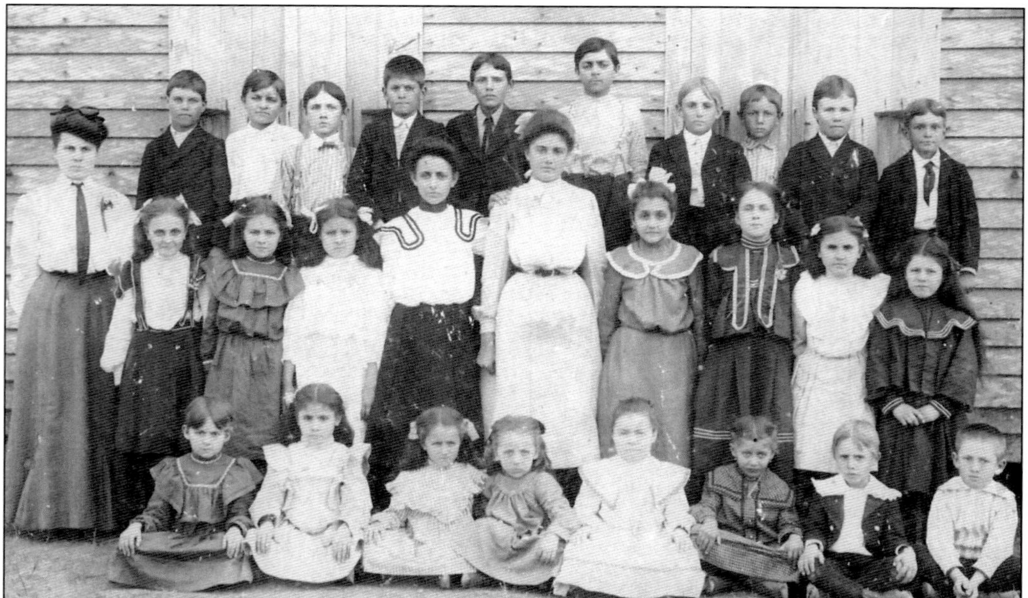

Pictured here in 1904 with their teacher Mrs. Reeves are Willie Garber, J. Melancon, A. Melancon, L. Fabre, M. Thomassie, O. Melancon, Eraste Landry, ? Melancon, O. Girouard, E. Bourque, E. Melancon, S. Smith, N. Melancon, A. Cabral, M. Thomassie, ? Fabre, E. Landry, L. Smith, C. Vallot, C. Melancon, L. Landry, I. Melancon, Lelia Morvant, B. Garber, U.B. Landry, Allen Fabre, and one unidentified young woman. (Anita Legget.)

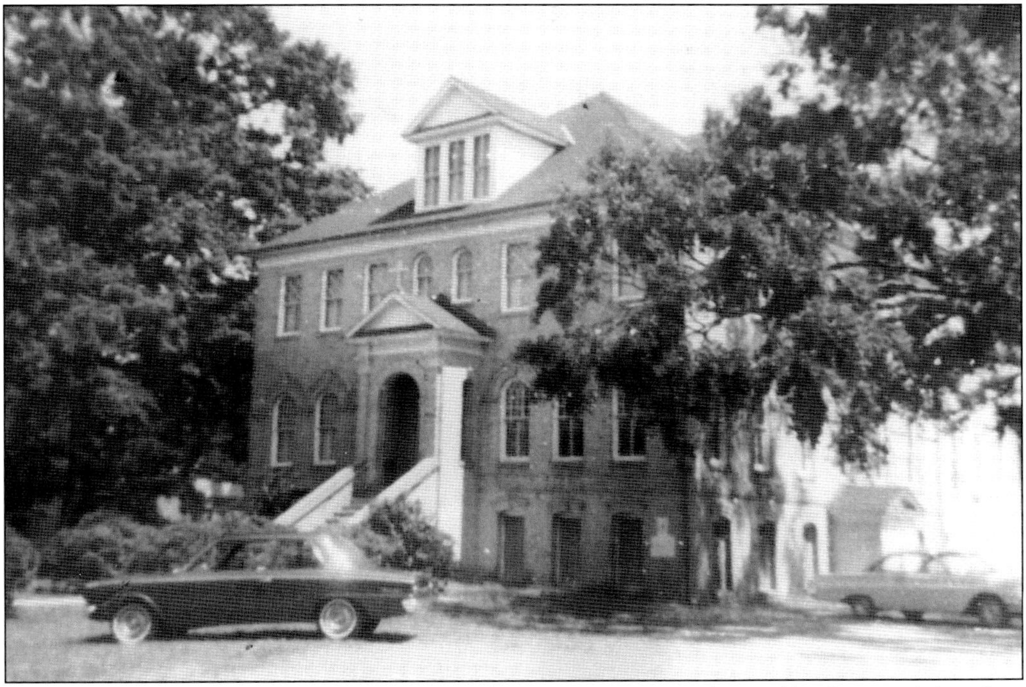

St. Cecilia School was built in 1909 at a cost of $25,000, on property donated by the town's founding father, Valsin Broussard. The Billeaud Company and family members have been benefactors of the school's chapel since the 1800s. (Author's collection.)

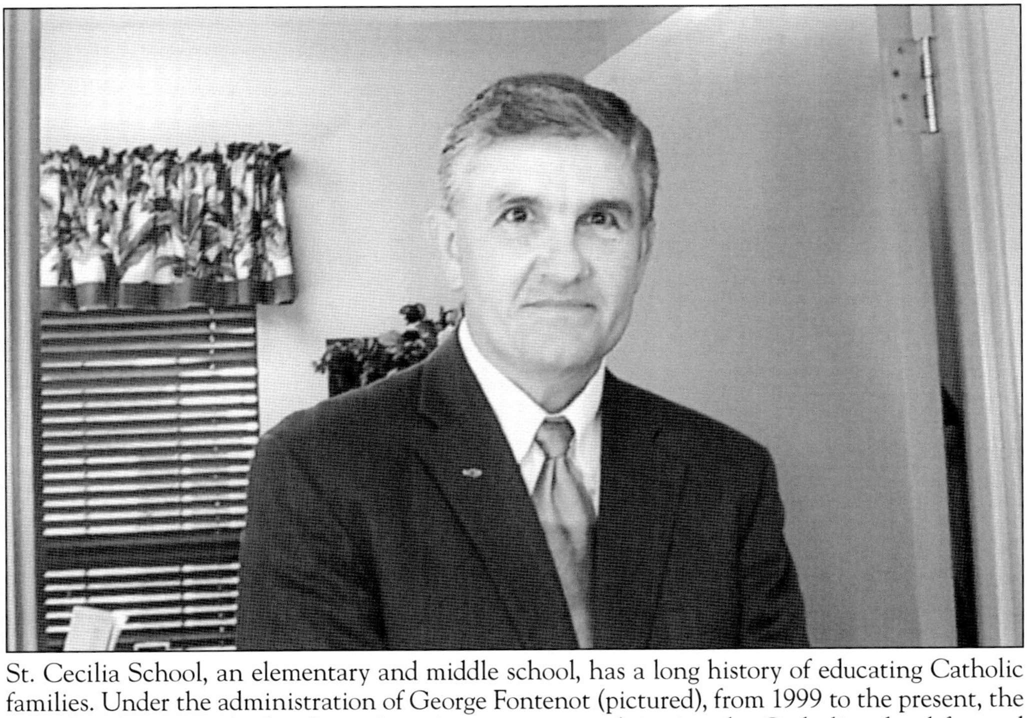

St. Cecilia School, an elementary and middle school, has a long history of educating Catholic families. Under the administration of George Fontenot (pictured), from 1999 to the present, the school underwent a $4.5-million, four-phase expansion, bringing the Catholic school forward into the 21st century. (Author's collection.)

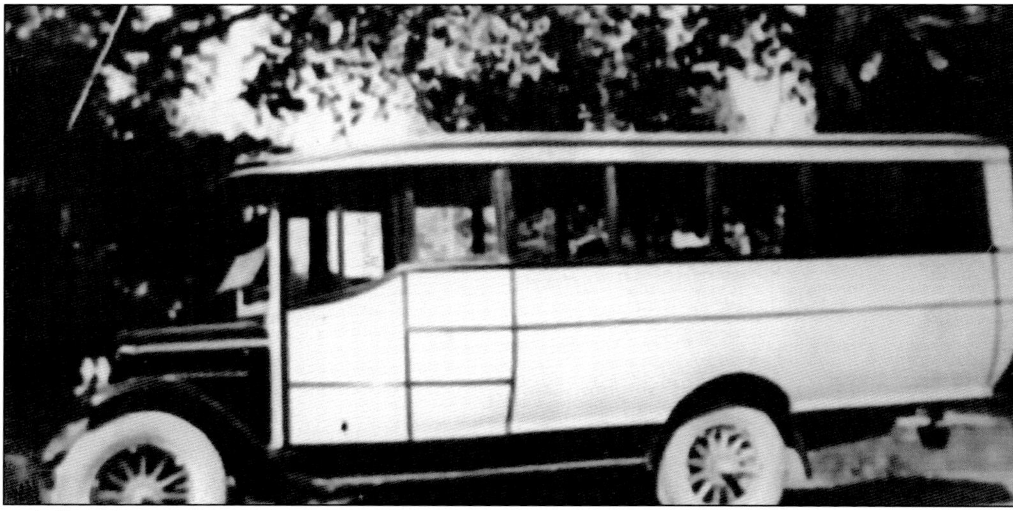

Cabill and Leo Boumans were owners of Boumans Lumber Yard, one of two lumber companies operating in downtown Broussard before World War II. Cabill built the first wooden school bus in 1930, which transported public school students. (Phyllis Boumans.)

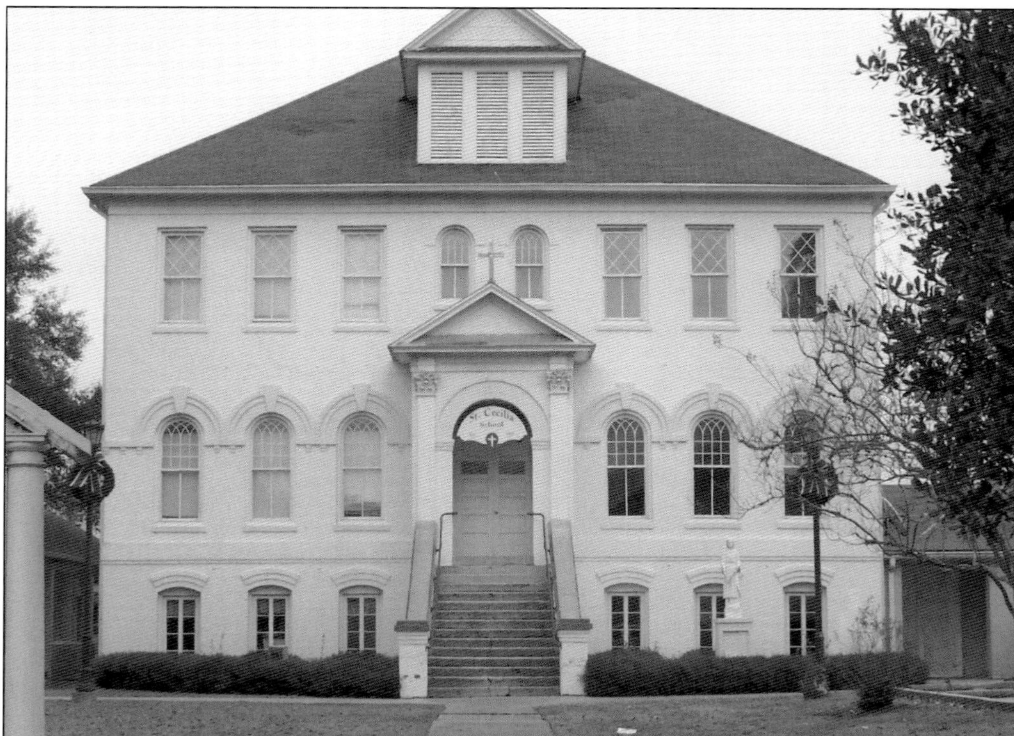

Listed in the National Register of Historic Places, Broussard's only Catholic elementary and middle school, St. Cecilia's, is located Main Street. St. Cecilia School remains open to this day. In 1964, the high school department was shut down by order of the bishop of Lafayette in an initiative to consolidate all Catholic high schools. The Sisters of Divine Providence remained on staff until 1974, at which time they returned to San Antonio, Texas, and lay teachers took over for elementary and middle school classes. (Author's collection.)

Sister Edwina, a nun of the Order of Divine Providence, is pictured here on the grounds of Sacred Heart Church with Bernard Duhon in February 1958 during a rare event for Louisiana—fluffy snow that actually stuck to the ground. Emma Bernard Hollier fondly recalls Sister Edwina as having taught her in first grade at St. Cecilia. Sister Edwina eventually left to teach elsewhere, returning during Hollier's senior year, again as her teacher. (Emma Bernard Hollier.)

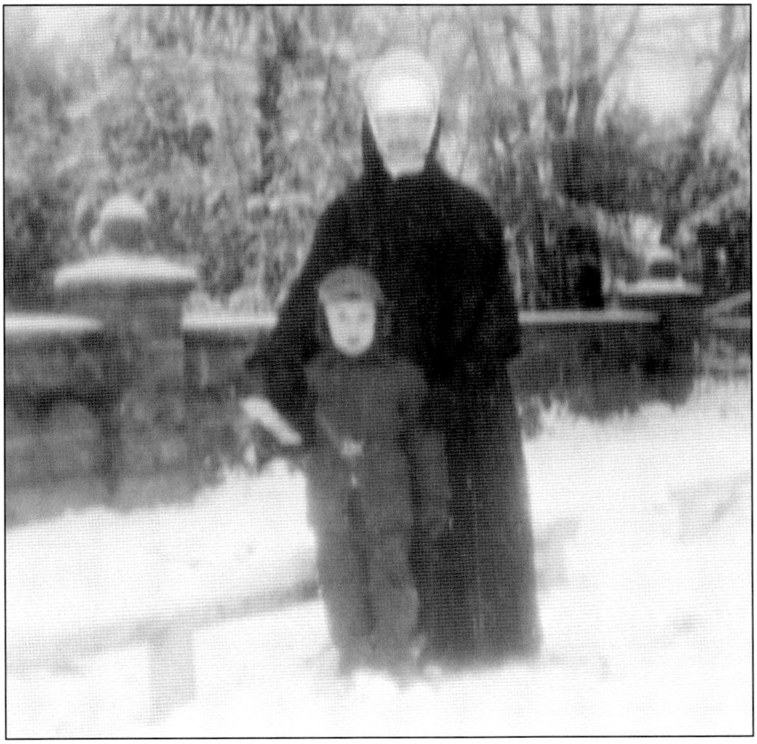

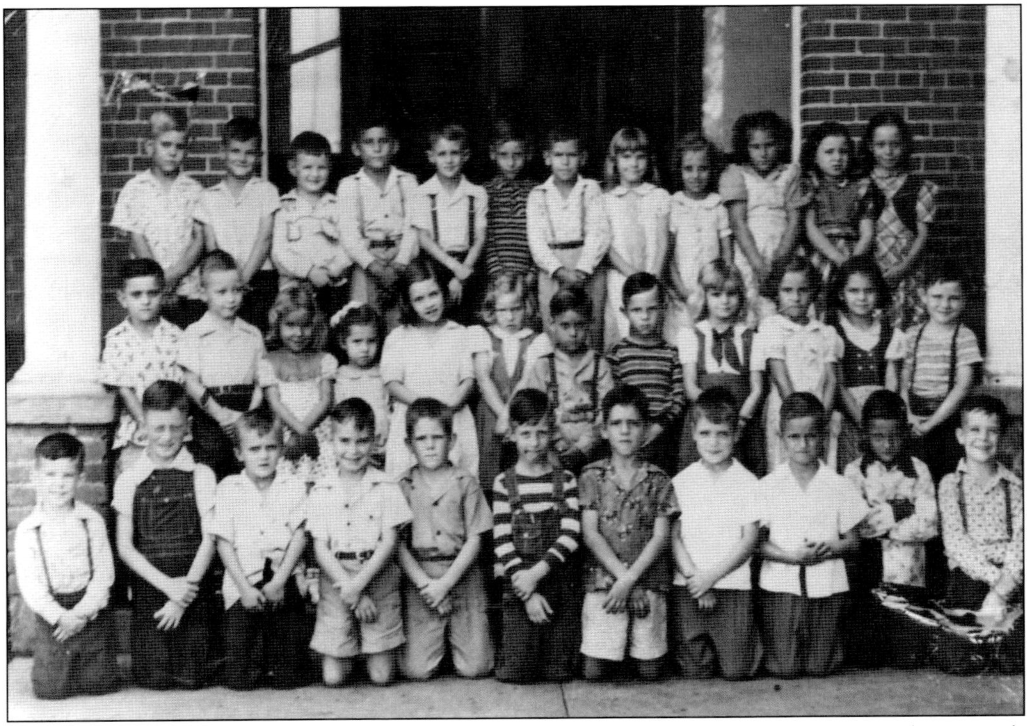

The 1947 Broussard Junior High class is pictured here. Joseph Trahan is on the second row, sixth from the right; and Ulysses Trahan is fourth from left on the third row. The other students in the photograph are not identified. (Courtesy Lafayette Parish Clerk of Court Louis J. Perret.)

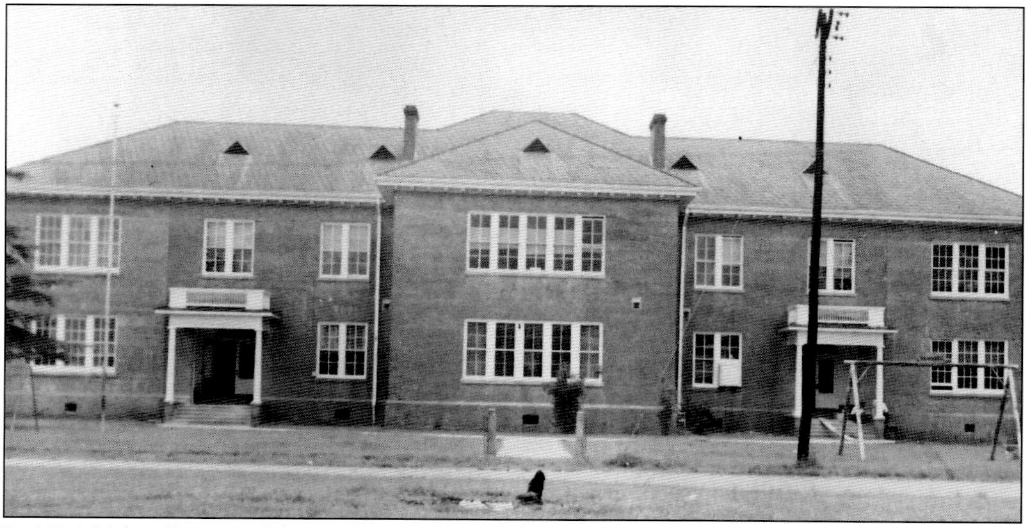

In 1884, Valsin Broussard donated property on East Main Street for Broussard's first public school. The two-room public school building was donated by the Farmers Alliance. J.W. Faulk was the school's first principal and later became Lafayette Parish's superintendent of schools. In the beginning there were two teachers; as attendance grew, a larger building and a plot of land were acquired, but at a different location, 406 East Madison. By 1916, that two-story frame building was at capacity. After a spirited contest, a bond issue for $30,000 passed for a new building. In 1983, pressure of student population and modernization necessitated building a new school on Morgan Street. (City of Broussard archives.)

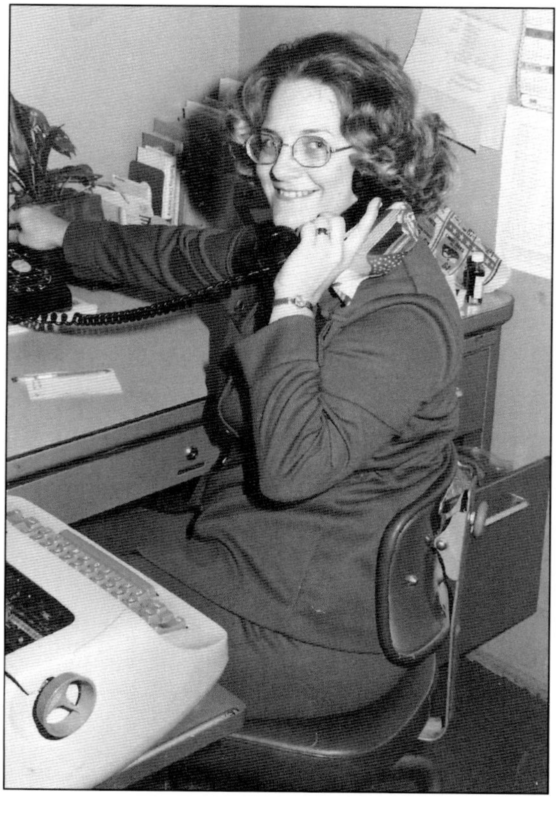

Velma Langlinais Reaux, a graduate of St. Cecilia School, served as Broussard Middle School's secretary from 1965 to 1995. She worked under principal A.J. Antoine's administration. Velma's father, Louis Langlinais, was once the chief of the Broussard Fire Department. (Velma L. Reaux.)

Louis Billeaud and his wife, Lucile Corne Billeaud, were the parents of 10 children—nine girls and one boy. Of the nine girls, five became nuns, three of whom belonged to the order of Sisters of Divine Providence and taught at St. Cecilia School. The other two girls joined a cloistered order. (City of Broussard archives.)

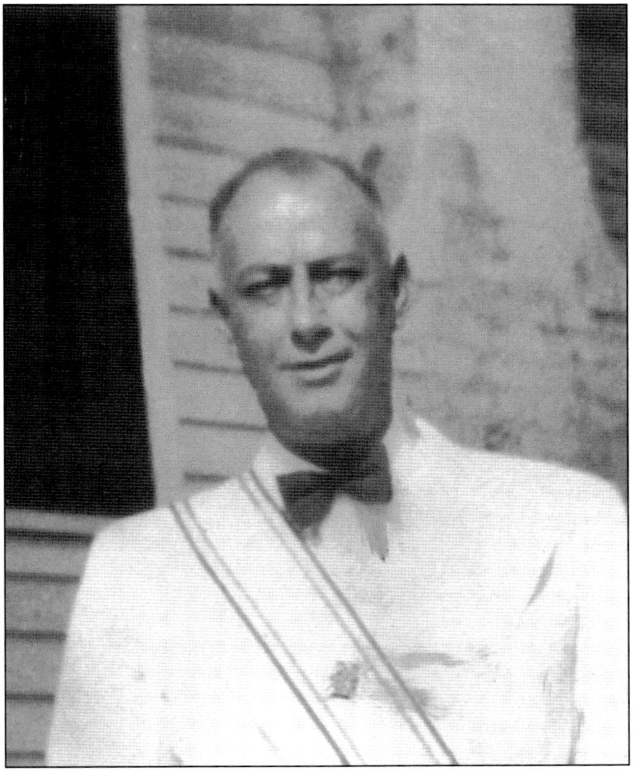

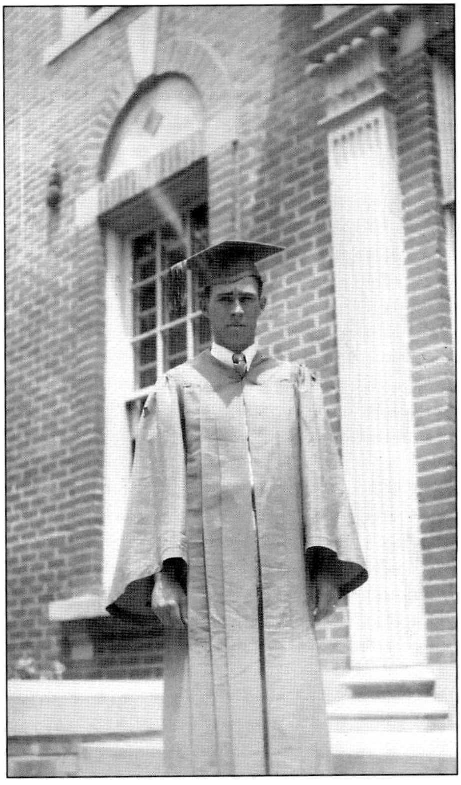

Henry Langlinais, born on February 19, 1921, graduated from Broussard High School. He later operated a dairy farm for many years in the La Neuville area. Following his retirement, Langlinais worked as a custodian for 19 years at Comeaux High School. Ellis Savoy, a cousin of his, was the school principal during those years. (Author's collection.)

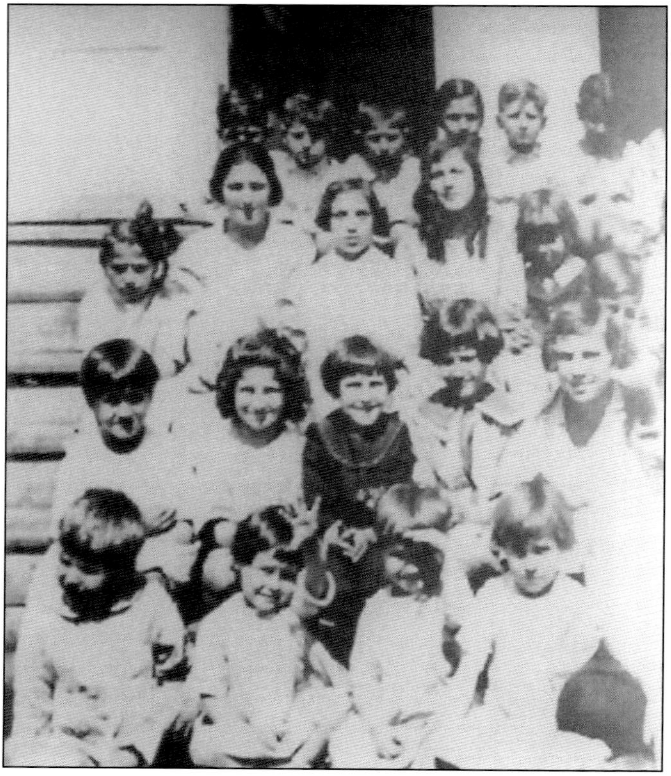

Attie Talbot Girouard (second row, second from left) attended grammar school in the Pillette community in a one-room schoolhouse between Lafayette and Broussard, now along the Verot School Road. Homework was done by the light of a kerosene lantern. Attie later married Charles Girouard, Broussard's mayor for 16 years. (Attie Talbot Girouard.)

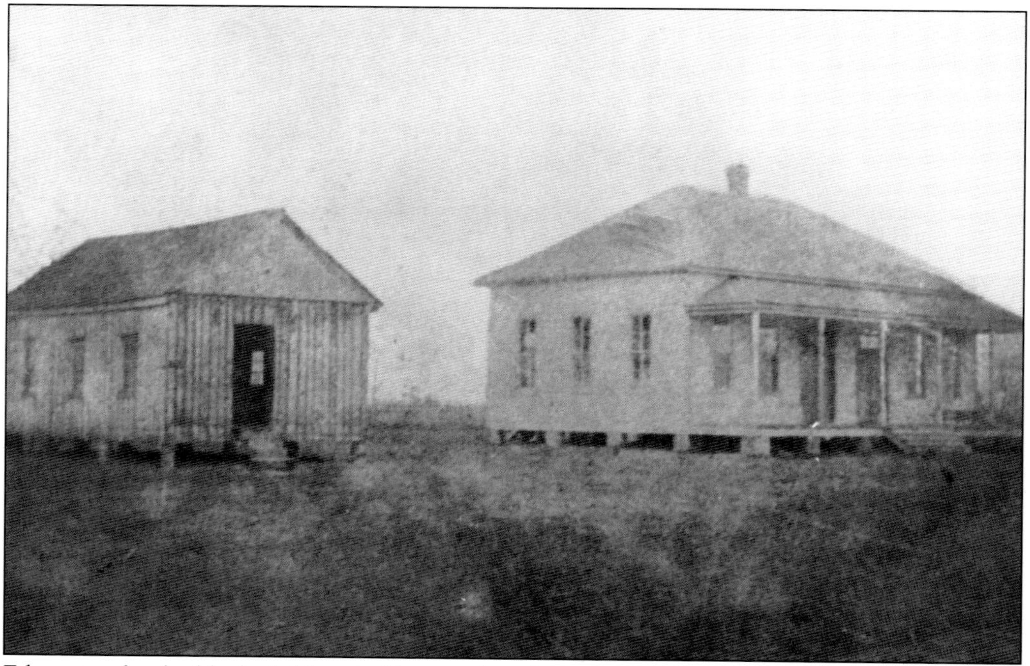

Education for the black children in Broussard made its appearance in the late 1920s with an old schoolhouse on Tolson Road. The earliest prototype of homeschooling took place at the home of Anna Flugence, where her family and others received tutoring twice a week. (Lafayette Parish Clerk of Court Louis J. Perret.)

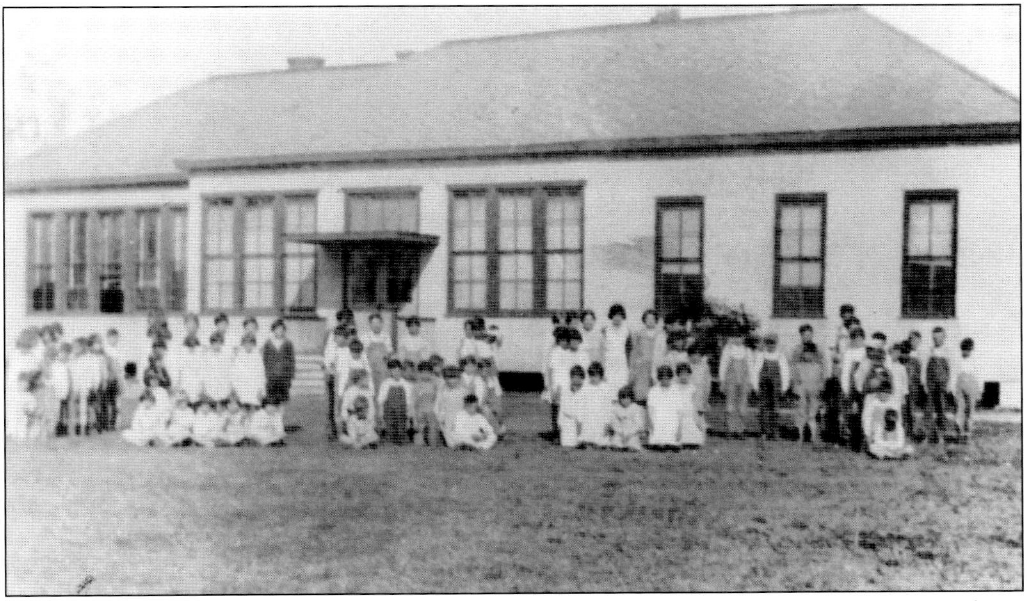

A small wood-frame school existed on Verot School Road from 1915 to 1940. The students shown here attended in the 1930s. The school was located on the corner of Verot School Road and New Flanders Road (now Ambassador Caffery Parkway). (Lafayette Parish Clerk of Court Louis J. Perret.)

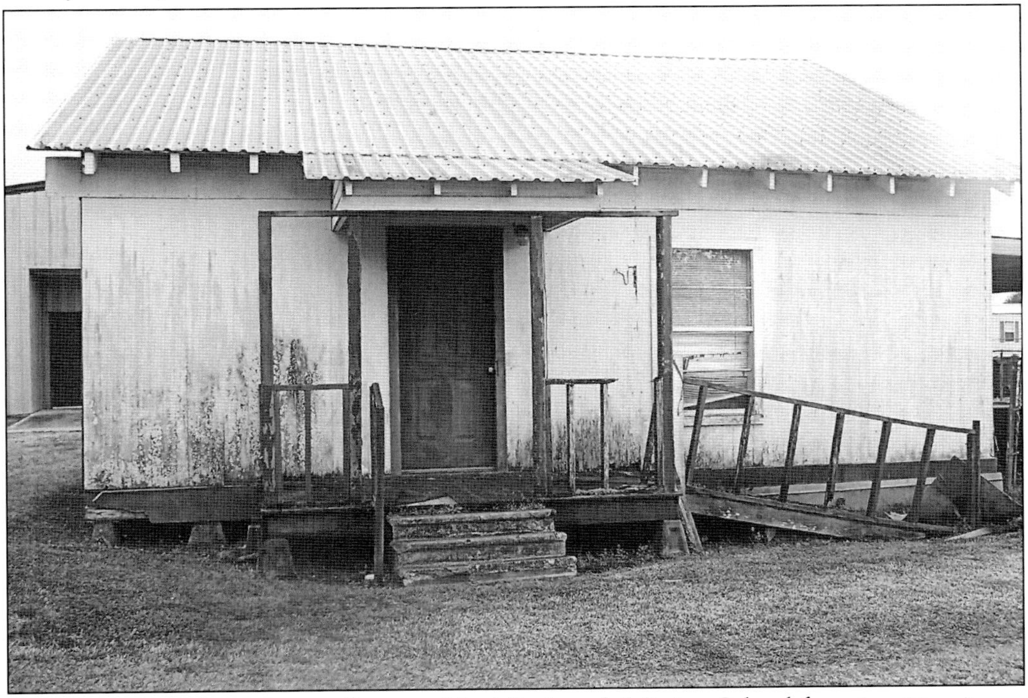

Before the days of integration, Broussard had St. Joseph Mission School for minorities; it was built on the grounds of Sacred Heart parish through the efforts of Mother Katherine Drexel. The small building was moved to St. Joseph parish in 1953. At that time, a rectory was constructed on the grounds along with another building donated by Drexel that was moved to the new site. (Author's collection.)

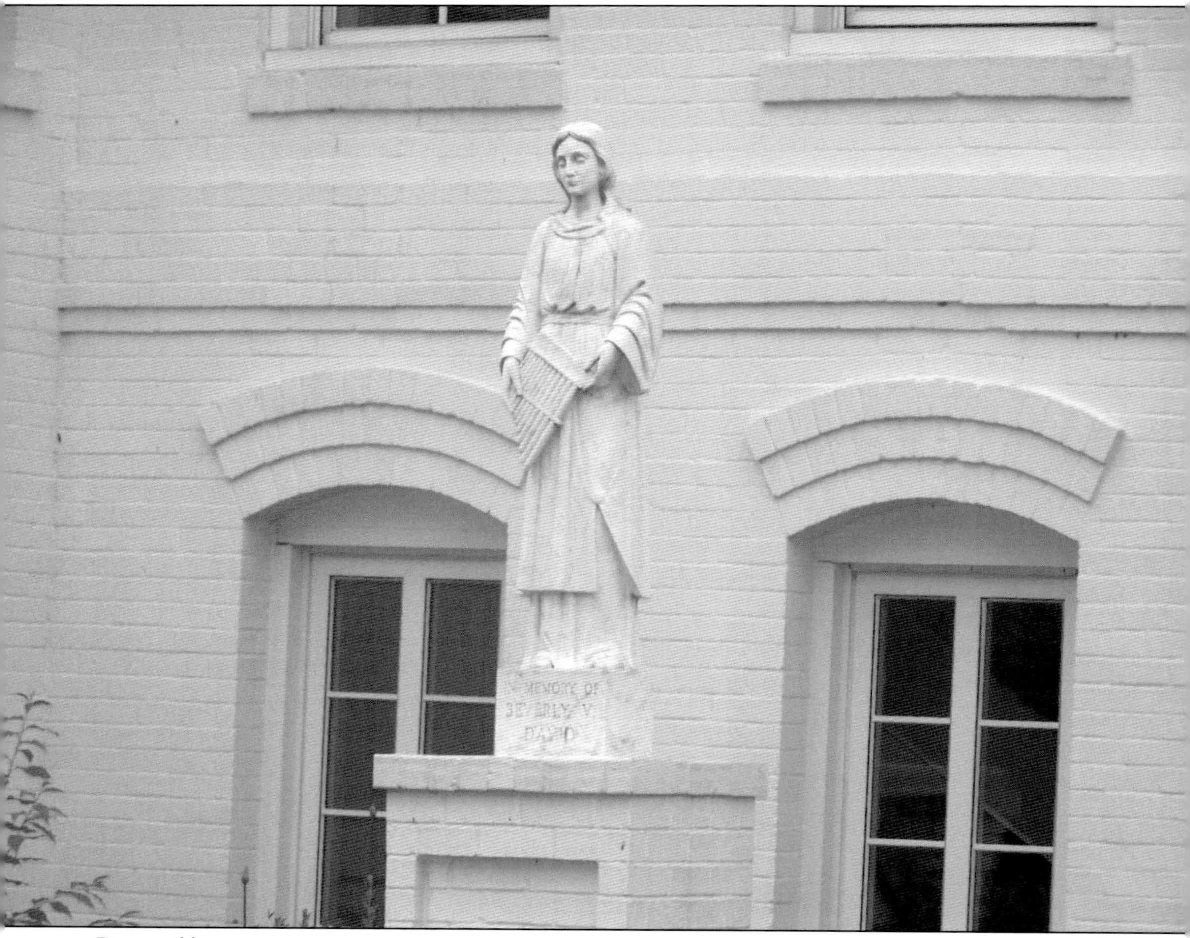

Pictured here is a monument representing St. Cecilia erected on the St. Cecilia School grounds in memory of Beverly V. David. St. Cecilia, a Christian from birth, was born in the second or third century; at an early age, she dedicated her life to God and made a vow of chastity. Cecilia was forced to marry the pagan Valerian. Cecilia's prayers were answered on her wedding day, as both Valerian and his brother Tiburtius were converted to Christianity and baptized by Pope Urban I. The Romans executed them, as Christianity was illegal. The executioners made two attempts to take her life. She is the acclaimed patron saint of both music and the blind, although it is not known whether or not she was blind herself. The Catholic Church commemorates her feast day on November 22. (Author's collection.)

Five

Commerce in New Broussardville

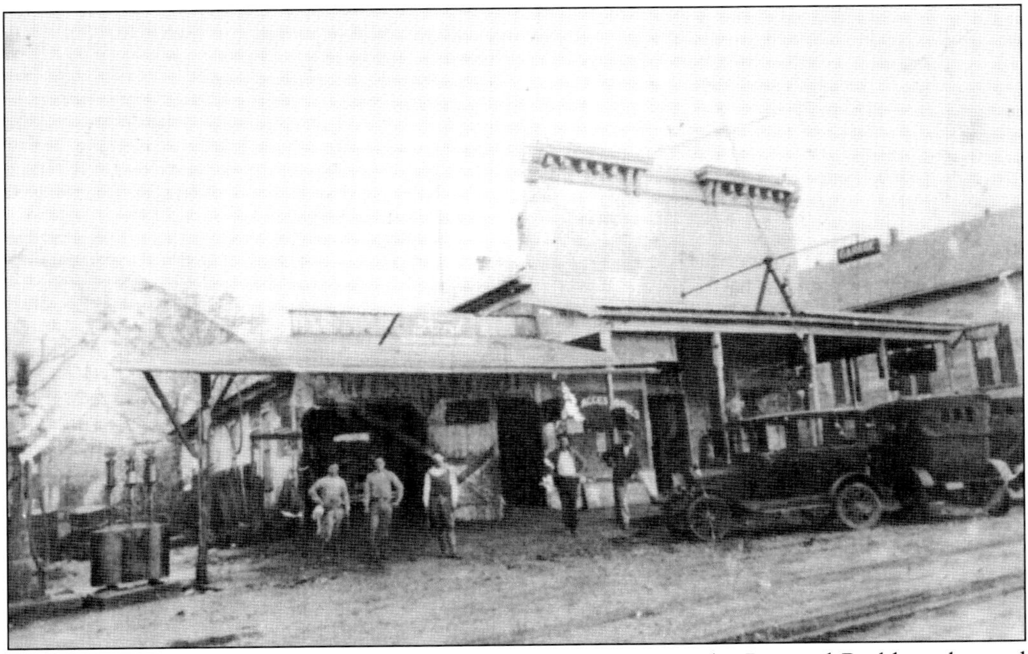

The city of Broussard's oldest standing commercial structure is the Bernard Building, located on Main Street. Its owner, Demas Guillaume "William" Bernard, and his descendants have continuously run enterprises from the building since 1902. (City of Broussard archives.)

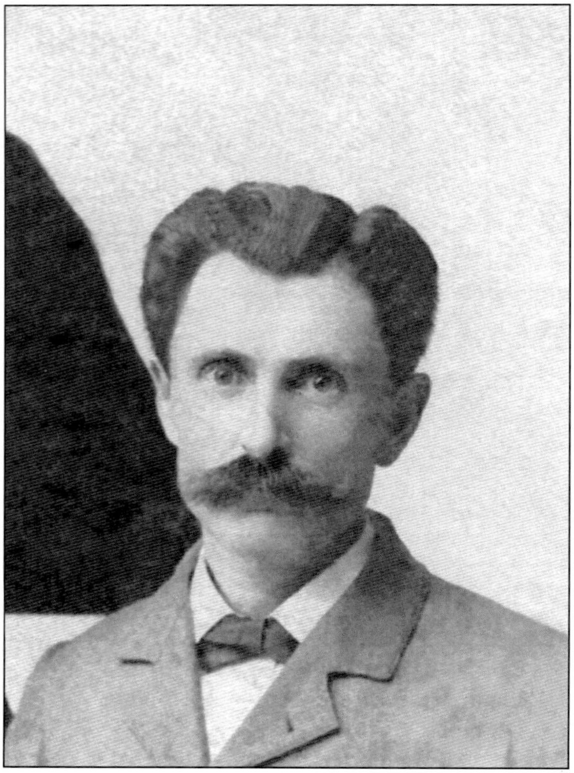

Demas Guillaume "William" Bernard built one of the first general stores in 1902, with an attached blacksmith shop in the rear. Upon Bernard's death in the 1920s, his son-in-law Denis Bernard purchased the store. In order to service the needs of the townspeople, Denis added a gas station, small repair shop, and saloon that were connected to the original structure. (City of Broussard archives.)

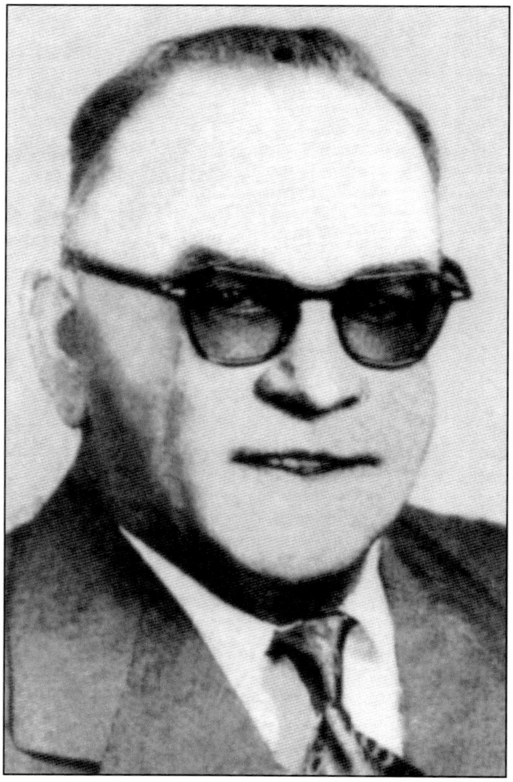

The Bernard family legacy passed down from Demas Guillaume "William" Bernard to son-in-law Denis Bernard (1893–1960) and on down the line to his son Louis Denis "L.D." Bernard (1919–2005), who is pictured here. Currently, David Bernard, an architect, is the fourth-generation business owner working in the Bernard Building. (City of Broussard archives.)

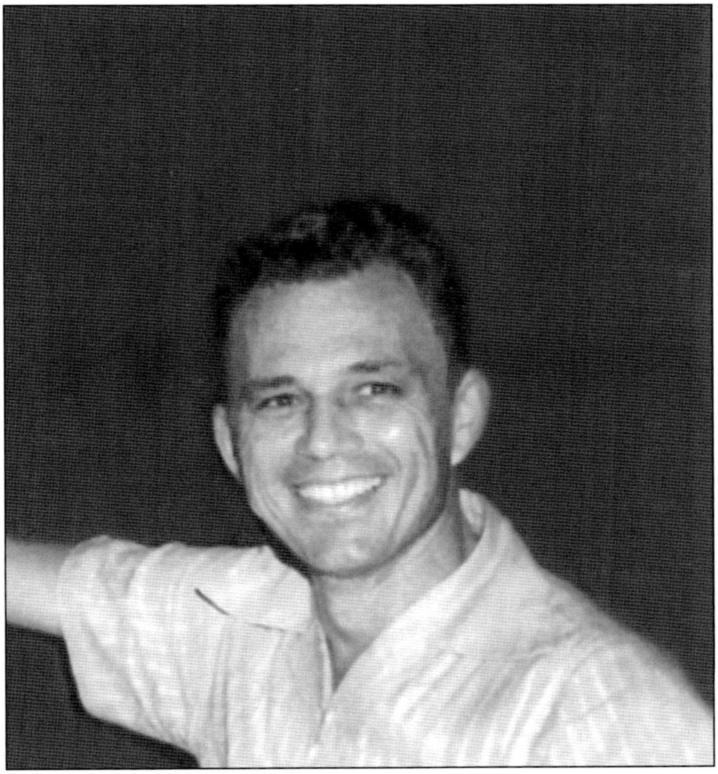

L.D. Bernard was the third of eight children, and an only boy quite spoiled by his siblings. He is the father of David Bernard and married to Linda Bell Bernard, whose mother, Marian Billeaud Bernard, was the third child in a family of eight and the only girl. Coincidences abound in those families. (City of Broussard archives.)

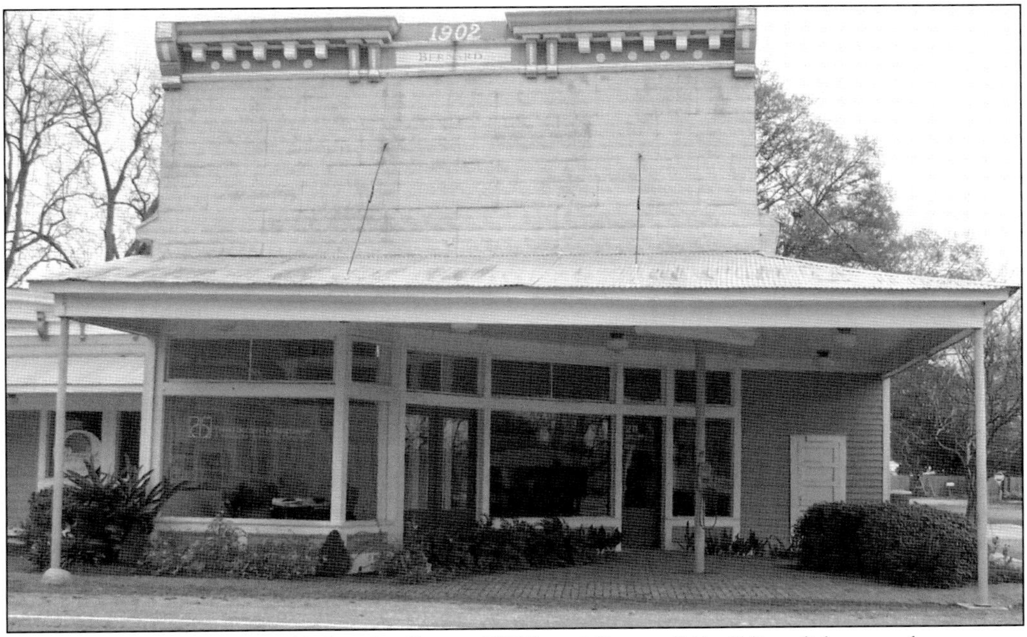

David Bernard's great-grandfather Guillaume "William" Bernard's' building did not undergo many physical changes over the years. In 1930, the front part of the structure and its corners were cut out, and some damage to the embossed tin was replaced but with a different gauge. In 2014, the building received a fresh coat of paint and an additional office that serves as rental property for an insurance agency. (Author's collection.)

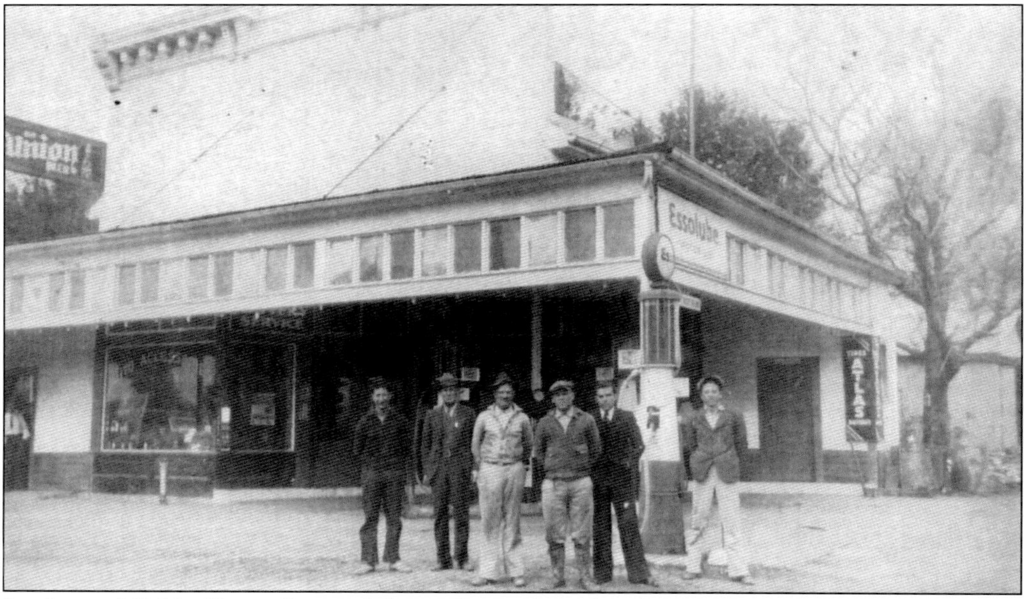

In the mid-1930s, Denis Bernard (center) stands with a few men outside Bernard's Service Station, a one-stop shop for gasoline and automobile repair. The Esso gasoline pumps had clear glass domes so customers could gauge the amount of fuel being pumped. Back then, customers purchased motor lube packaged in metal cans and could purchase Atlas tires and batteries as well. (Mark Ste Marie.)

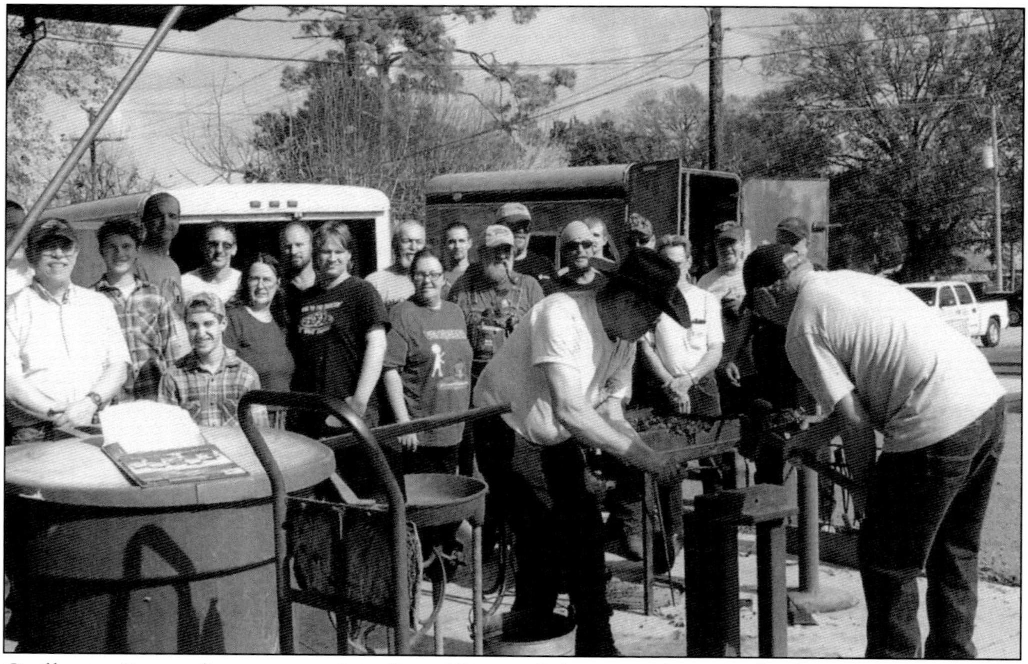

Guillaume Bernard's great-grandson David Bernard also traces his roots back to Valsin Broussard, the town founder. The buildings erected in 1902 aptly serve as David's architectural firm, and the still-operable blacksmith shop fulfills the need for David to practice his ancient craft, as he is a skilled blacksmith and metalworker. David, in cap and glasses on far left, looks on as Jerry Baker, local blacksmith, teaches a weekend hammer workshop. (Author's collection.)

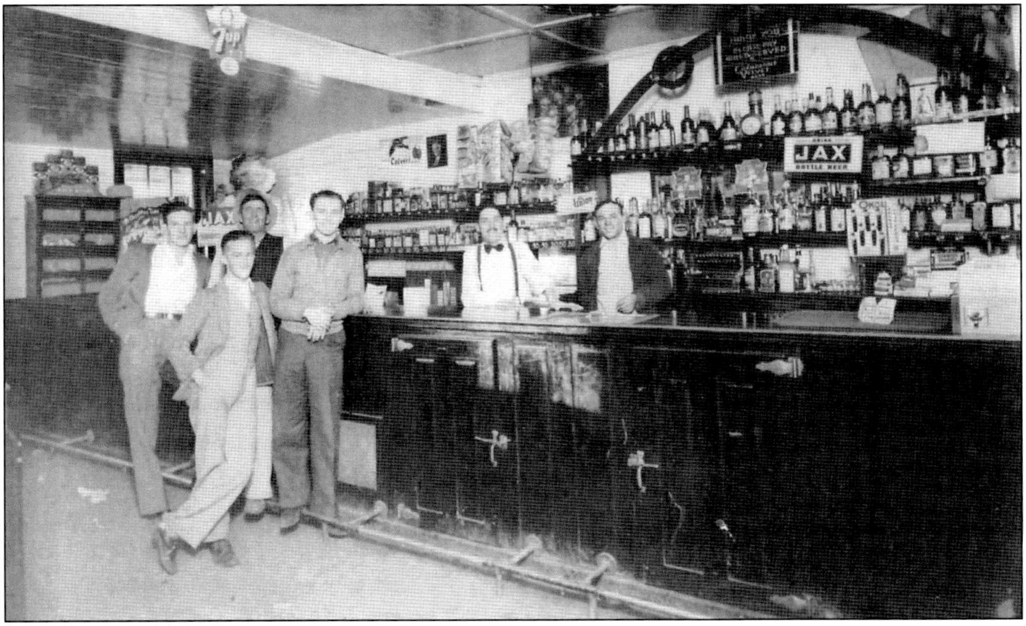

After working hours, menfolk would stop by Bernard's Saloon, operated by Denis Bernard on the opposite side of Bernard's Auto Supply, to enjoy a cold bottle of Union beer and play a game or two of pool. Bernard is to the right of the unidentified bartender in 1937; note the Jax beer sign, advertising another popular beer back in the day, brewed in New Orleans, Louisiana. The brass foot rail provided a rest for weary feet. (Mark Ste. Marie.)

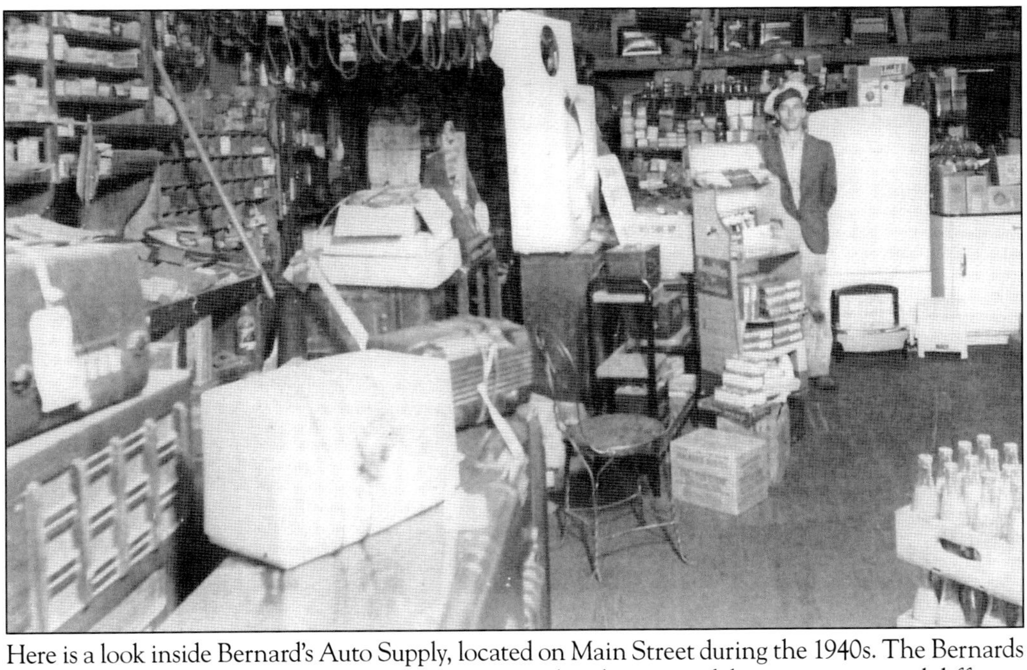

Here is a look inside Bernard's Auto Supply, located on Main Street during the 1940s. The Bernards were a resourceful bunch of guys who did what it took to be successful, operating several different types of businesses, from a mechanic shop and small engine repair to lawn mower rental and repair and the first telephone company in town. The town taxi, owned by Aniston Ewing, would stay parked in front of the building while waiting for a call out. (Mark Ste. Marie.)

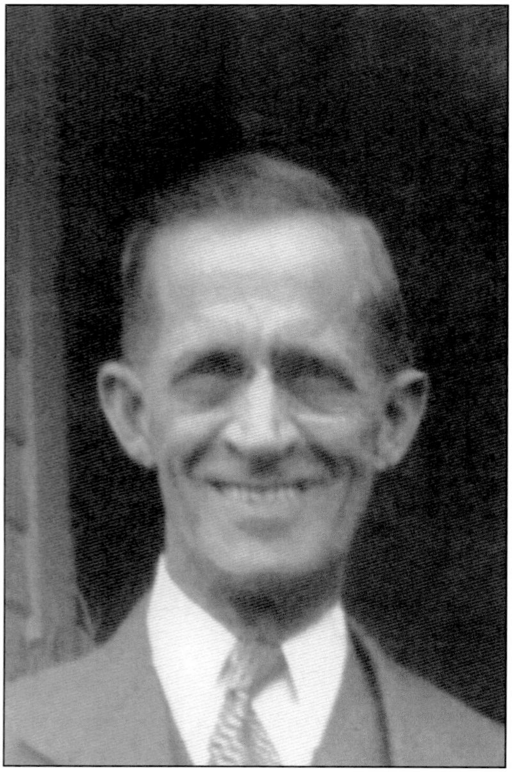

The Ducrest Building, at 101 West Main Street, was constructed by Gustave St. Julien and Edmond Comeaux, who owned and operated it as a general store until 1910. Pictured is Thomas Lucien "Nonc Jack" Ducrest, Broussard's first pharmacist, reopened the building in 1924, and it also served as a post office for many years. The building was later bought out by Lucien's son Francis, who leased it to George Debaillon, a pharmacist. (Lafayette Parish Clerk of Court Louis J. Perret.)

Felix Ducrest stands beside a poster of his uncle and doppelgänger Louis Felix Ducrest, who was the first casualty from Broussard in World War II—a sailor aboard the USS *Arizona* who died at Pearl Harbor on December 7, 1941. Louis Felix is remembered as a happy-go-lucky boy, the eighth of 11 children born to Lucien Ducrest, Broussard town pharmacist and postmaster, and his wife, Regina St. Julien. American Legion Post No. 69 in Lafayette is named after Louis Felix Ducrest, a 1937 graduate of St. Cecilia School. (Author's collection.)

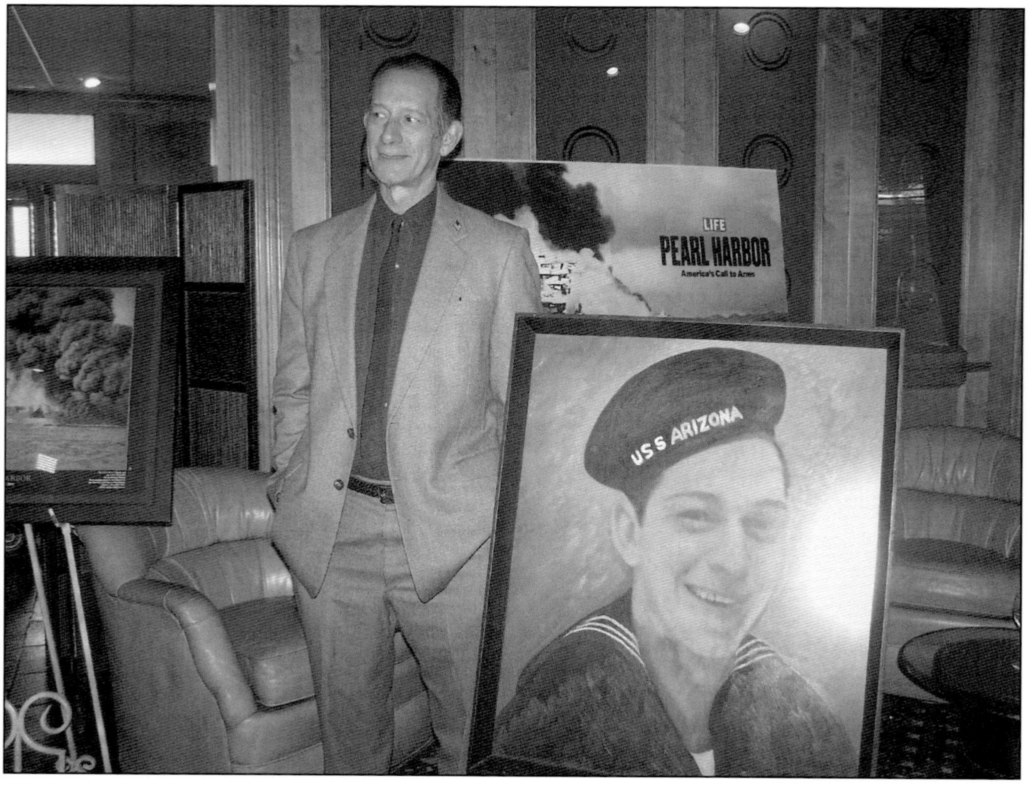

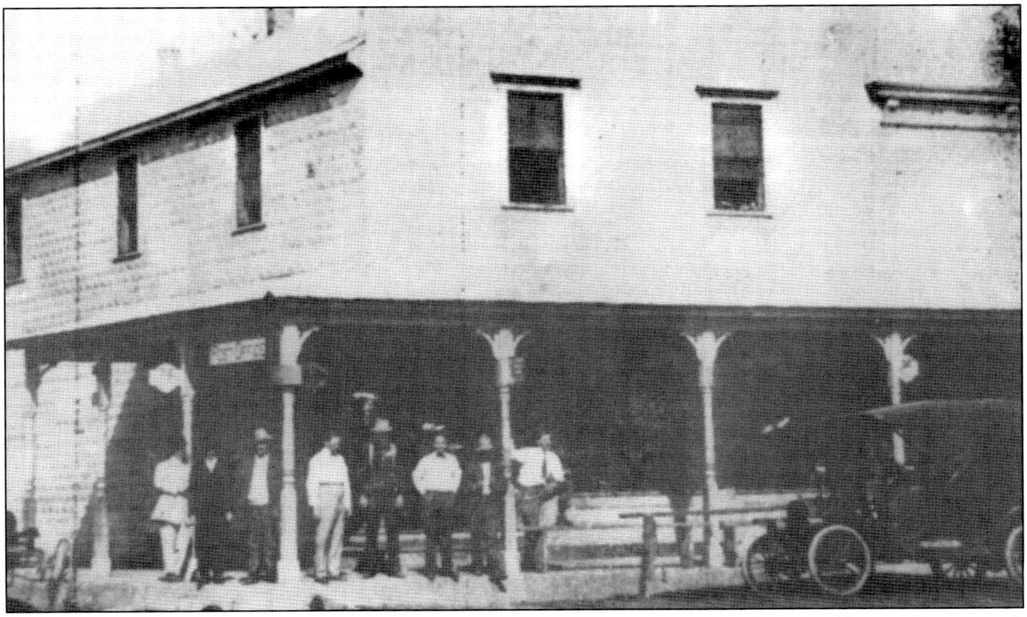

A group of menfolk congregates in front of the Ducrest Drugstore and post office in Broussard. The town's first post office was established in 1878 with J.B. Malagarie as the first postmaster. This scene took place in 1903, as one can tell by Martin Girouard's Ford Model T driving down Morgan Avenue, which was just a dirt road. The post office, barbershop, and saloons were popular gathering places to shoot the breeze. (Lafayette Parish Clerk of Court Louis J. Perret.)

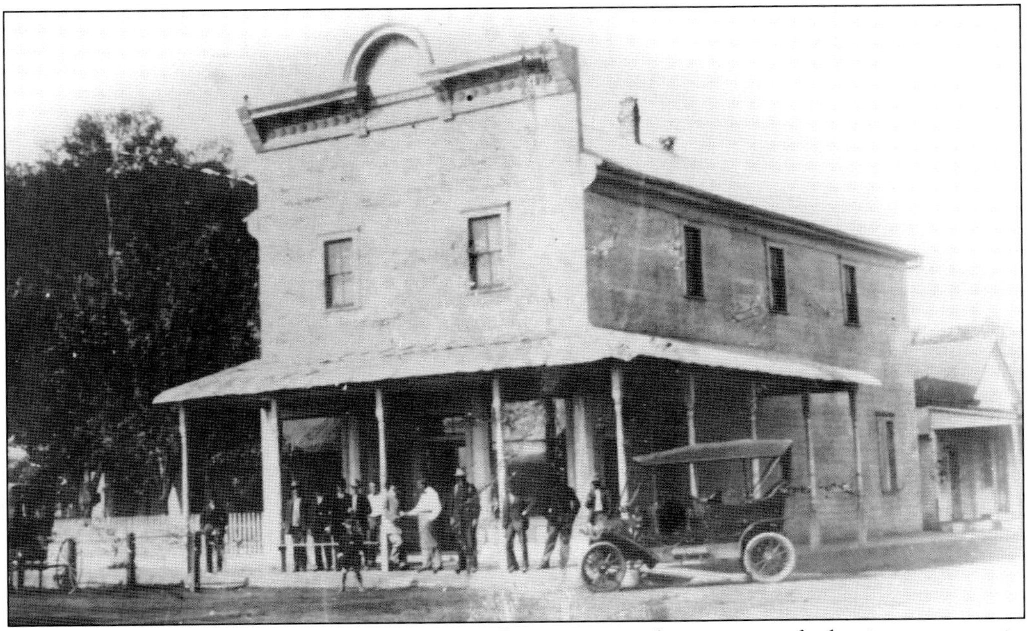

The L.J. Landry building was popular as an early-morning gathering space for business owners in the early 1900s. Pictured here are, from left to right, Joseph LeBlanc (merchant), Raoul Malagarie, L.J. Landry (store owner), Clement Bernard (owner of the Model T Ford), Edmond Comeaux Sr., Drozin Dubois, Eulice Bernard, L. Duhon (small boy), and Maxie Landry. (Lafayette Parish Clerk of Court Louis J. Perret.)

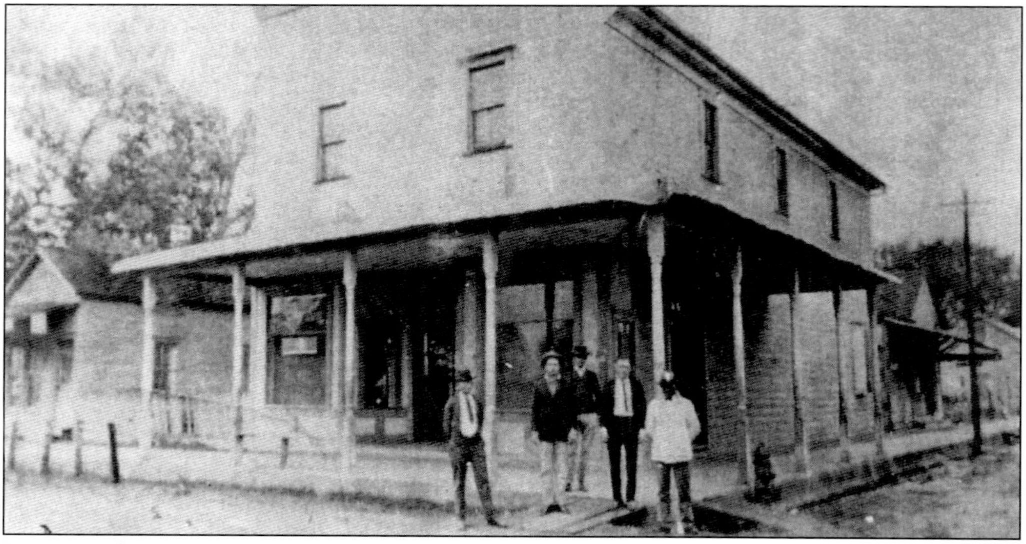

In 1903, Thomas Lucien Ducrest constructed the Ducrest Building, located at 101 West Main Street, which served as a general store owned and operated by J. Gustave St. Julien and Edmond Comeaux until 1910. Ducrest reopened the building in 1924 for his practice as the first town pharmacist. The building also served the community as home to the local post office for many years. It was later bought out by Thomas Ducrest's son Francis Ducrest, who leased to another pharmacist. Gloria Ducrest's family leased it to the Lafayette Parish Library as the Broussard Branch until 2015, when the parish built a larger library on La Neuville Road. (Both, Lafayette Parish Clerk of Court Louis J. Perret.)

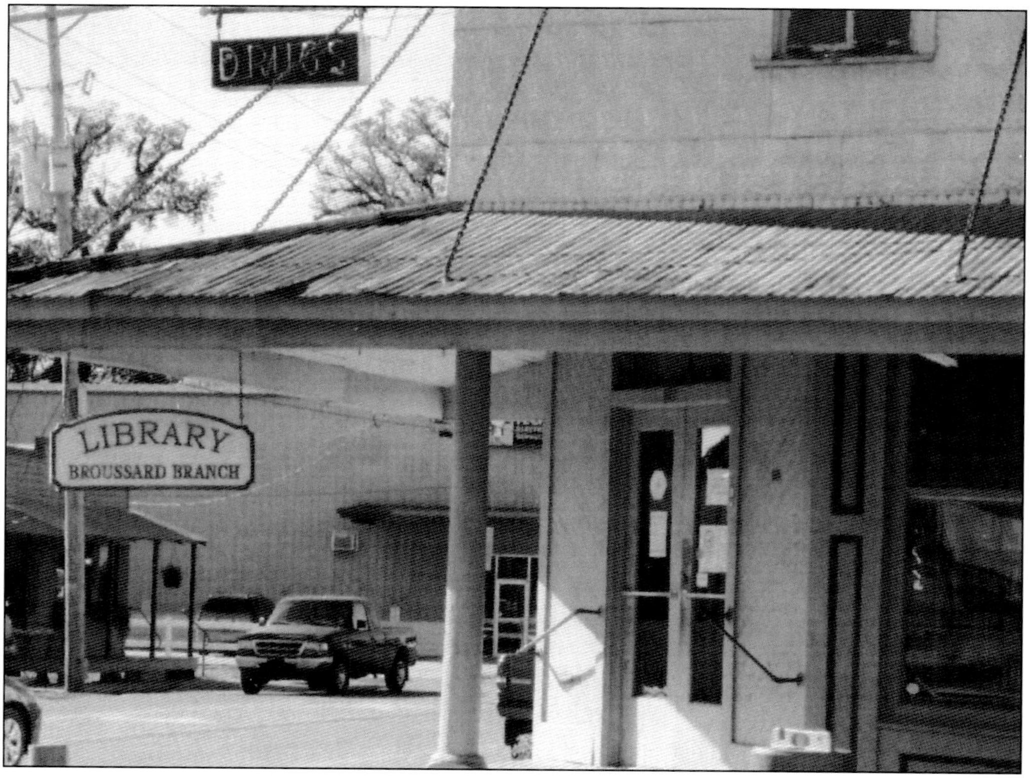

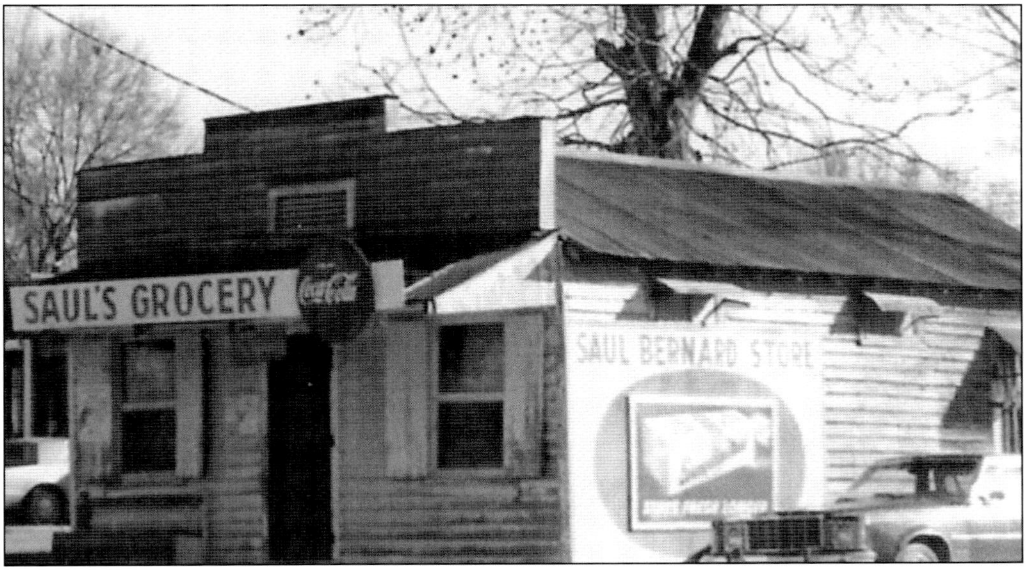

Saul Bernard and his wife, Agnes Reaux Bernard, were longtime proprietors of Saul's Grocery, which was adjacent to Bonin's Oak Bar on Main Street. Much of the quaintness and charm of Broussard was reflected in this small business establishment. The general merchandise store kept a well-stocked candy counter, which proved to be a delight for youngsters coming into the shop with their parents after school. Saul's Grocery sold everything from groceries to piece goods. It was probably the first fast-food outlet in town, as the grocery also sold cold-cut sandwiches. (Liz Girard.)

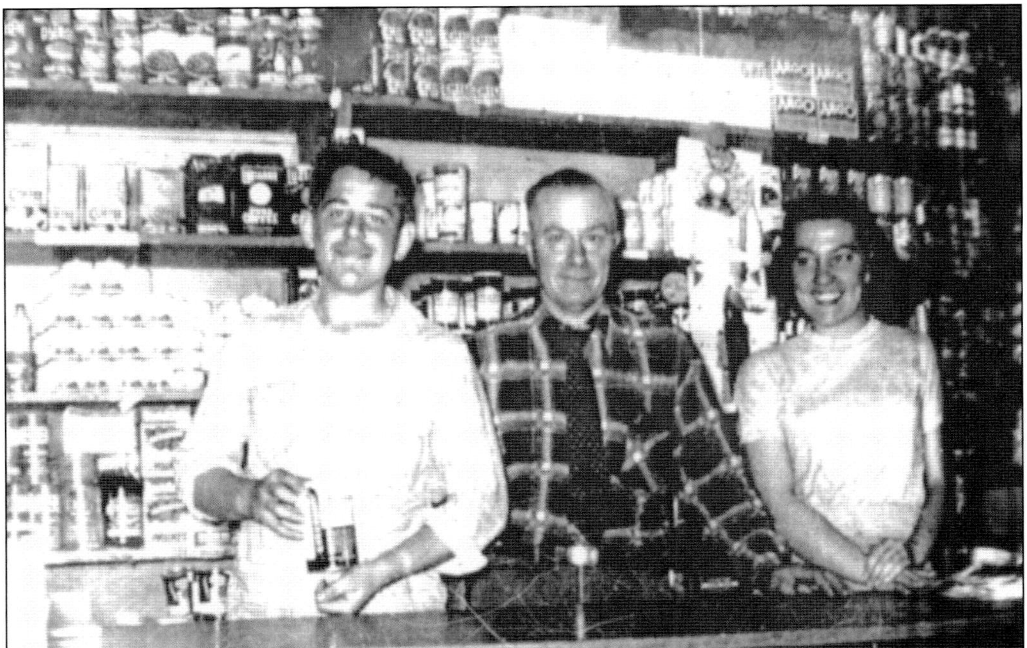

Saul G. Bernard, his wife, Agnes Bernard, and their son Huey Jude Bernard are pictured here inside their family-run mercantile store located on Highway 182, known today as Main Street. The shelving behind Huey's head holds canned goods and local coffees Mello Joy and Luzianne, popular brands still found on supermarket shelves. (Liz Girard.)

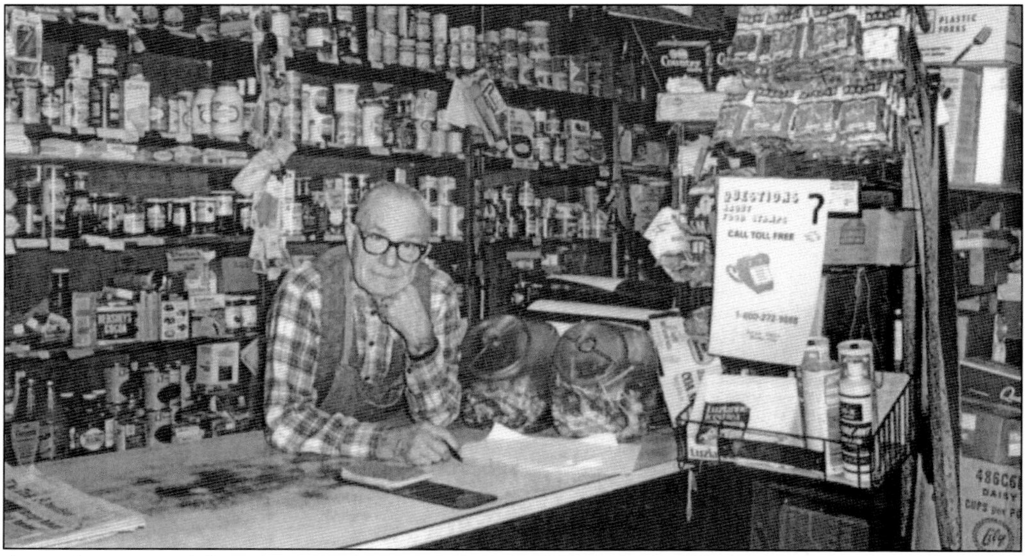

An informational flyer seen on the counter at Saul Bernard's Main Street grocery lists a phone number to call with any questions concerning enrollment in the pilot food-stamp program. In 1964, Pres. Lyndon Johnson signed into law the Food Stamp Program to provide for low-income families' nutritional needs. After Saul's death, the family leased out the little gray building; its first lessee, OldeTyme Ice Cream Parlor, sold only Borden's ice cream, an all-time favorite since 1940. (Liz Girard.)

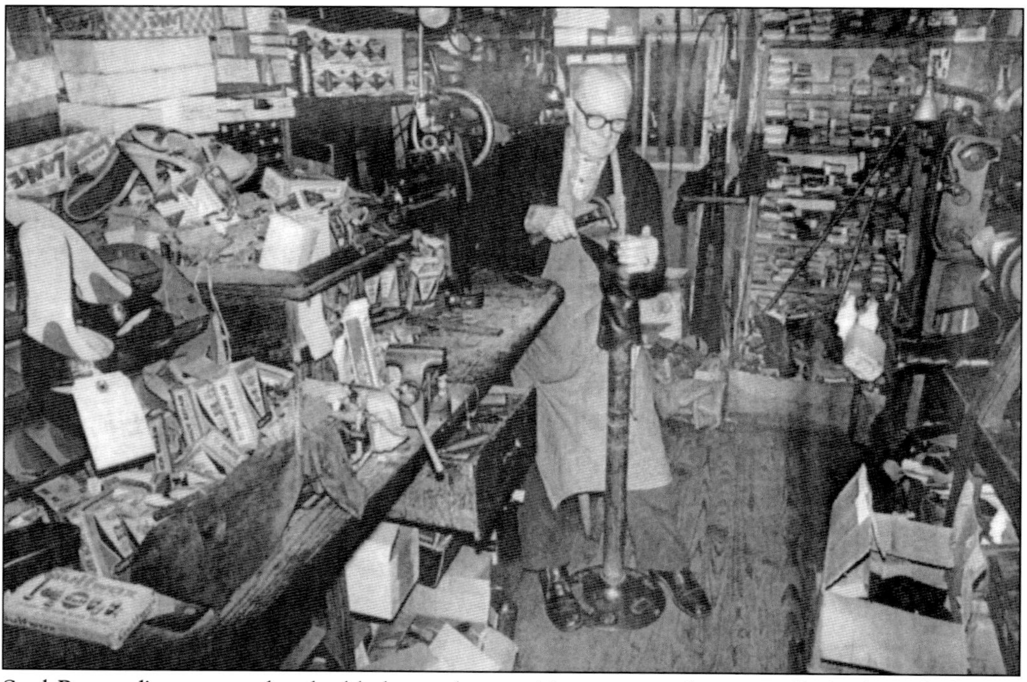

Saul Bernard's grocery also doubled as a shoe and boot repair shop as well. Saul resoled many women's high-heeled shoes and boots, seen in a bin either waiting for repair or pickup. Many different types of machinery were necessary for the skilled artisan to make quality repairs. The boxes of Gulf wax on the table would have been used to slick the edges of leather on the boot Bernard is resoling. (Liz Girard.)

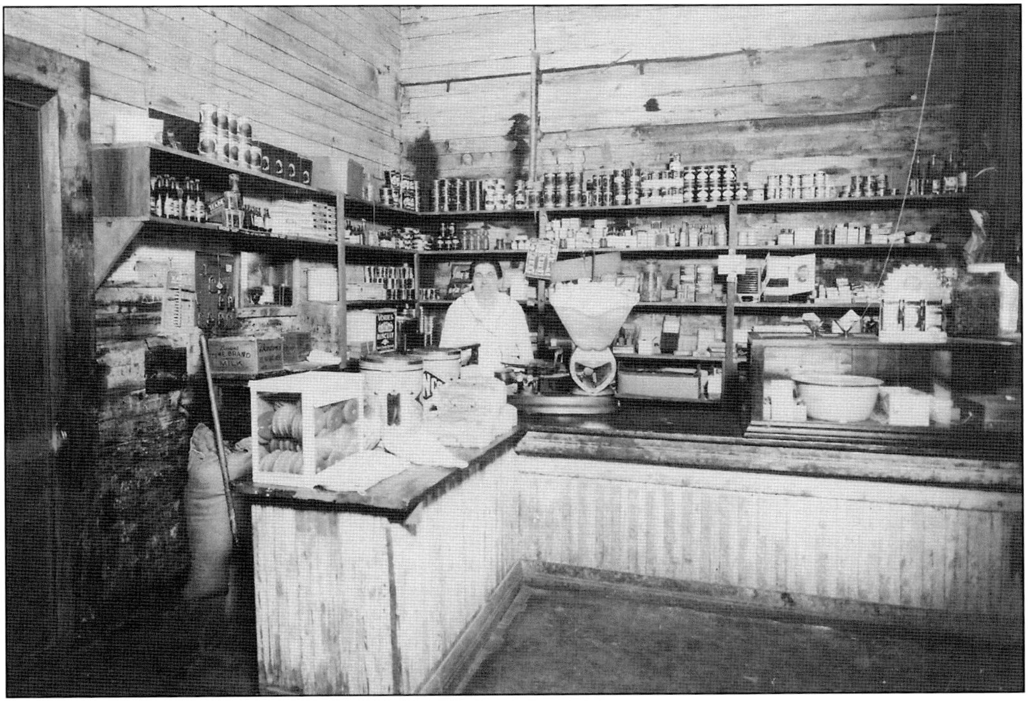

During World War II, families were issued ration stamps to purchase gasoline, meat, canned goods, flour, and sugar. Marie Richard Bernard operated one of several mom-and-pop groceries in Broussard. She is shown near a scale used for weighing sugar, which was the first staple item to be rationed, from 1942 to 1947. (Velma L. Reaux.)

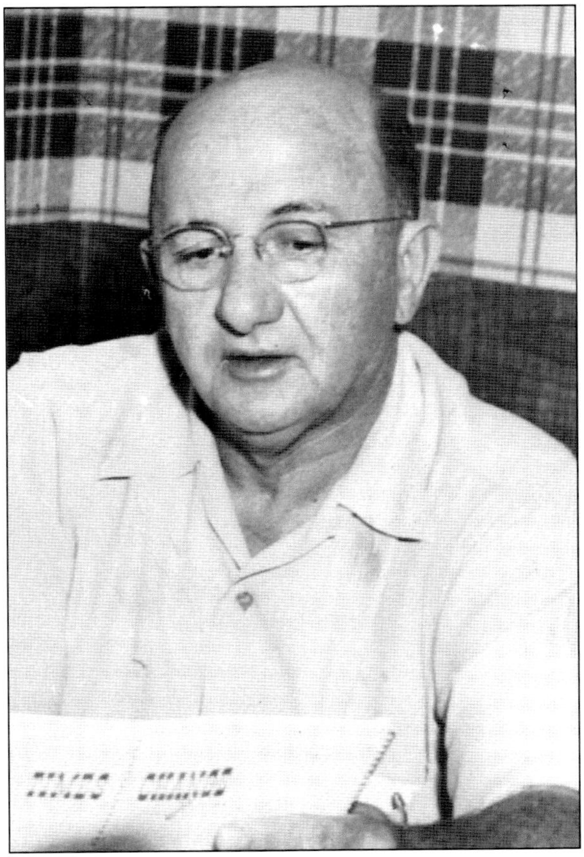

Joseph Huval, founder of Evangeline Maid Bread, was born in 1897. He began baking and delivering bread in 1937. Evangeline Maid Bread became a Louisiana staple; it is the one with the logo showing a little maiden dressed in blue and white. The model for the bread wrapper was none other than Joseph and Lorena Landry Huval's daughter Mary Helen Huval Guchereau (1919–2011). (Lafayette Parish Clerk of Court Louis J. Perret.)

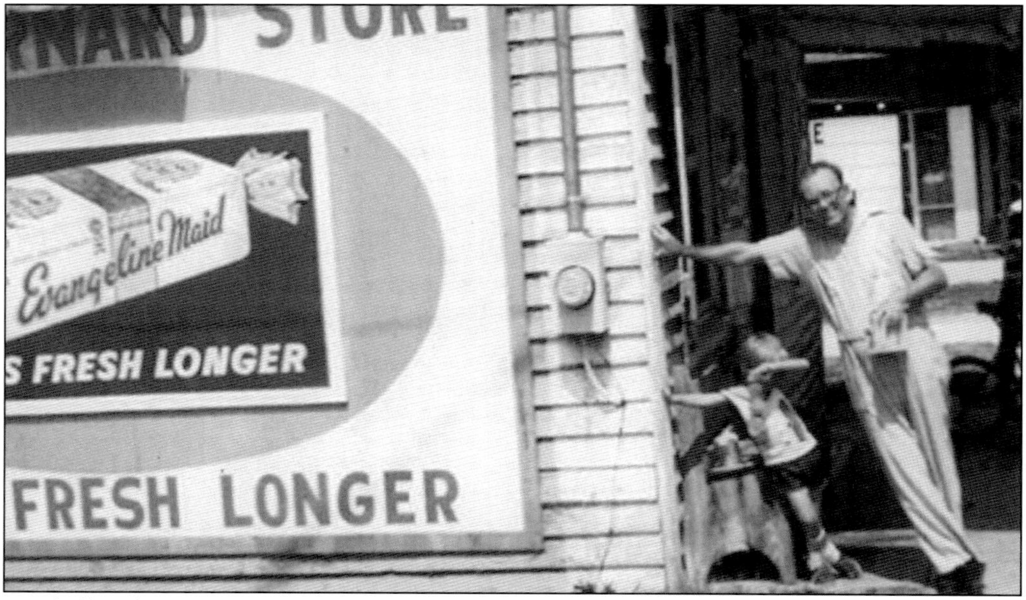

Mitchell Duhon is pictured here as a young boy with his uncle L.D. Bernard, a jack-of-all-trades. Bernard was an excellent woodcarver and in his spare time made wooden pull toys and rocking horses for his nieces and nephews. Among Bernard's business accomplishments was being the owner of a service station that repaired small engines and televisions until tubes went out of use. He then went to work for the postal service. Today, Duhon is cooking up burgers at Poppa D's Hamburgers—and he uses Evangeline Maid buns. (Mark Ste. Marie.)

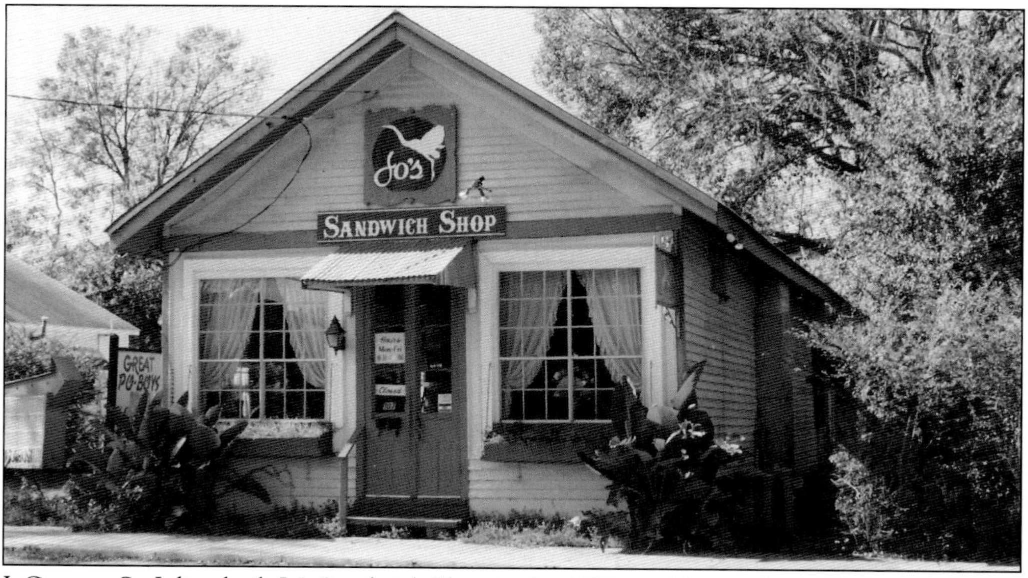

J. Gustave St. Julien built Jo's Sandwich Shop in the 1900s on Morgan Street for his son L.F. St. Julien and daughter-in-law, Regina. L.F. used the building as a drugstore and post office and also shared the space with Roy Billeaud while his grocery was being built on Main Street. Harry Conrad also used the building as a warehouse for the overflow of used furniture and appliances from his furniture store. L.F.'s sister Cecile and her husband, Edmond Comeau, are the grandparents of Walter Comeaux, the first city-parish president in Lafayette. (Lafayette Parish Clerk of Court Louis J. Perret.)

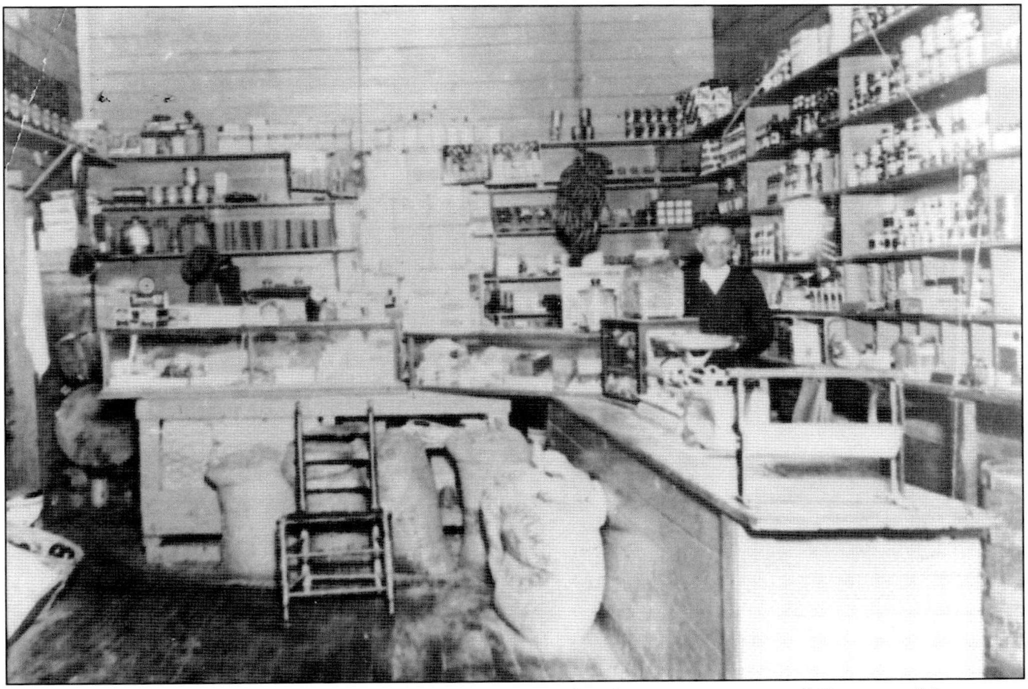

There were five or six general stores operating in the downtown area of Broussard between Morgan and Main Streets in the early 1900s. By the late 1960s, only a few of the old groceries and mercantile stores were still in business. This storekeeper, possibly Adonis Bernard, stands behind the counter of his well-stocked store waiting for customers. (Lafayette Parish Clerk of Court Louis J. Perret.)

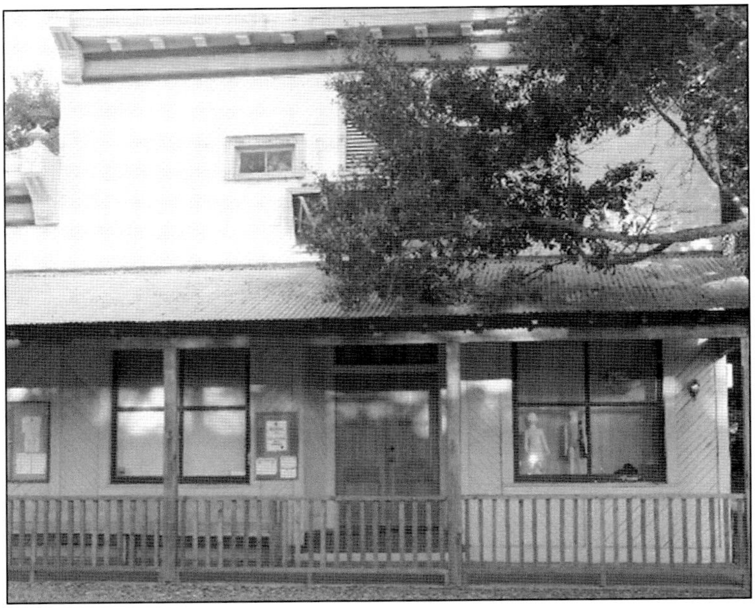

The Janin Store, a general merchandise business, was built in the 1890s by Joseph Oscar Girouard and his son-in-law François Janin. The business was family-run until 1970, at which time the building was partially leased to a stained-glass studio. Over the years, several other businesses have occupied the building, and it currently houses a children's dance studio. (Author's collection.)

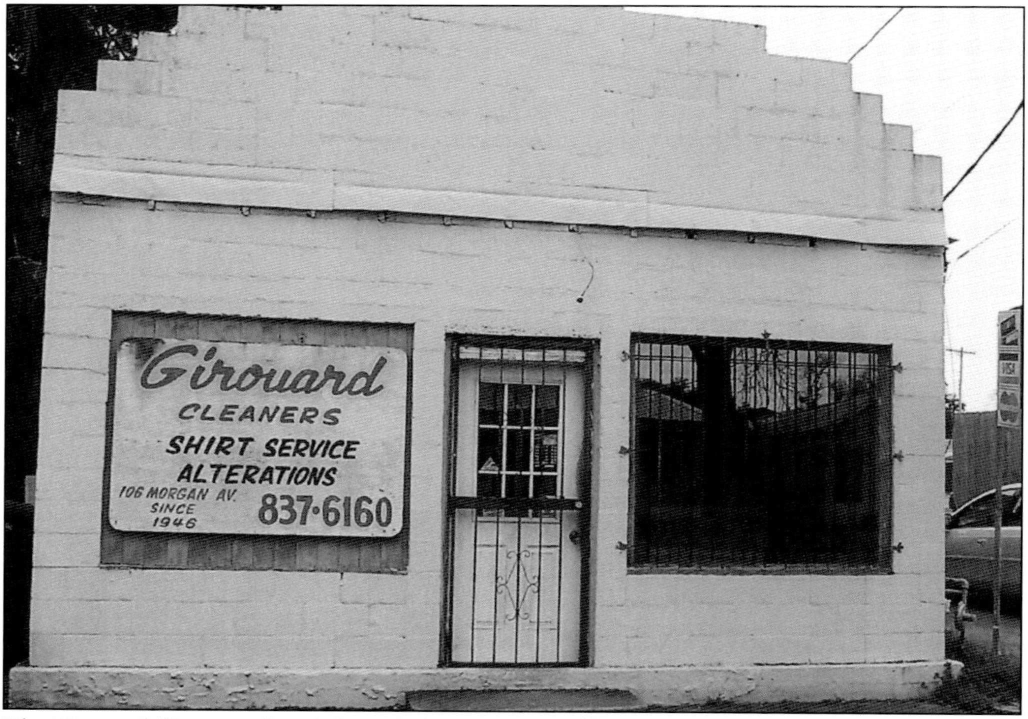

The Girouard Cleaners, founded in 1946, was co-owned by Frank Girouard Jr. and his brother Lee Girouard, grandsons of Joseph Oscar Girouard, a prominent planter. Glen Babineaux and his wife, Elizabeth Girouard Babineaux, are second-generation owners of the full-service dry cleaning business that continues to serve Broussard families laundry needs to this day. (Elizabeth Babineaux.)

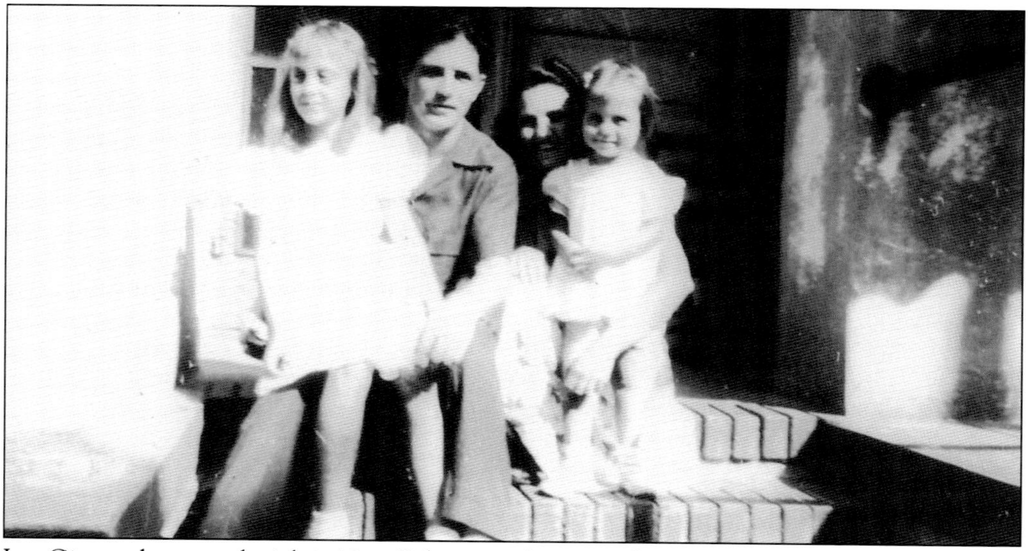

Lee Girouard accepted a job in New Orleans working at a shipyard building boats during World War II, as he was not able to enlist. Lee is pictured with his wife, Adele, and their two children, Jacqueline Girouard (Hollier), left, and Emma Lee Girouard (Hollier). The sisters married cousins. After the war, Lee and his brother Frank opened the Girouard Cleaners, which is still serving the needs of the citizens of Broussard. (Emma Lee Hollier.)

Lee Girouard, co-owner with his brother Frank Girouard Jr. of Girouard Cleaners, takes a break from the heat inside the cleaners. To save on the business's electricity bill, the customers' laundry was hung outdoors to line dry behind the cleaners. (Elizabeth Babineaux.)

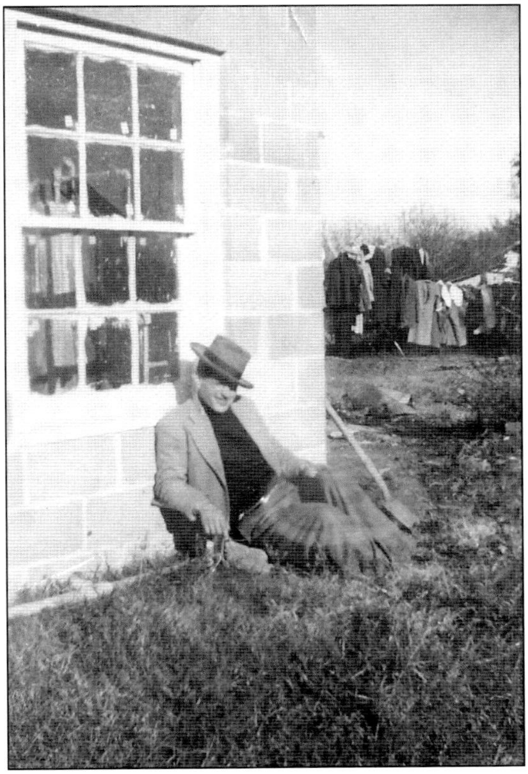

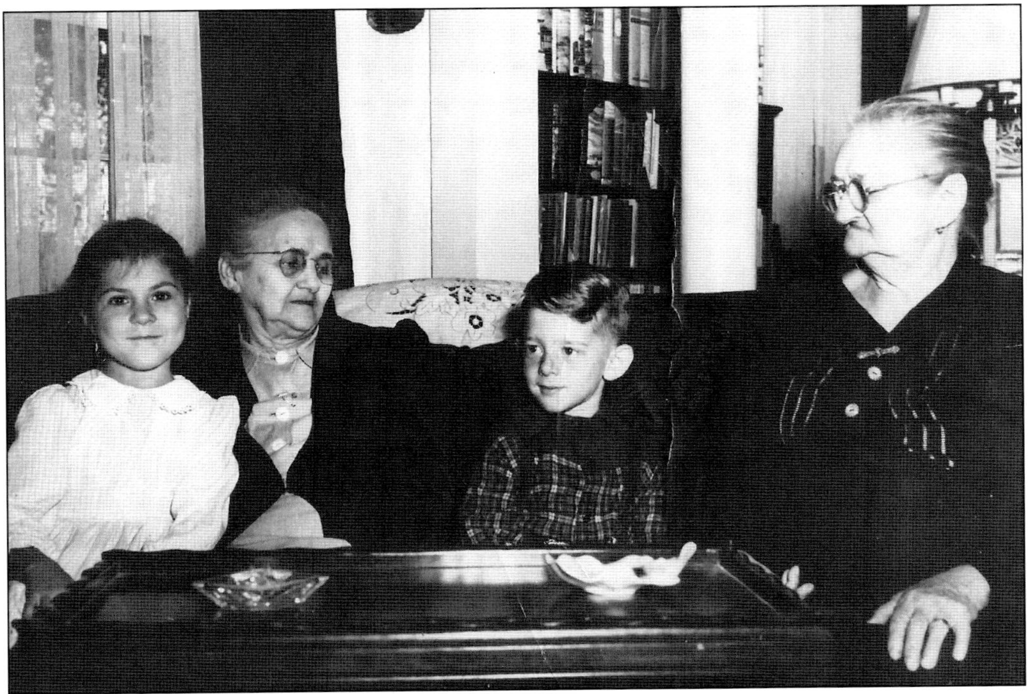

Emma Lee Hollier (left), daughter of Lee Girouard, is pictured here with Clara "Mom" Broussard Bernard (second from left), her son Emile Bernard, and Cecile "Dadoone" Broussard Breaux inside the Broussards' home parlor in 1949. (Emma Lee Bernard Hollier.)

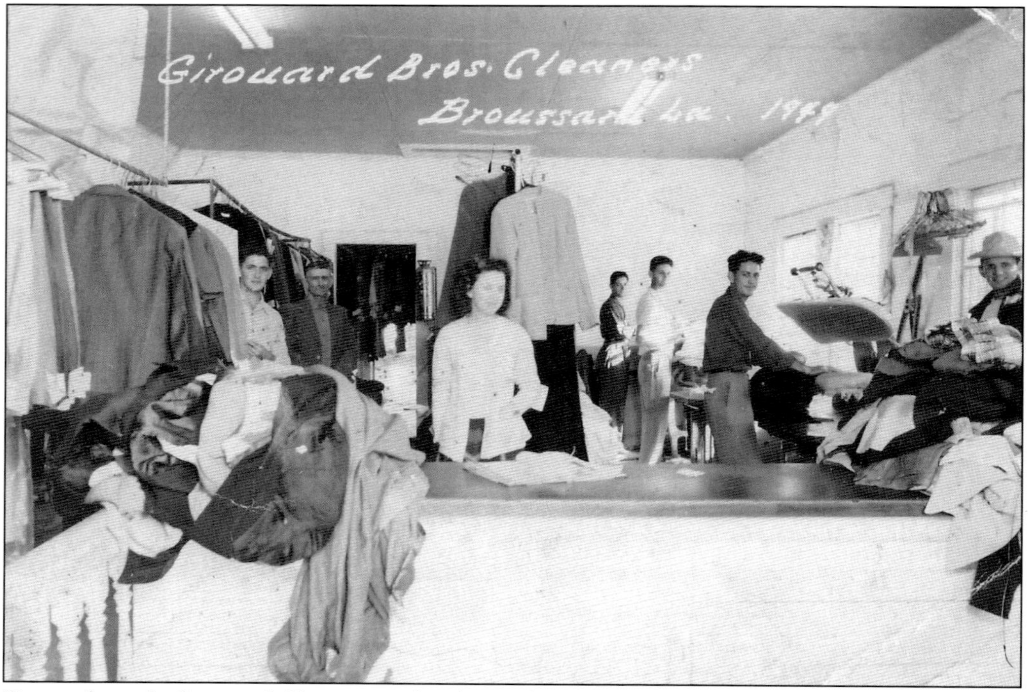

Pictured inside Girouard Cleaners, a family-run business, are, from left to right, Ed Girouard, unidentified, Ida Belle Girouard Pesson, Charles Smith, Lee Joseph, and twin brothers Frank and Maxim Girouard. (Emma Lee Girouard Hollier.)

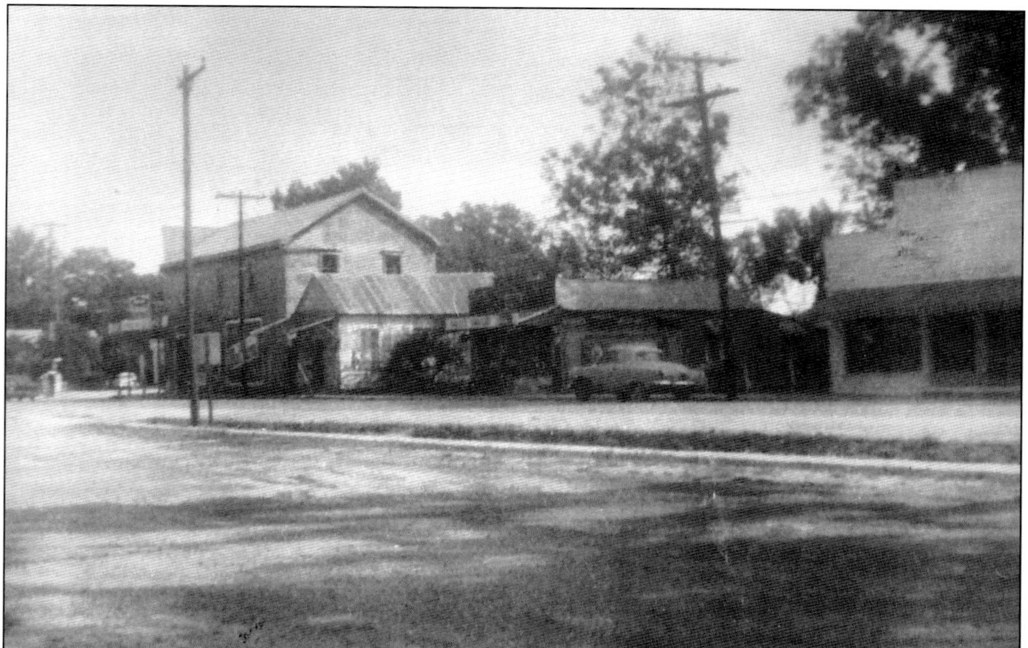

This view of Morgan Avenue from around the 1950s shows a few businesses such as Harry Conrad Furniture, which sold both furniture and appliances. By 1962, more change came to Broussard with the construction of US Highway 90. Transient traffic through town was therefore greatly reduced. (City of Broussard archives.)

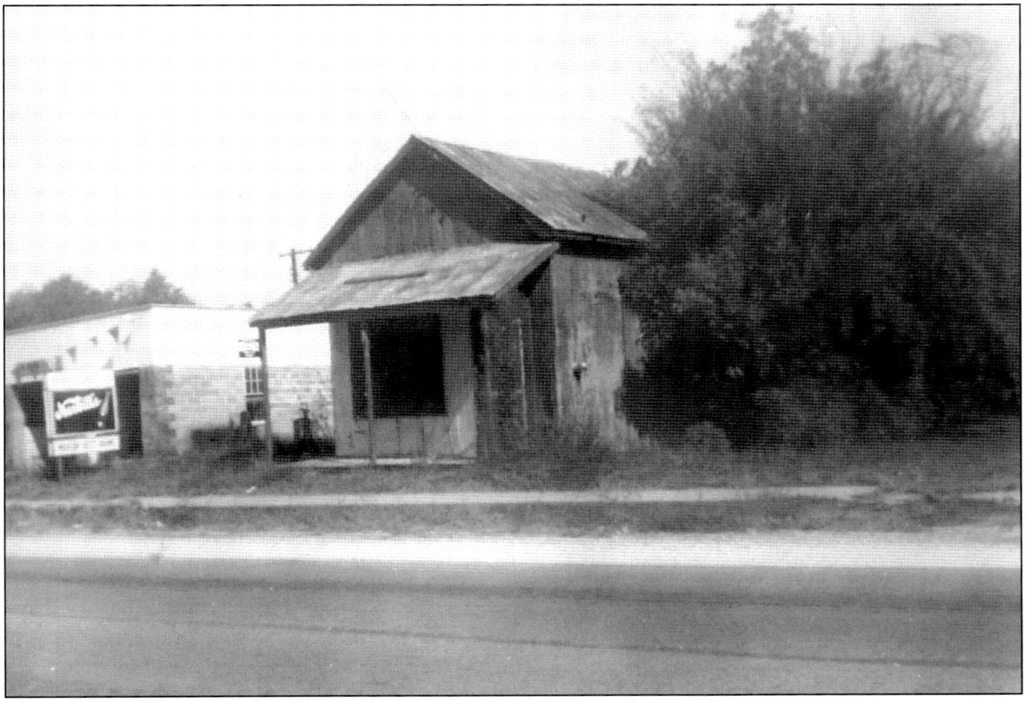

Pictured here is Augustin "Gros" Richards's small butcher shop and meat market that served the townsfolk in Broussard during the 1940s. Augustin's sister-in-law Marie Richard also operated a grocery on Main Street for many years. (City of Broussard archives.)

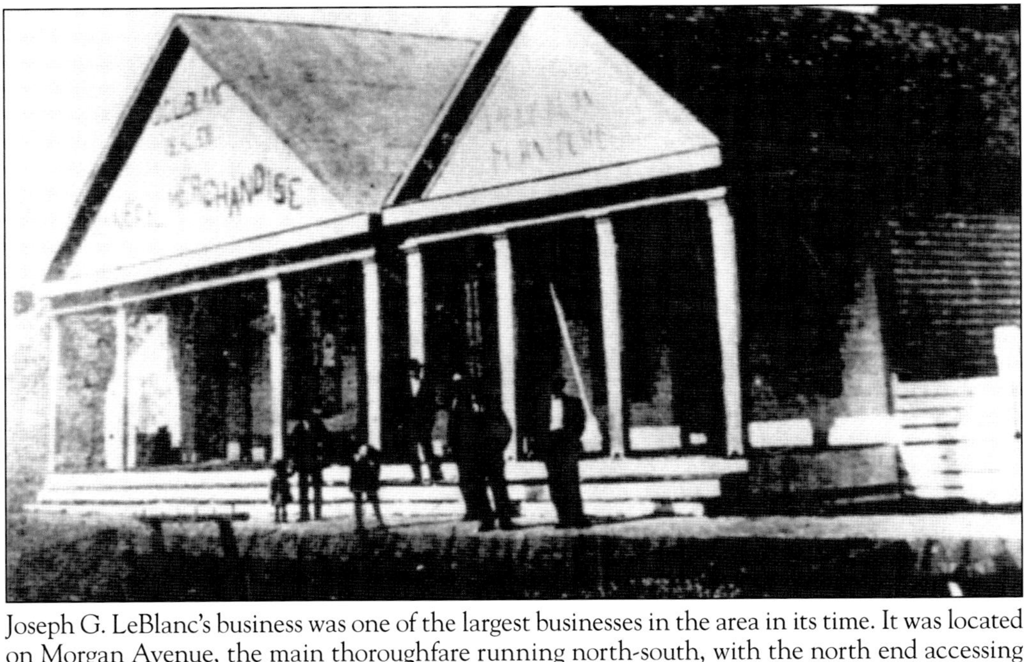

Joseph G. LeBlanc's business was one of the largest businesses in the area in its time. It was located on Morgan Avenue, the main thoroughfare running north-south, with the north end accessing the railroad depot. LeBlanc's general merchandising store was one of several businesses that continued to prosper following the Civil War. (City of Broussard archives.)

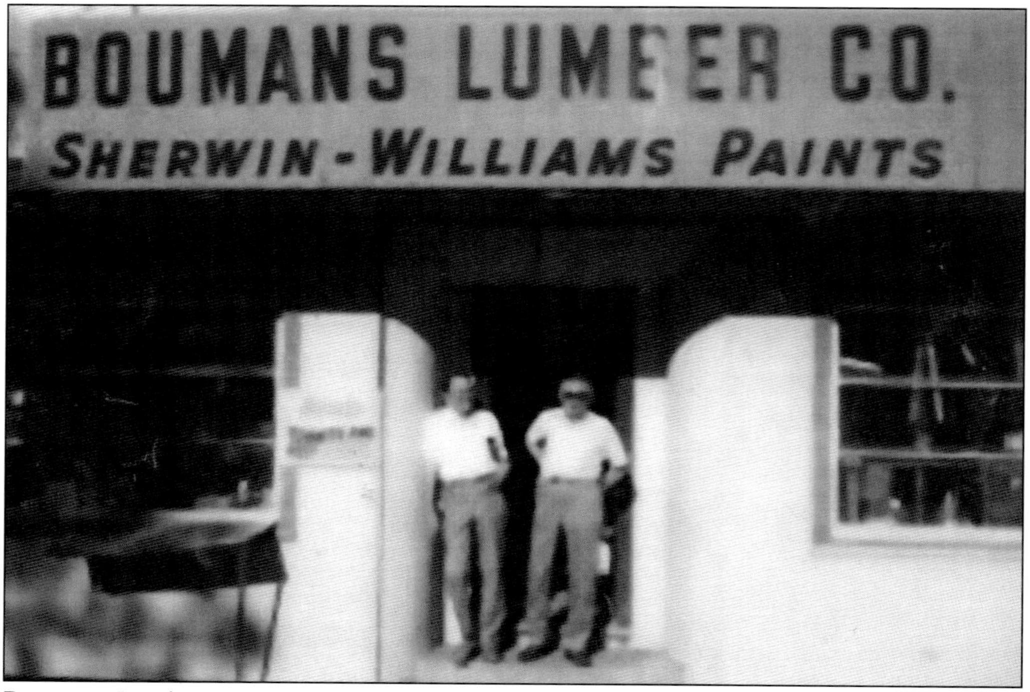

Boumans Lumber Company, a Sherwin-Williams paint distributor, was one of two lumber companies operating in Broussard before World War II. Pictured here are BLC owners Leo and William "Cabill" Boumans. (Phyllis Boumans.)

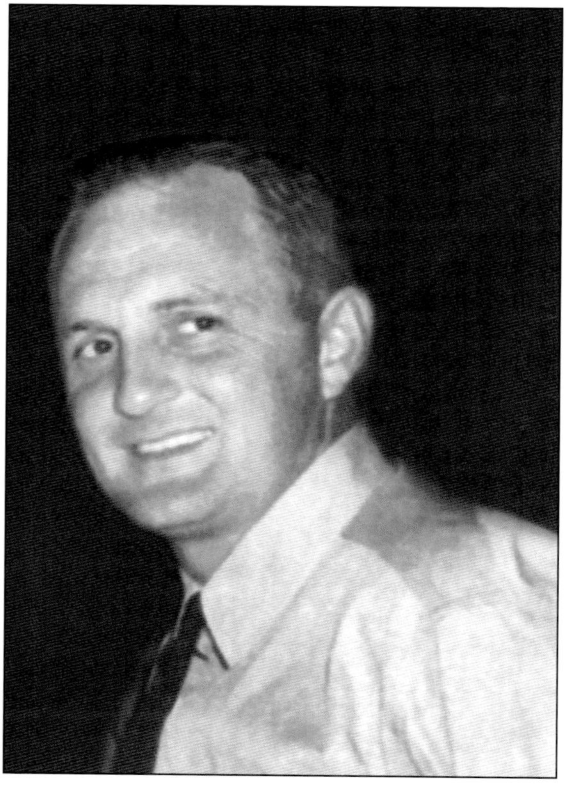

Leo and Cabill Boumans owned and operated Boumans Company from the early 1950s until it closed in 1985. An old building that served as an office for the lumberyard is currently being used by First Baptist Church for its Lighthouse ministry. Pictured here is a young Cabill Boumans. (Phyllis Boumans.)

Cabill Boumans was a master carpenter, and he built the first Christmas parade float in the area around 1955. The town of Broussard has always been a big supporter of community events such as putting on Christmas and Mardi Gras parades. In order to avoid a hardship for families with children participating in holiday events in recent times, the Mardi Gras parades are held in the city of Youngsville. (Phyllis Boumans.)

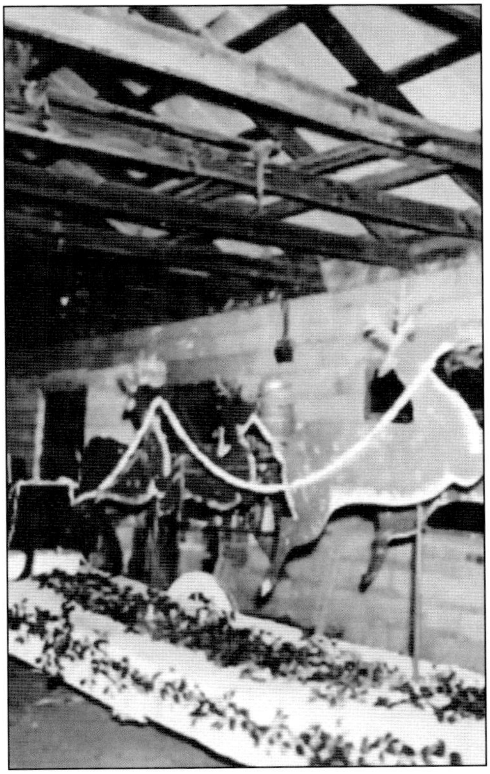

Prominent families such as those of Martial Billeaud, J. Gustave St. Julien, François Janin, and Joseph LeBlanc ran some of these businesses on Morgan Avenue. Downtown Broussard had one bank—Bank of Broussard—two hotels, a railway express, and a passenger depot. As seen in this c. 1900 image, this was still considered the horse-and-buggy era, as automobiles were considered a luxury. Broussard was duly incorporated in 1884, with Valsin Broussard donating much land to lay out the town. (City of Broussard archives.)

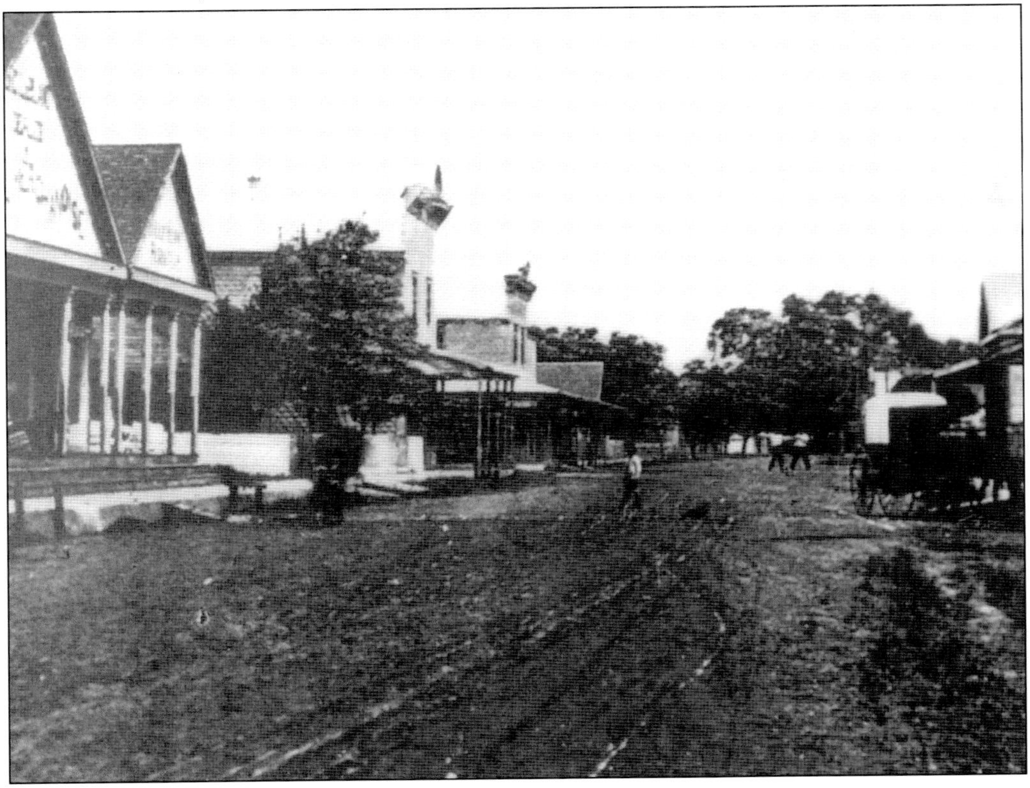

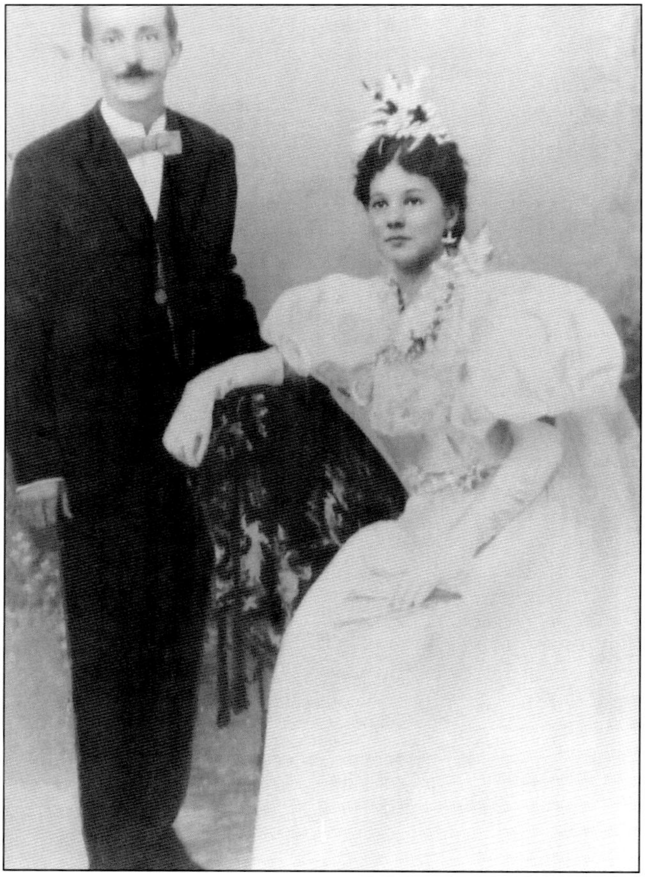

As the town of Broussard grew and prospered, prominent merchant Joseph Germaine LeBlanc and his wife, Ninette Angelina Gauthe, raised a family of 10 children: son Joseph G. LeBlanc Jr., and nine daughters—Mazie LeBlanc (Lewis), Inez (Stomer), Hazel (Mouton), Margo (McKey), Adele (Peck), Sylvia (Langlinais), Jeanne (Boudreaux), Corinne (Comeaux), and Therese (Latour). Joseph and his wife, Ninette, started a tradition of holding a family reunion on New Year's Day. Sylvia married Charles K. Langlinais Jr., father of Charles E. Langlinais, Broussard's current mayor, who has served in that capacity since defeating Leroy Miguez in December 1990. (Carolyn Langlinais.)

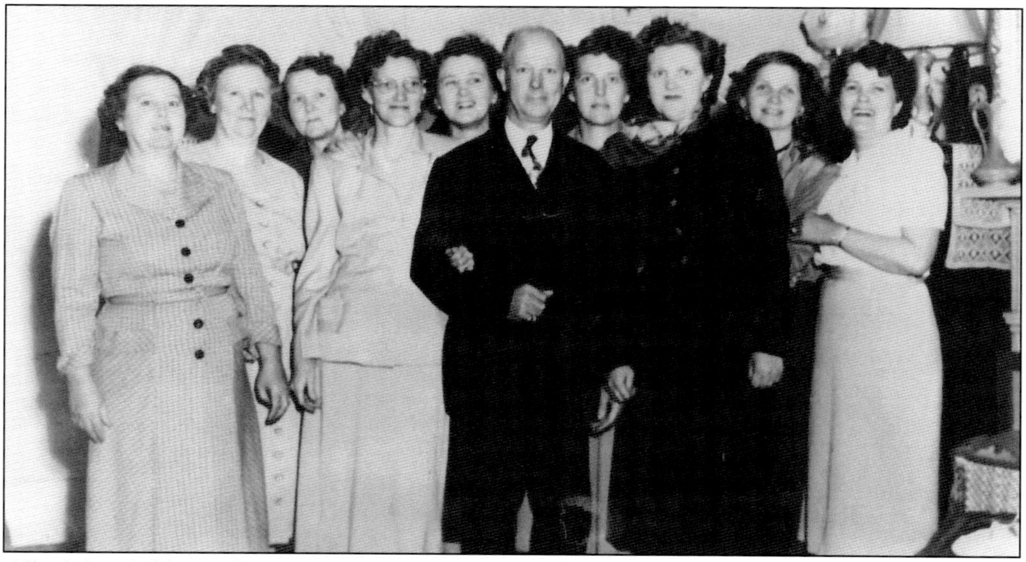

All of the children of prominent merchant Joseph G. LeBlanc Sr. are pictured at their annual New Year's Day reunion in 1949. From left to right are Mazie LeBlanc Lewis, Inez Stomer, Hazel Mouton, Margo McKey, Adele Peck, J.G. LeBlanc Jr., Sylvia Langlinais, Jeanne Boudreaux, Corinne Comeaux, and Therese Latour. (Lafayette Parish Clerk of Court Louis J. Perret.)

Joseph G. LeBlanc is pictured later in life walking to work. The LeBlanc family home was in proximity to Joseph's mercantile business and Sacred Heart Church, which the family attended. (Carolyn Langlinais.)

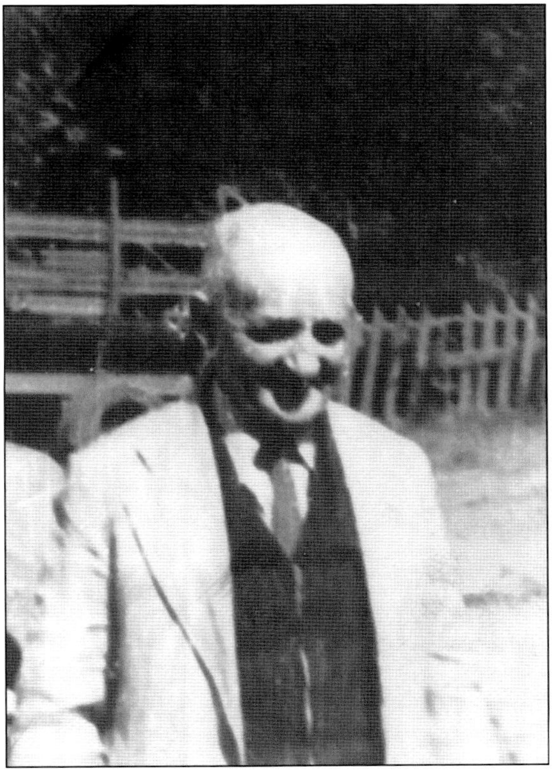

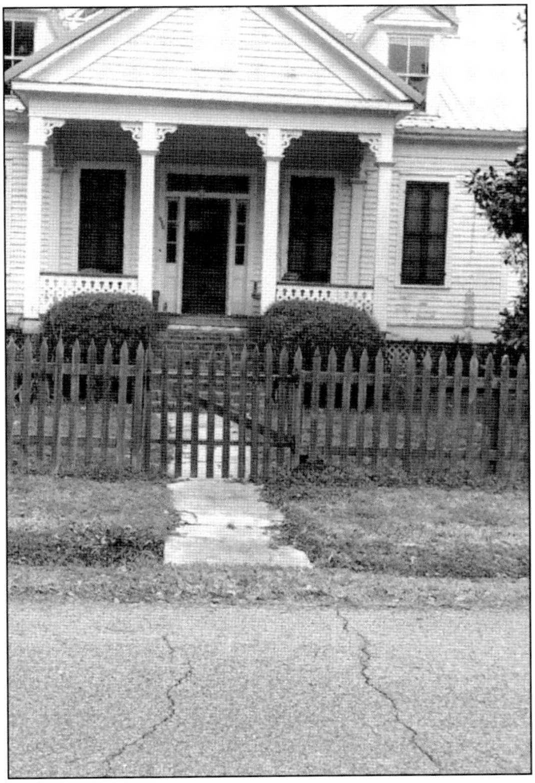

Joseph G. LeBlanc, a Broussard merchant, purchased the Joseph Arthur Roy home at 105 St. Pierre Street in 1889. The well-proportioned Palladian portico dominates the facade; symmetry and proportion were prime design elements of the structure, indicating a neoclassical influence. It is reported the house had the first interior bathroom in Broussard. (Carolyn Langlinais.)

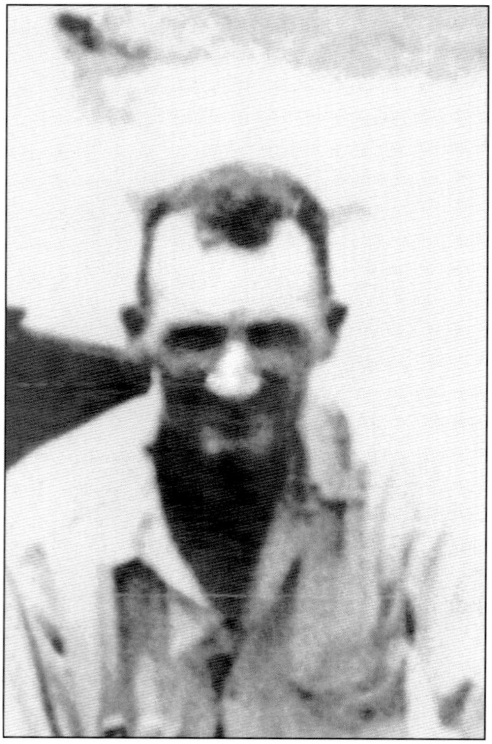

Emile Choplin, a carpenter by trade, helped with construction of many homes and businesses during his lifetime. He is seen here crossing Morgan Avenue, a main thoroughfare. His grandson Alexander "Brother" asserts that Emile loved to fish and could catch them by hand. (City of Broussard archives.)

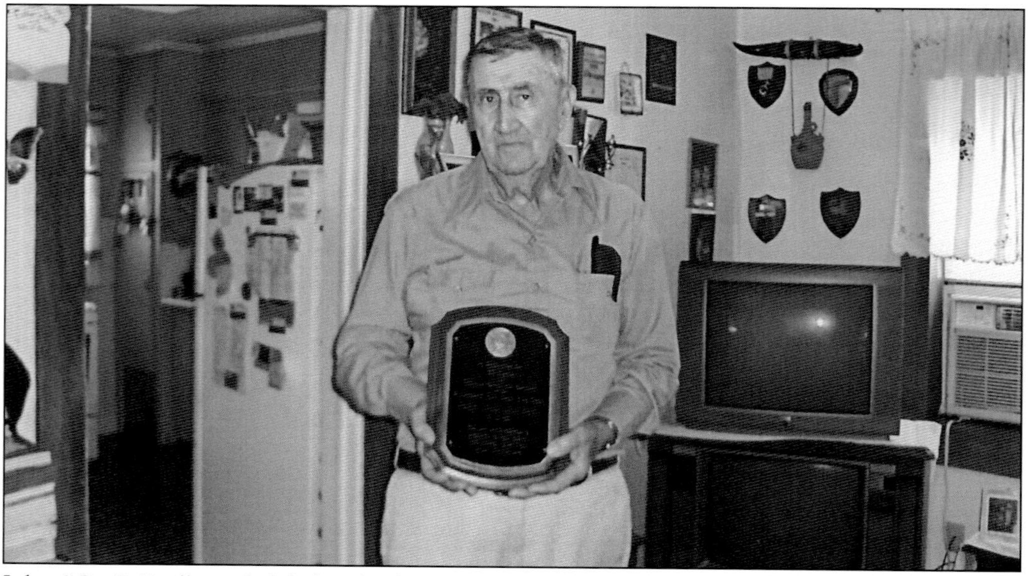

John "Gus" Guilbeau left behind a legacy of civic pride and volunteerism. For over 25 years, Guilbeau was town marshal and also volunteered with the Broussard Fire Department; he also drove a school bus from 1973 to 1988, served as a cook for events at Sacred Heart Church, and was a lifetime member of Woodmen of the World Insurance Company. During his years coaching and umpiring back in the 1960s and 1970s, Guilbeau remembers Ron Guidry (of New York Yankees fame) during Guidry's freshman year on the University of Southwest Louisiana junior varsity team: the future star's wild pitches and how hard he could throw scared Guilbeau. (Author's collection.)

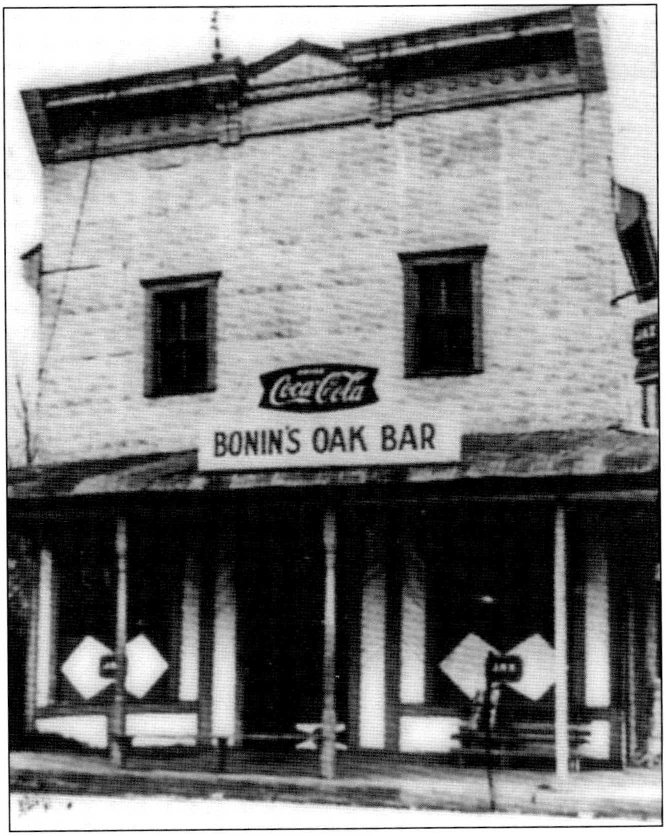

Bonin's Oak Bar, on the corner of Morgan Avenue and Highway 182/Main Street, was a favorite hangout in the 1950s. Andre Ste. Marie rented the old general merchandising store after Martial "Red" Bernard died. Following Ste. Marie's death, Patrick Bonin took ownership, running a bar locals dubbed Matt Dillion's Saloon, a rowdy place where men played a mean game of bourré, dominoes, and pool. Frequently, fights occurred when men drank too much wine or beer, and city marshal John Guilbeau rode in on horseback to keep the peace. Before segregation, the black patrons had a separate room attached to the building, but they were allowed on the white side. There was also a walk-up service window for customers. (Lafayette Parish Clerk of Court Louis J. Perret.)

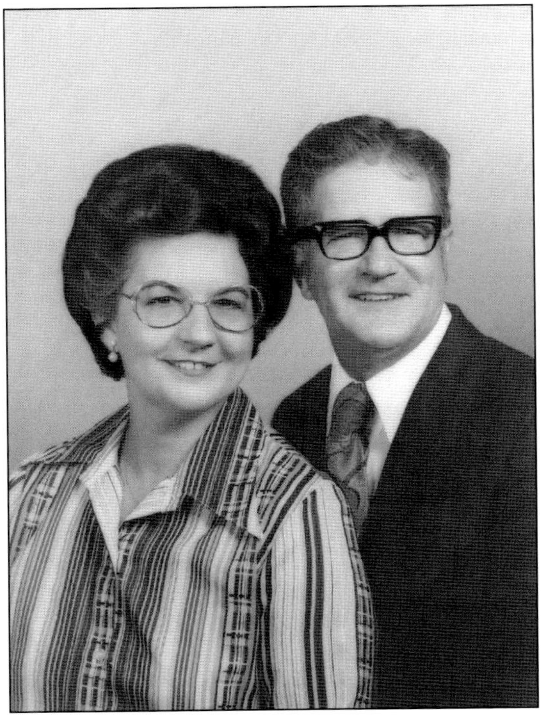

Joseph and Cecile Brugere Girouard's many descendants continue to carry on their roles in the 21st-century business community of Broussard. Pictured here are Alton Girouard and Rose Molbert Girouard, who opened Ton's Drive Inn on West Main Street in 1963. The iconic restaurant still caters to a daily lunch crowd. (Author's collection.)

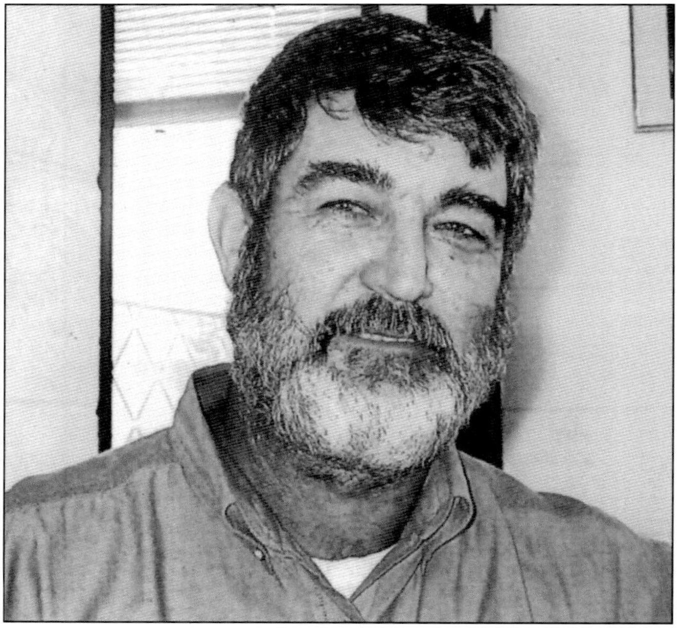

Ton's Restaurant, 101 West Main Street, is a second generation–run family business and celebrated its 50th anniversary on May 11, 2013, with the whole community coming out to support Karl (pictured) and Juanita Girouard. In its infancy, Ton's served up the best hamburgers and fries around town in a small green building, which was located across from the present establishment. (Author's collection.)

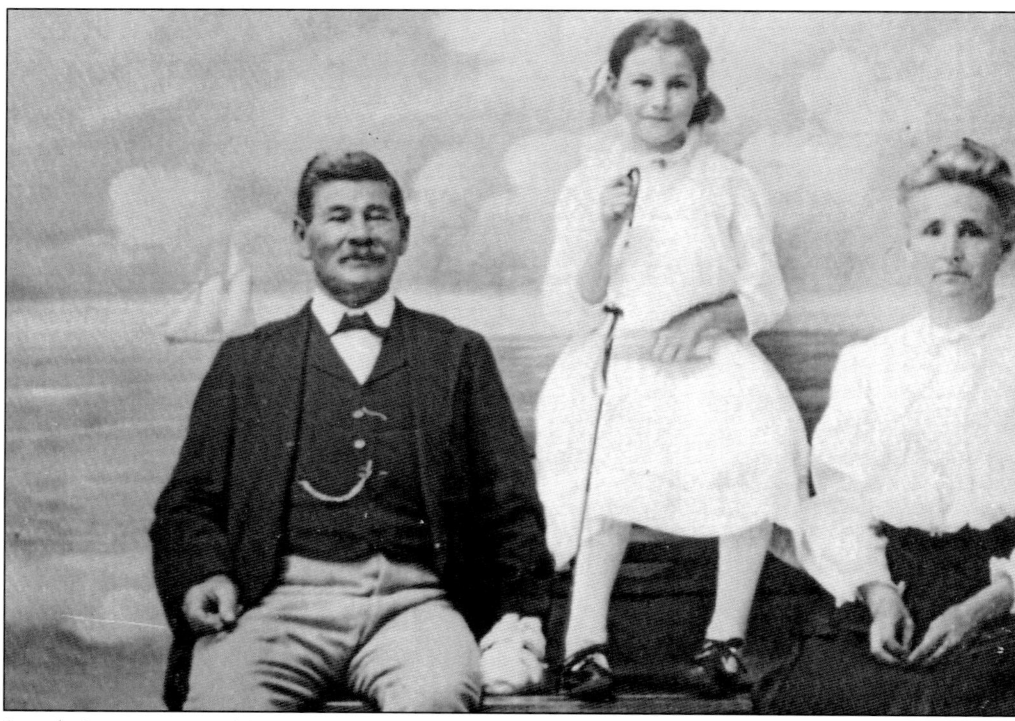

Joseph Oscar Girouard (1839–1916), a wealthy planter and community leader in Broussard following the Civil War, is pictured here around 1905 with his second wife, Cecile Brugere Girouard, and their youngest daughter, Stella Girouard Hebert. The couple raised 13 children in a lovely plantation-style home situated in a hilly area on Bayou Tortue Road. Joseph raised hogs, cattle, horses, mules, and 400 chickens. Joseph died in 1916, with his son Frank receiving the house and 44 acres that he later sold. In recent years, the home was moved across the highway from its original site, restored, and renovated by owner Terry Girouard. (Gail Hebert.)

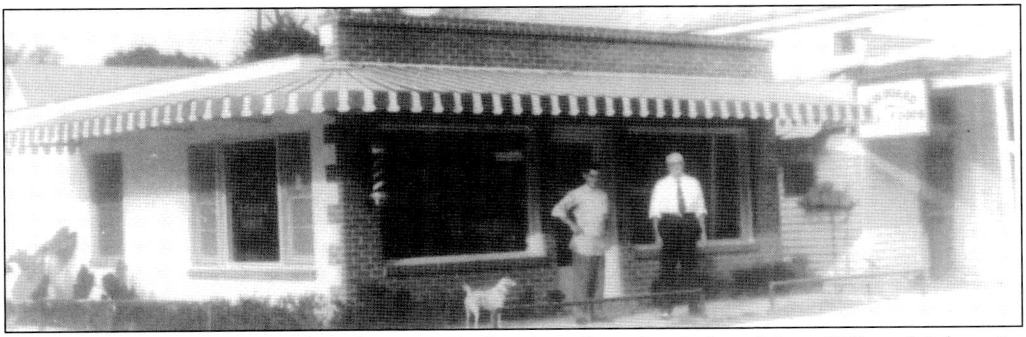

Charles Malagarie inherited Malagarie's Barbershop from his father, Marc Gilbert Malagarie. The shop was on Main Street adjacent to where Ton's Restaurant is today. Charles, a barber, and his wife, Shirley, a beautician, opened Malagarie Barber & Beauty Shop in 1963. Later in life, Charles went to work as a mail carrier for the postal service. (Bill Malagarie.)

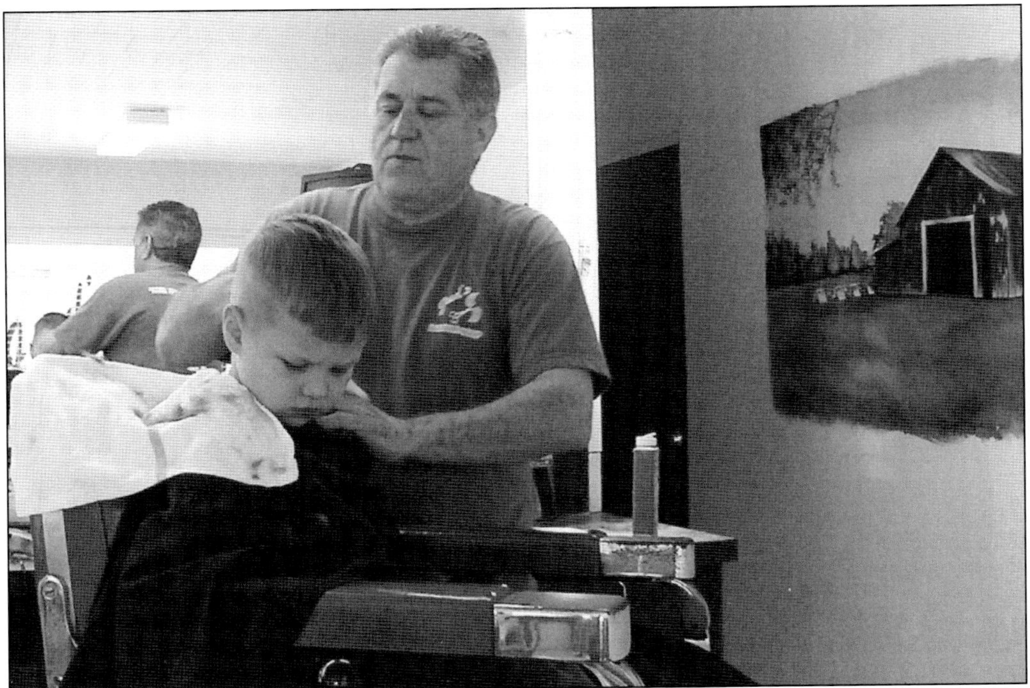

Alexander "Brother" Choplin, walked right into his future profession in the 1950s at Malagarie's Barbershop when barber Charles Malagarie offered him a job, which he accepted on the spot. The rest is history; after completing a barbering course at Moler Institute of Barbering in New Orleans, Brother came back to Broussard and worked two years in New Iberia until 1962, when Gilbert Malagarie opened a new shop on East Main Street. It has been nearly 55 years, and the menfolk still love getting haircuts along with a neck and shoulder massage, at no extra charge, from Brother Choplin. (Author's collection.)

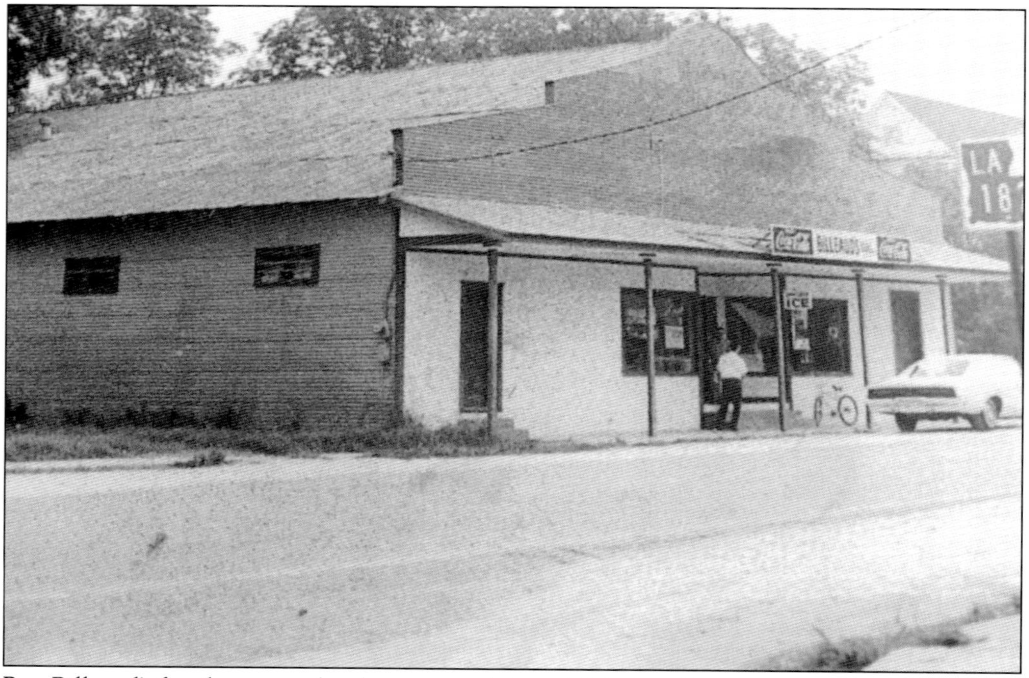

Roy Billeaud's family grocery has been around since 1889. An older store was renovated in 1956 and moved farther back onto property that faced Highway 82. At right is a glimpse of the Louisiana highway sign. (Lafayette Parish Clerk of Court Louis J. Perret.)

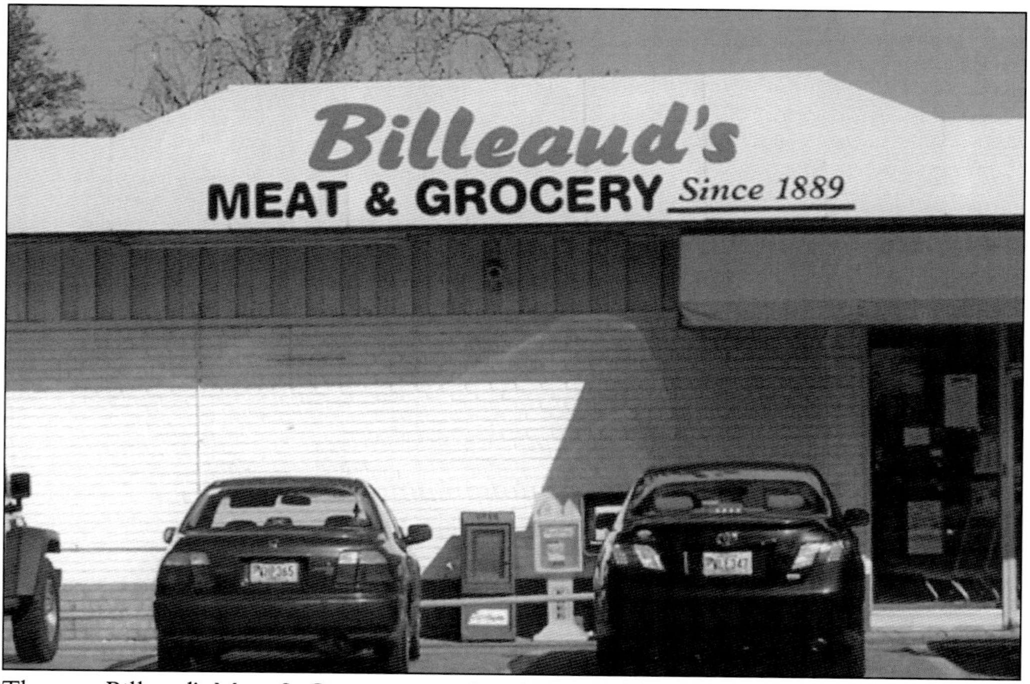

The new Billeaud's Meat & Grocery, owned and operated by Billy Billeaud, a third-generation grocer, is not hard to miss: just look for the big yellow-and-black sign. Inside are friendly cashiers and the grocery's award-winning boudin, which is shipped across the United States. (Author's collection.)

Six

Dairy Farming, a Way of Life

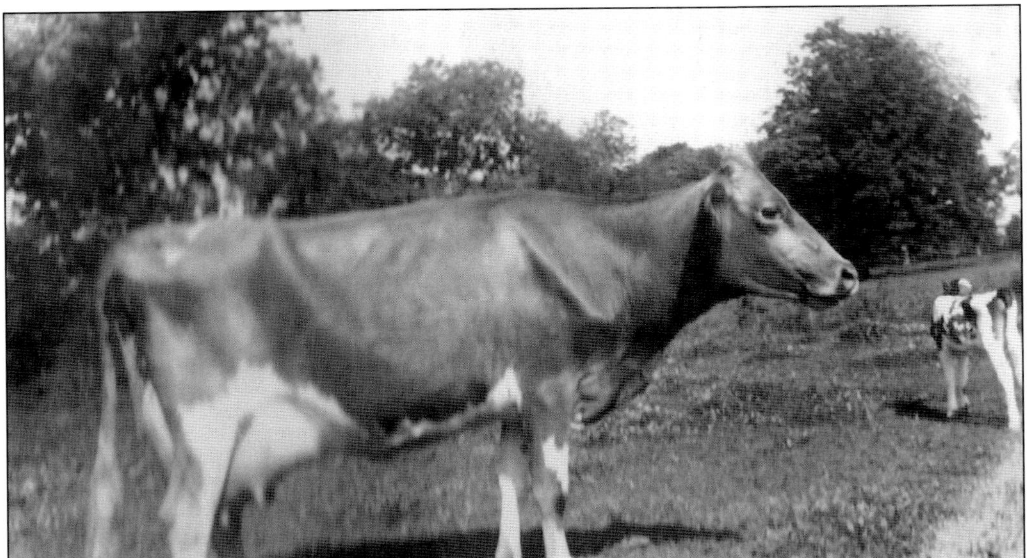

Producing dairies operating in Louisiana in the 1970s went down to 150 from a high of 1,700. There were several dairy-farming families operating in and around Broussard during the late 1940s through early 1970s—Minus Breaux, Lawrence Girouard, Maxie Girouard, Frank Garber, William Menard, and Henry Langlinais. Dairy farmers belonged to a number of local producer-owner cooperatives. Dairy farmer Ralph Racca milked for a neighbor and was actively involved with Dairy Herd Improvements from 1977 to 1984. (Ralph and Sarah Racca.)

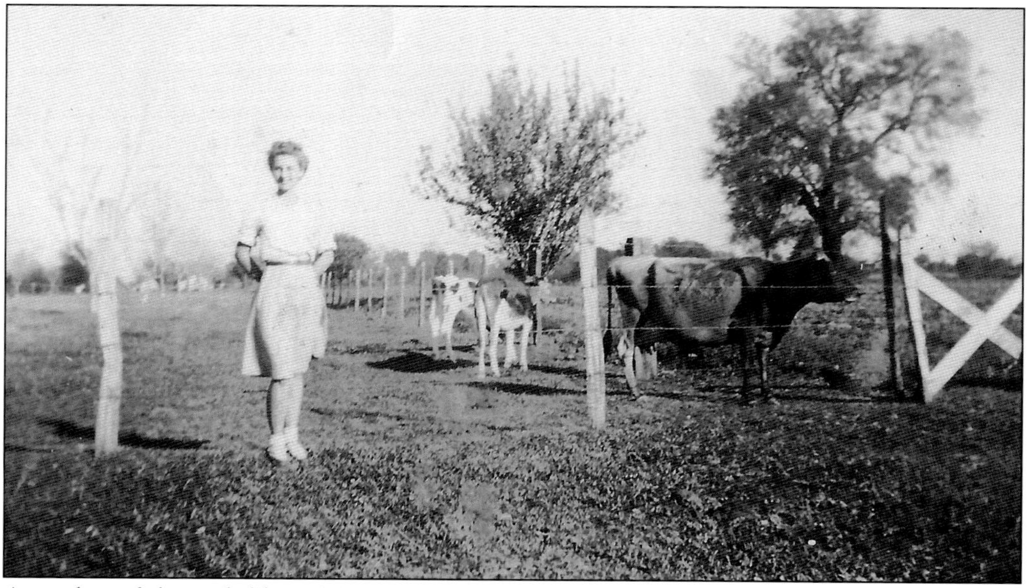

A mother of three children, Margaret "Nonie" Morvant Gondron, like most dairy farmwives during the World War II era, had to do extra chores with milking and feeding the cows. Dairy farming was a staple of life, and an assurance of providing fresh milk and cheese for families. LeeRoy Gondron, manager of Southwest Cooperative, grew corn and baled hay as feed for the cattle. (Jimmy Gondron.)

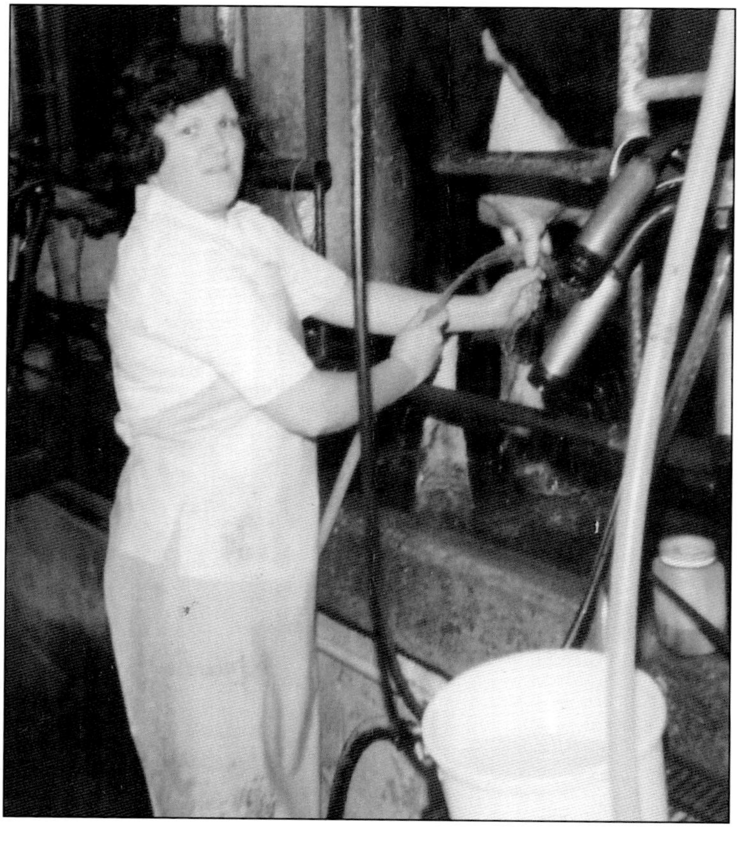

In the 1940s and1950s, women were helping hands and partners with their husbands on family dairy farms. Although milking cows become mechanized in the 21st century, not all small farms could afford the equipment. Sarah Guidry Racca juggled duties of child rearing and cooking meals while tending to the chore of milking the cows. (Ralph Racca.)

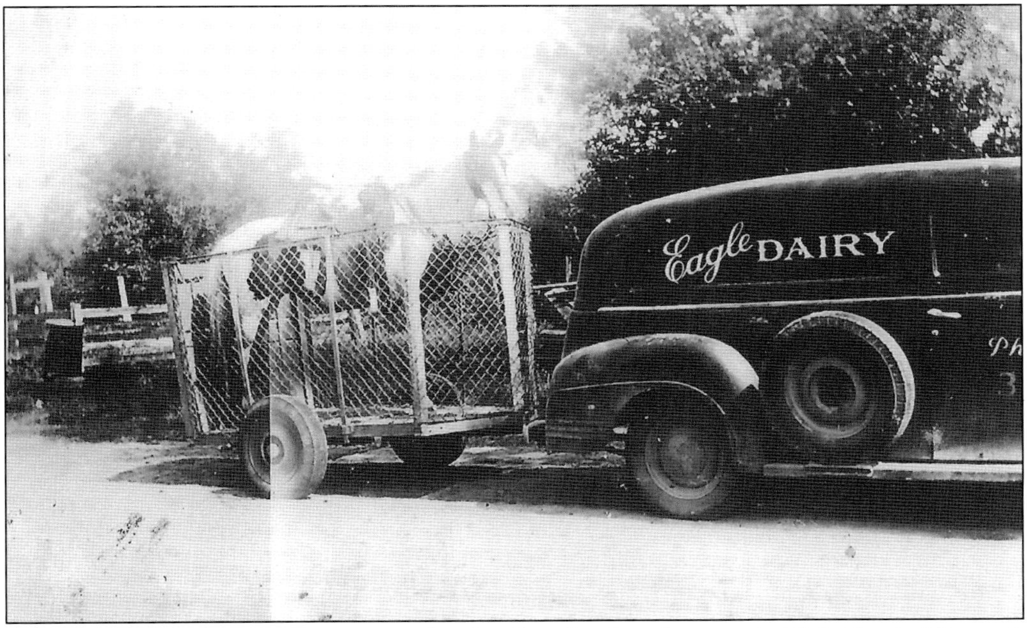

In 1943, Southwestern Cooperative members LeeRoy Gondron (manager), Alidie Tauzin (director), William Menard, and others traveled to Wisconsin to purchase the first Holstein cows (known as quantity milk producers) brought to the area, for their dairy farms. At that time, other farmers raised Jersey (a small reddish-brown breed) and Guernsey cows as milk producers. (Jimmy Gondron.)

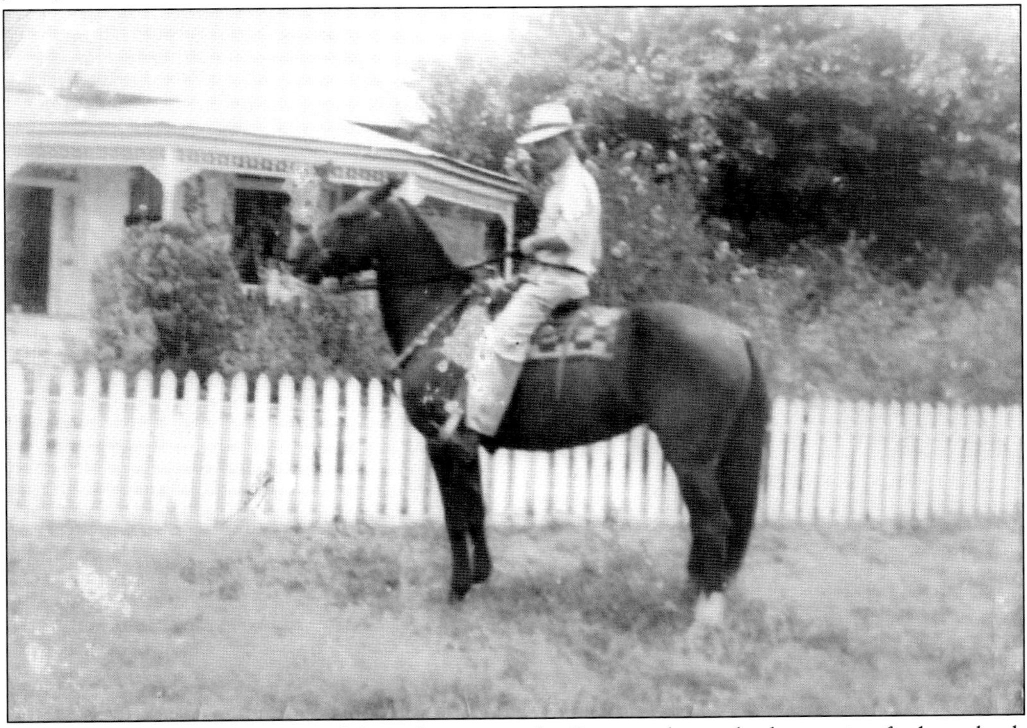

Gaston Gondron, one of several dairy farmers in the Broussard area, had a passion for horseback riding. Every year, Gondron participated in the town's annual Christmas parade on his prized stallion Black Beauty while carrying the American flag. (Jimmy Gondron.)

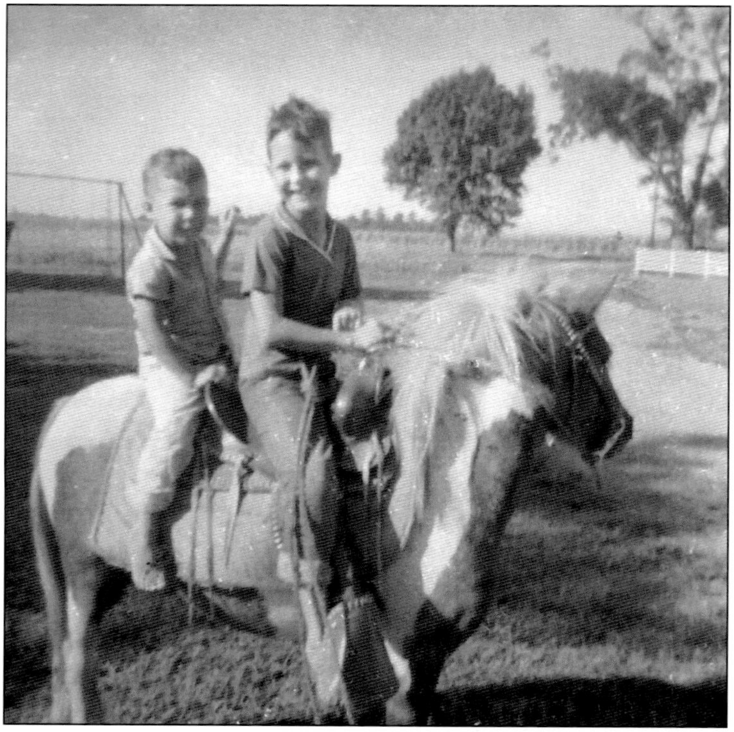

Brothers Donald "Donnie" (holding reins) and Stanley "Stan" Dutile grew up on the ancestral dairy farm of Margaret and Durel Dutile located near the city limits of Broussard. Today, Donnie conducts research for furthering animal science at the Louisiana State University field office in Jeanerette, while Stan is the county extension agent. (Jackie Dutile Theriot.)

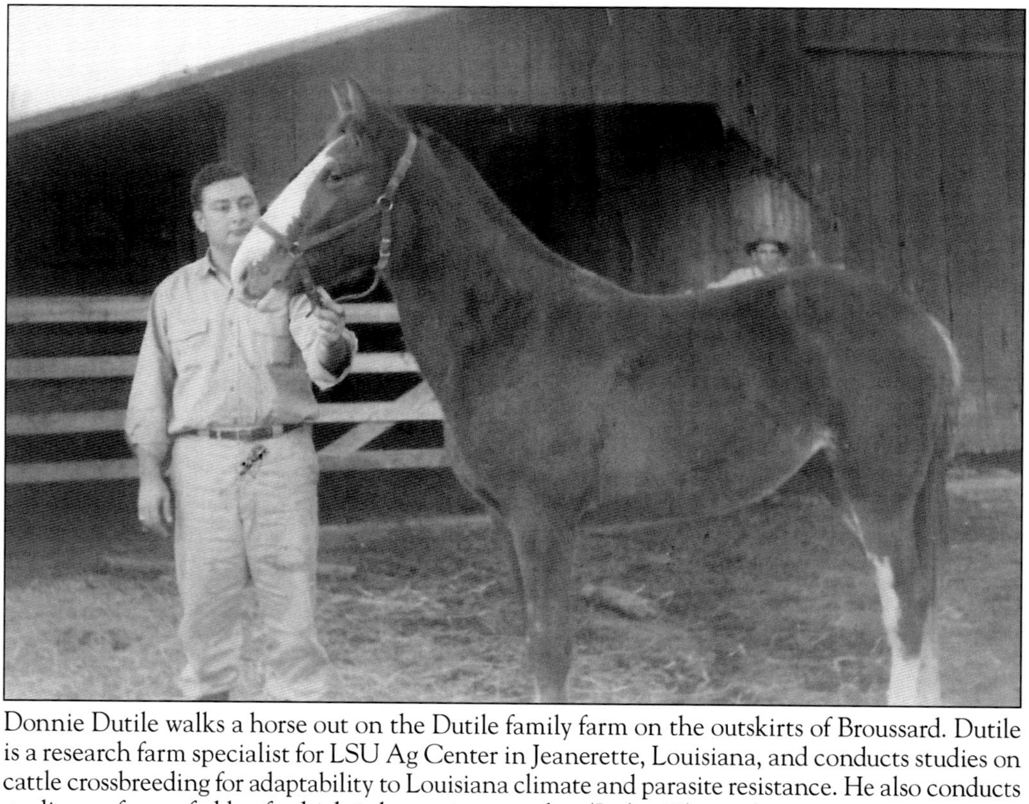

Donnie Dutile walks a horse out on the Dutile family farm on the outskirts of Broussard. Dutile is a research farm specialist for LSU Ag Center in Jeanerette, Louisiana, and conducts studies on cattle crossbreeding for adaptability to Louisiana climate and parasite resistance. He also conducts studies on forage-fed beef, which is becoming popular. (Jackie Theriot.)

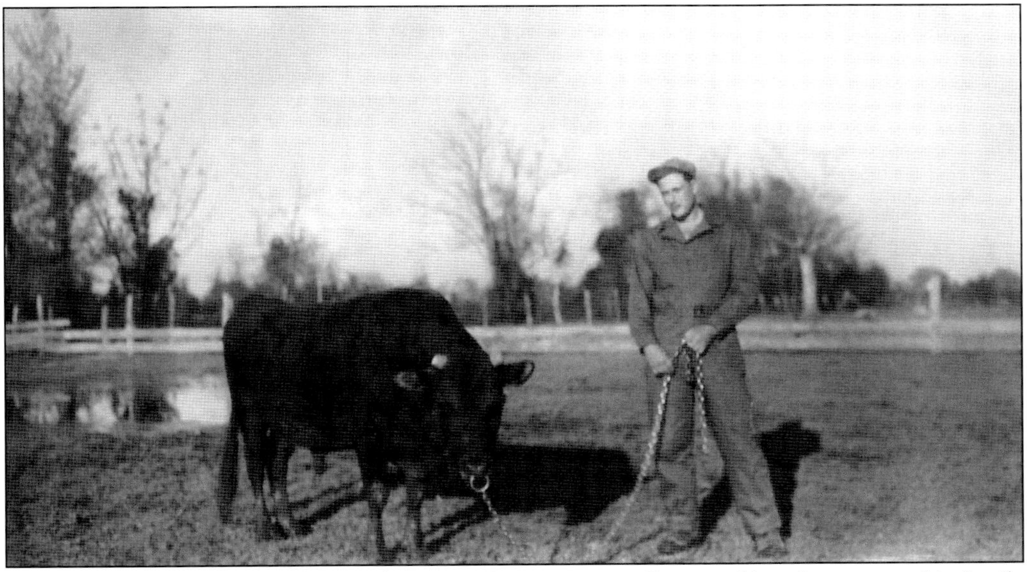

Gaston Gondron managed the Southwestern Cooperative in Broussard besides running his family farm, growing corn and baling hay to feed his grazing cattle herd. Shown here in the pasture, Gondron is training his prized bull. (Jimmy Gondron.)

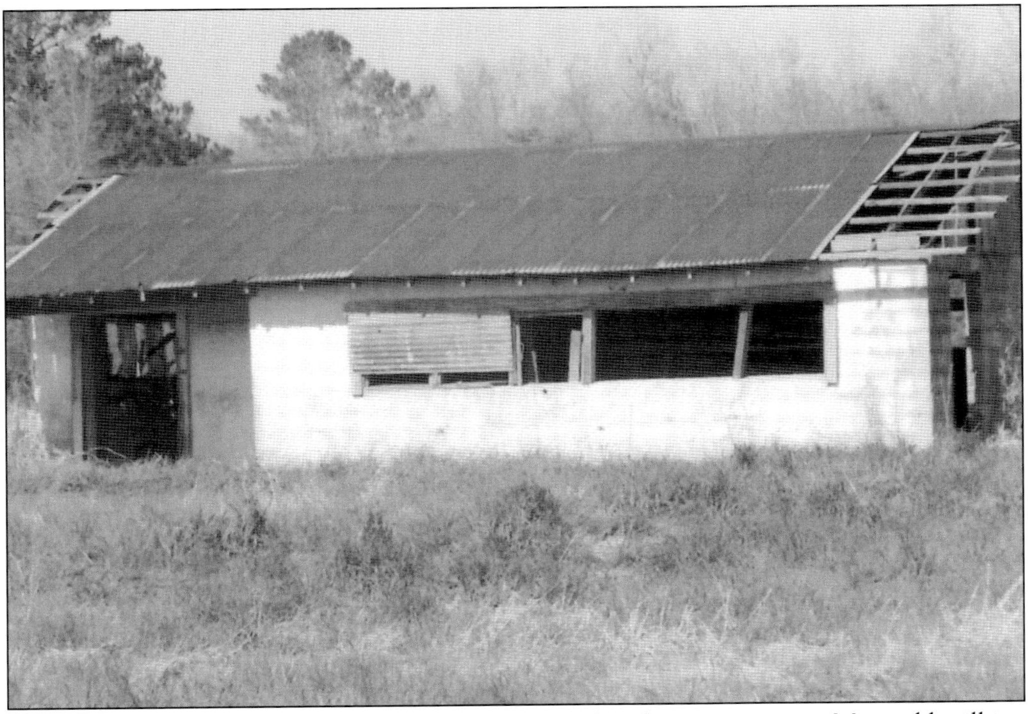

Onezine Langlinais's family dairy on Larriviere Road closed many years ago. Many old milking sheds still dot the landscape in rural areas of Broussard, a staunch testament to farming families whose livelihoods depended on dairy farming. (Author's collection.)

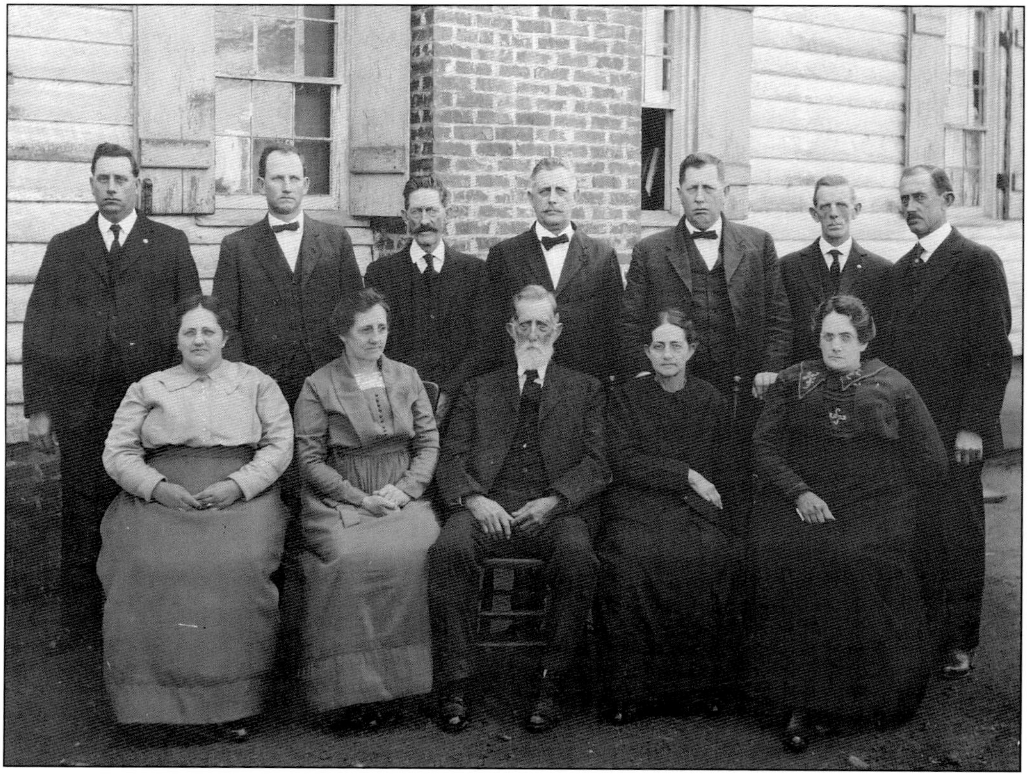

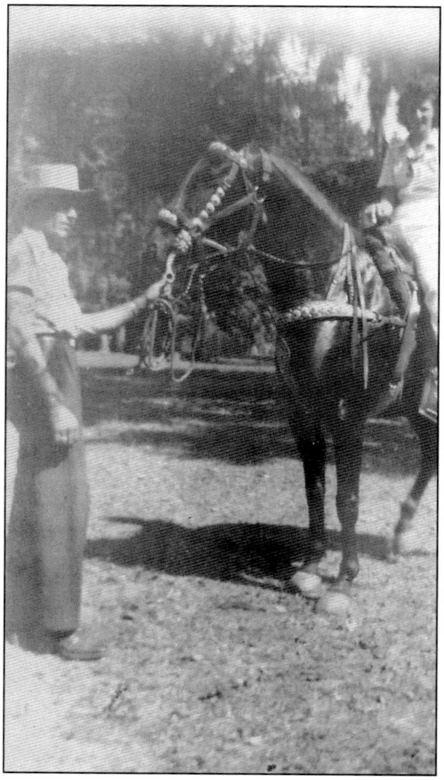

Born in 1889, Onezine Langlinais is shown with his siblings at his Broussard residence as they celebrated his 87th birthday on January 18, 1976. Two of Onezine's sisters never married and lived in the home until their deaths. (Doris Langlinais.)

Doris Langlinais Constantine, seated on her horse, was reared on Larriviere Road and to this day resides in the home her great-grandfather built. Onezine Langlinais's family home was moved onto the property by a team of oxen before the Civil War. Doris's parents, Guillaume and Blanche Langlinais, ran a dairy, where milking cows was a daily ritual that had to be performed at 2:00 a.m. and again at 4:00 p.m.—a task she loved doing. (Author's collection.)

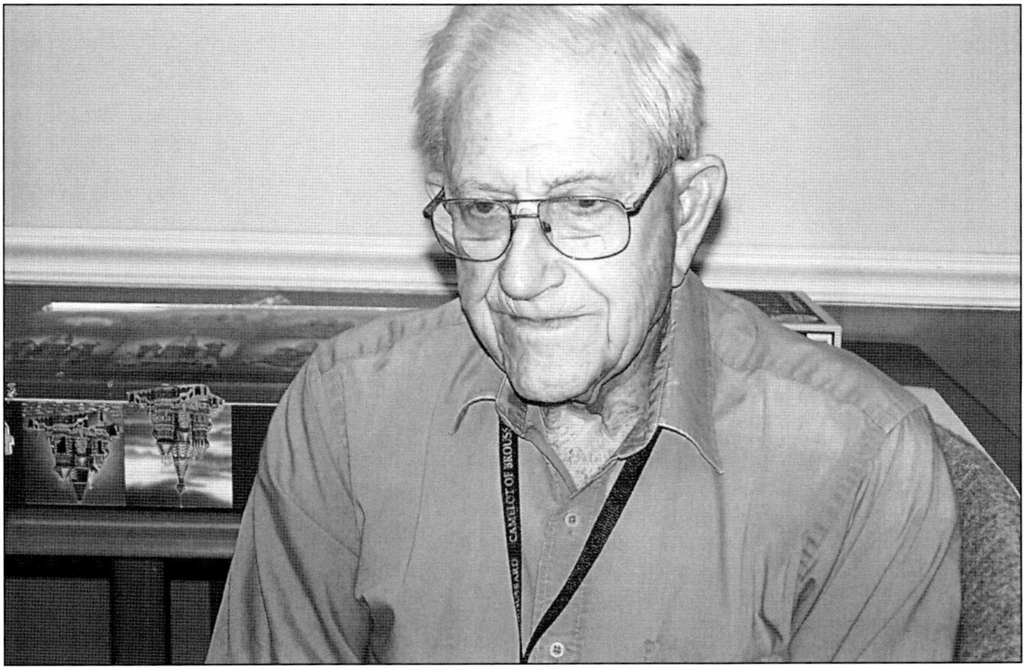

Henry Langlinais operated a dairy farm in the Long Plantation area for many years following his tour of duty in World War II, from June 1944 to 1946. As a private first class in the Army, Henry was part of a replacement battalion stationed in Germany during the Battle of the Bulge. After the war, Henry owned and operated a dairy farm until his retirement. He then decided to go back to work as a custodian at Comeaux High School for 19 years under principal Ellis Savoy. Now 94, Henry resides at Camelot of Broussard and regales visitors with stories from the past. (Author's collection.)

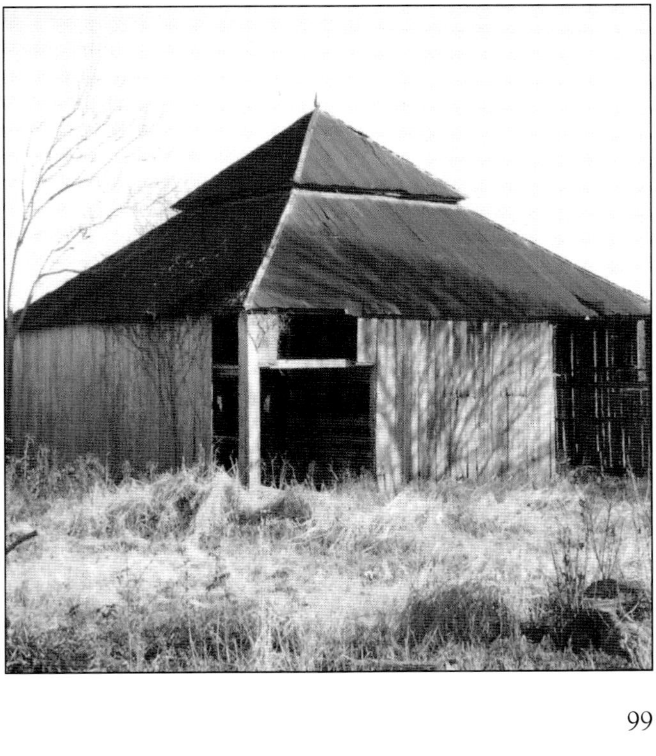

An oddly shaped barn on Rose St. Julien Larrivere's homestead is believed to be the oldest known structure in Broussard, dating back to 1784. Alexandre Barde, a tutor and news journalist who served briefly in the Civil War, is purported to have lived in the St. Julien home while writing his classic and controversial *L'histoire des comités de vigilance aux Attakapas* in 1861. (Author's collection.)

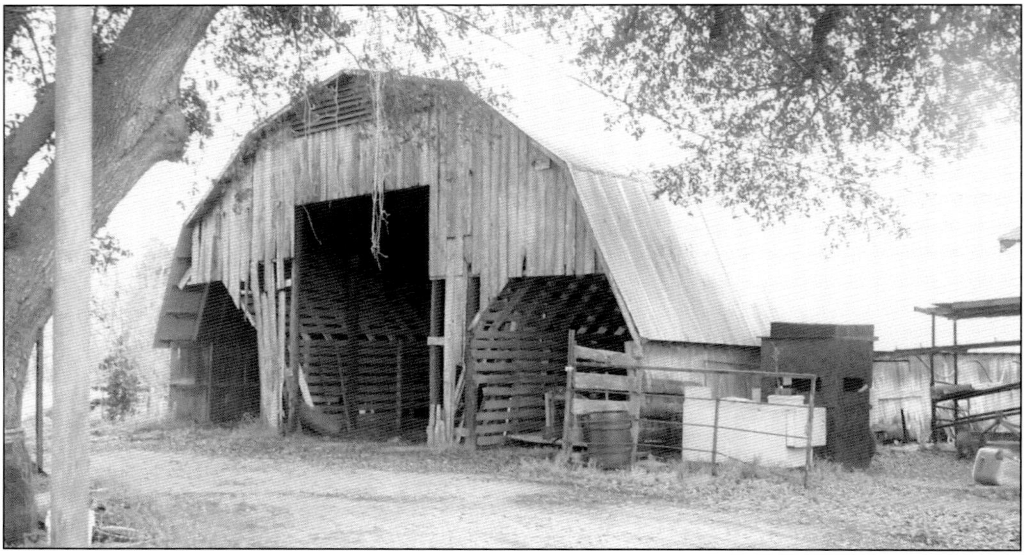

Ralph Racca, a lifelong dairy farmer, became involved with dairy-herd improvement from 1971 to 1984. Ralph and Sarah Guidry Racca live on and maintain farm property belonging to the J. Maxie Girouard family, where they raise assorted fowl. Ralph also drives a school bus for the Lafayette Parish School System. Maxie and his wife, Vida, operated one of the first family dairy farms in Lafayette Parish in 1951. Maxie was a board member for Dairymen, Incorporated, which was on Highway 90; its specialty was making mascarpone cheese for the pizza market. Maxie closed the dairy in 1971. Ralph also bales bay and helps his grandson raise chickens on the property. (Both, author's collection.)

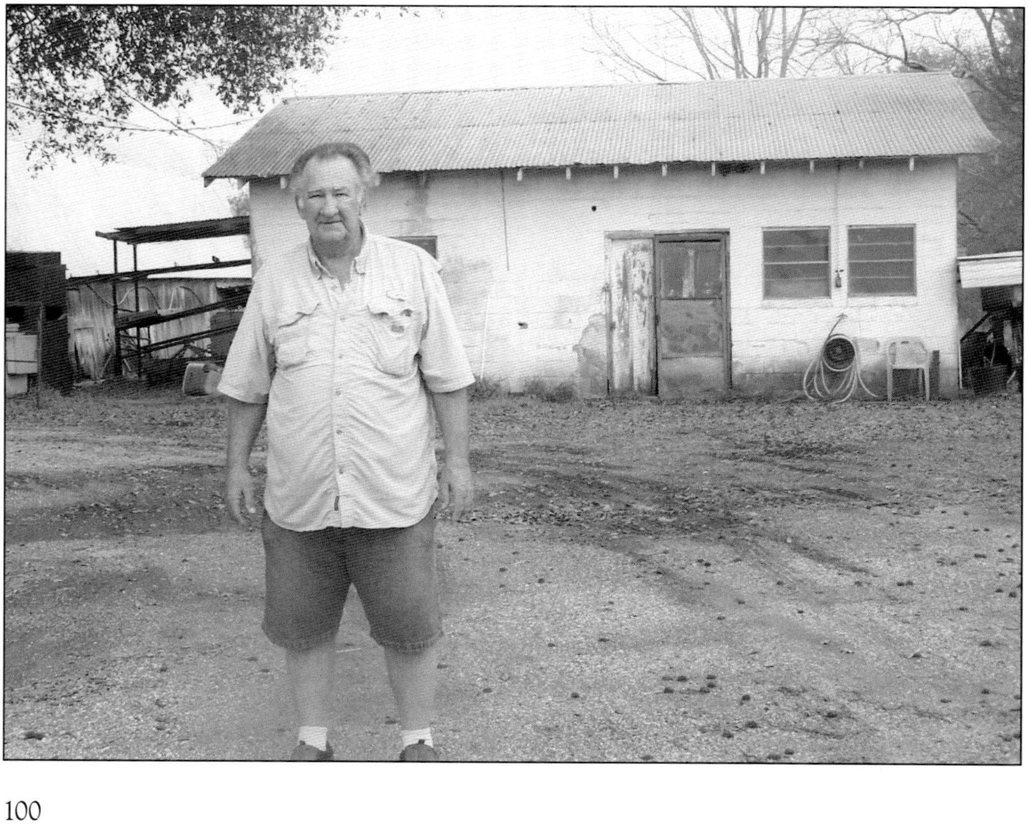

Seven

Dutiful Civil Servants and Military Figures

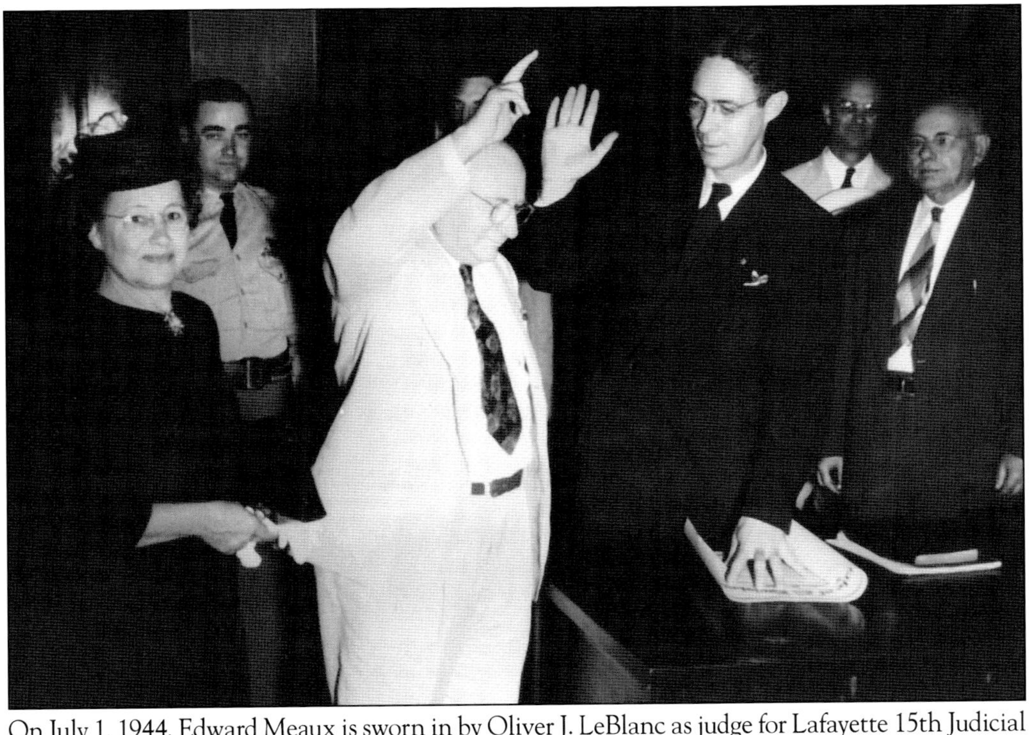

On July 1, 1944, Edward Meaux is sworn in by Oliver J. LeBlanc as judge for Lafayette 15th Judicial Court. With raised hand, Meaux swears to uphold his court duties, as witnessed by Ida Girouard Meaux, his smartly attired spouse, who is wearing a pillbox hat. In the rear are State Trooper Hundley, Don Labbe, and Valsin Benoit. (Lafayette Parish Clerk of Court Louis J. Perret.)

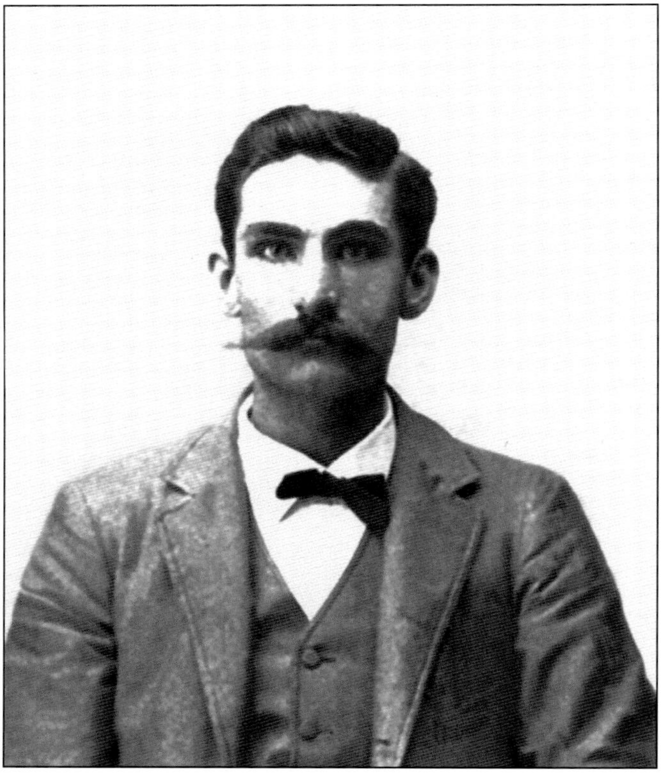

Joseph Breaux (pictured) built his Victorian home on Main Street in the later part of 1890, and it was purchased in 1915 by Joseph Oscar Girouard, who earned the rank of major during the Civil War. Over the years, the home underwent extensive remodeling and presently serves as Broussard City Hall. (City of Broussard archives.)

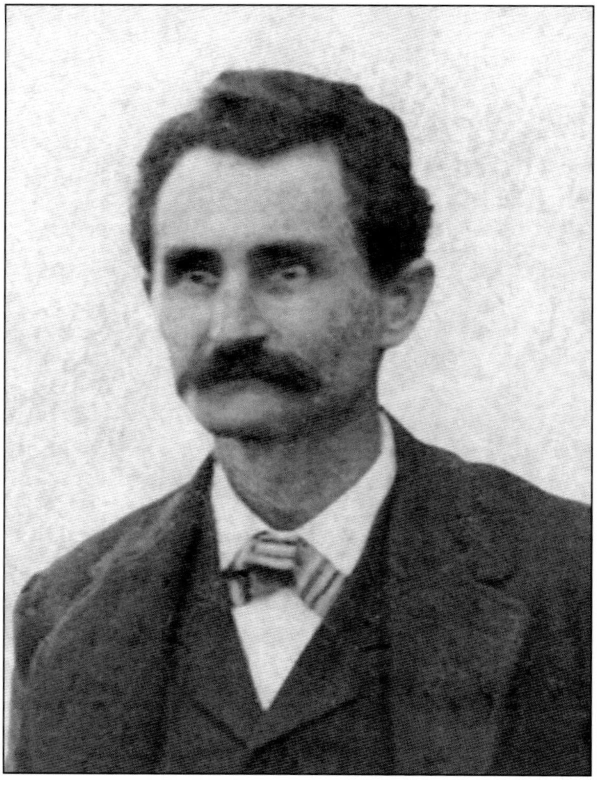

Romain Ulysses Bernard, the third of 11 mayors, served in that capacity from June 1922 to September 1923. Bernard married Helene Broussard, one of the daughters of the town's founder, Valsin Broussard. The Town of Broussard first incorporated in 1884 with a charter providing for a mayor, corporation council, town clerk, and town marshal. However, in 1886, the charter lapsed, as the people were discontent with their officials and government. Not until 1906 was the town reincorporated and a new government established. (City of Broussard archives.)

Eugene Edward Soulier, DDS, the town dentist, shared space in the Ducrest Drugstore and Broussard Post Office, where he provided for the dental needs in the community. Dr. Soulier also earned the respect of the townspeople as a four-term mayor, governing Broussard from 1910 to 1919. (City of Broussard archives.)

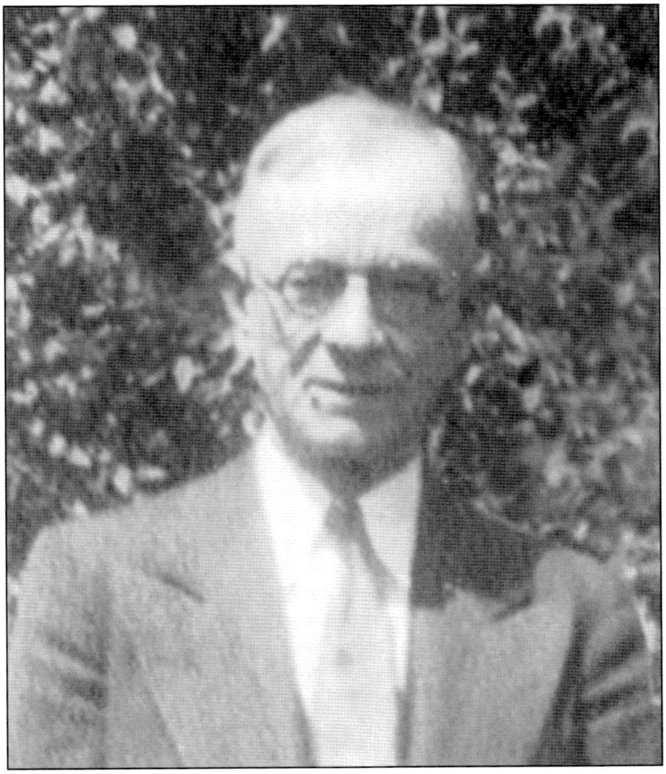

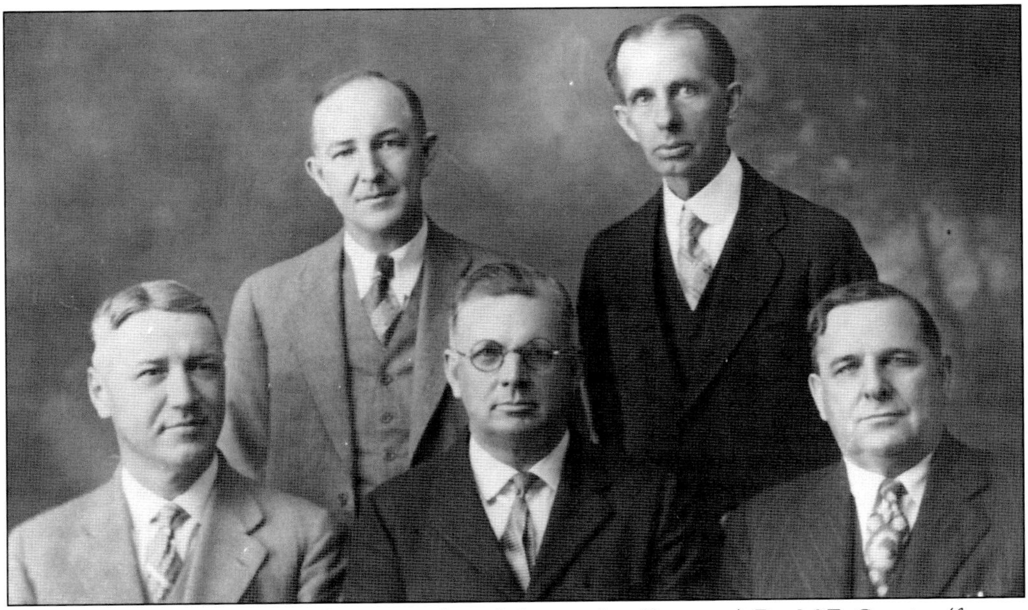

Lafayette Medical Society officers are, from left to right, (first row) Dr. M.E. Saucier (former president), Dr. A.J. Comeaux (president), and Dr. R.D. Voorhees (delegate to state convention); (second row) Dr. W.J. Youngue (secretary) and Dr. L.A. Prejean (vice president). Dr. Youngue married Goldie Billeaud, daughter of Charles Billeaud of the Billeaud Sugar Factory family. Since 1924, Dr. Youngue's unusual Bungalow-style home has had numerous owners. (Lafayette Parish clerk of court Louis Perret.)

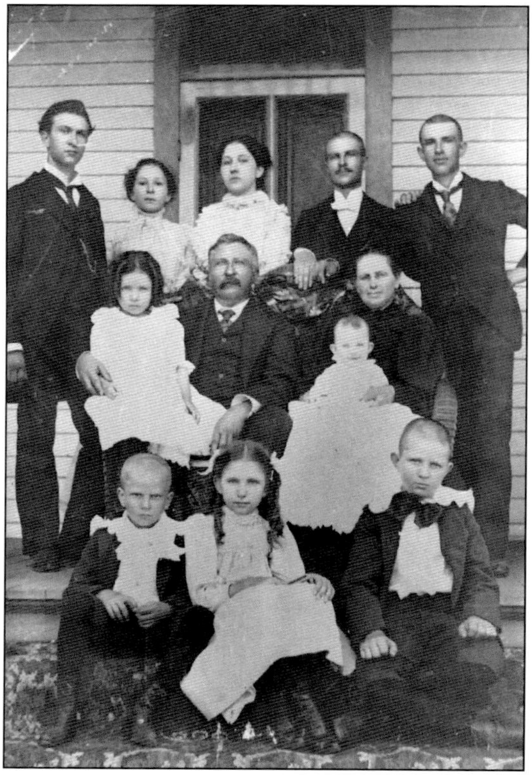

J. Gustave St. Julien and his wife, Marguerita Helena Roy, are pictured here in 1899. Both were natives of Lafayette Parish. J. Gustave left college at the outbreak of the Civil War and enlisted in the Confederate army, serving throughout the long conflict. The St. Julien and Roy families have long been identified with the agricultural, professional, and political interests of Lafayette Parish. (Lafayette Parish Clerk of Court Louis J. Perret.)

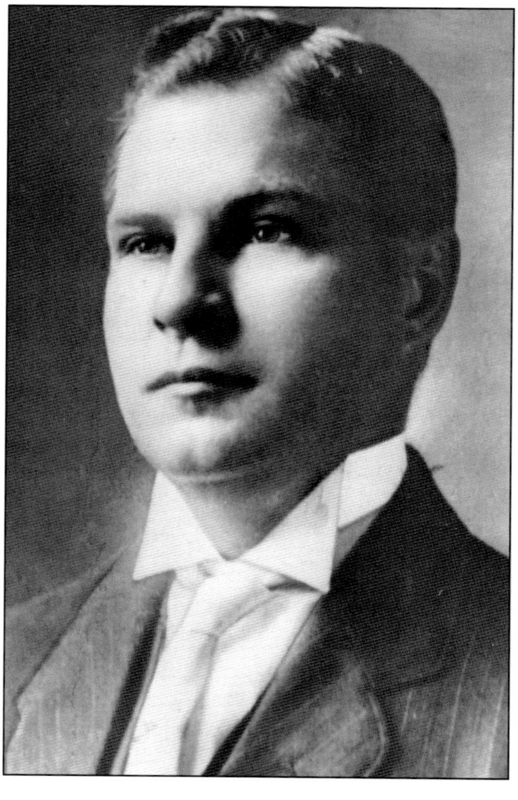

Gilbert St. Julien, son of J. Gustave and brother to Maj. Aurelien St. Julien, led the vigilante committee in Lafayette Parish after the close of the Civil War. Gilbert served on the police jury for 20 years, twice as president. After college, he ran Martial Billeaud Jr.'s general merchandise store in Broussard. In 1901, Gilbert served four years in the legislature. He married Idolie Girouard, one of Joseph Oscar Girouard's daughters, in 1905. (City of Broussard archives.)

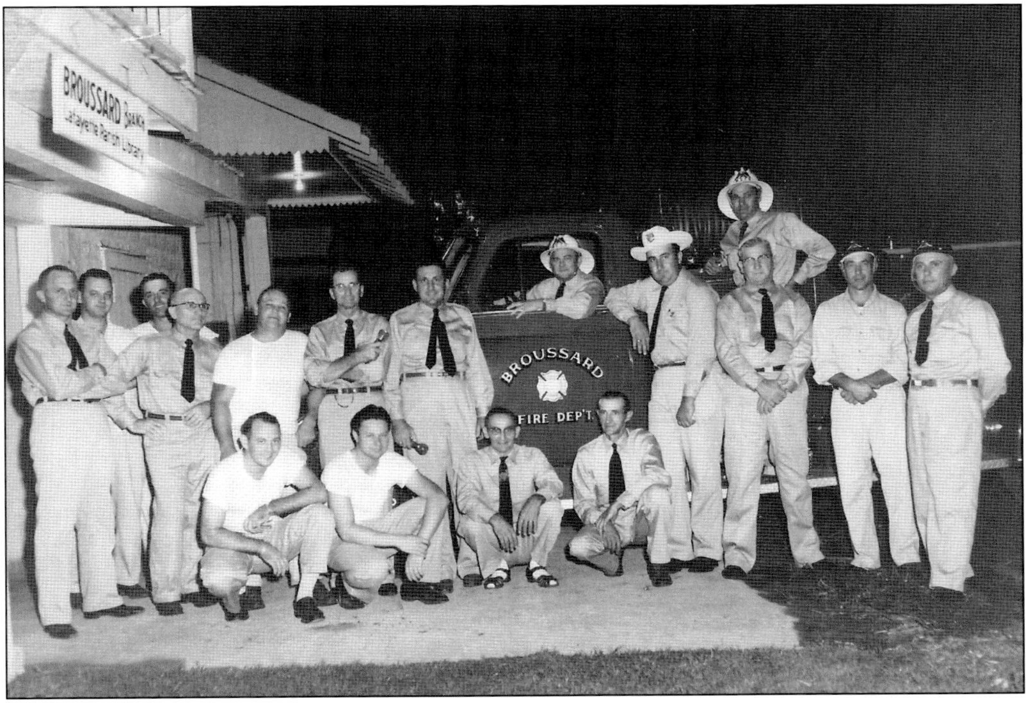

Broussard's old town hall and library is the backdrop in this photograph of the Broussard Volunteer Fire Department, which was located across Main Street from the present-day Broussard administrative offices. Pictured are, from left to right, (kneeling) Bootsie Morvant, Raymond Billeaud, and two unidentified; (standing) Cabill Boumans, two unidentified, Clarence Smith, Alsace Bernard, Donnie Gautreaux, Louis Felix "Crip" Malagarie, assistant chief John "Gus" Guilbeaux, Aniston Ewing (town taxi driver), assistant chief George Prejean (on running board), and two unidentified. Inside the cab of the fire truck is Chief Louis Langlinais. (Charlie Landry.)

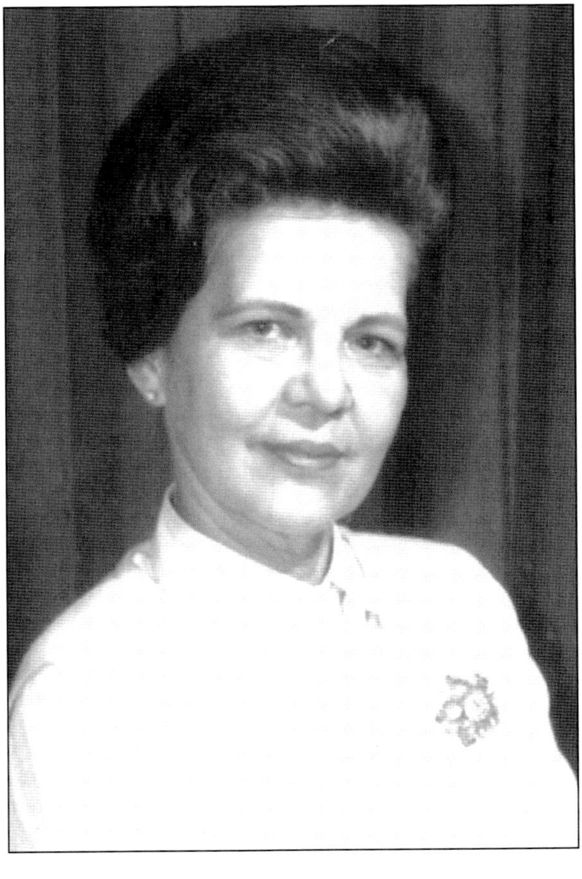

Annette Choplin Hollier Broussard served as the town clerk of Broussard during the administrations of Mayor Charles "Boy" Girouard and Mayor Leroy Miguez. Broussard was also the town's librarian. (City of Broussard archives.)

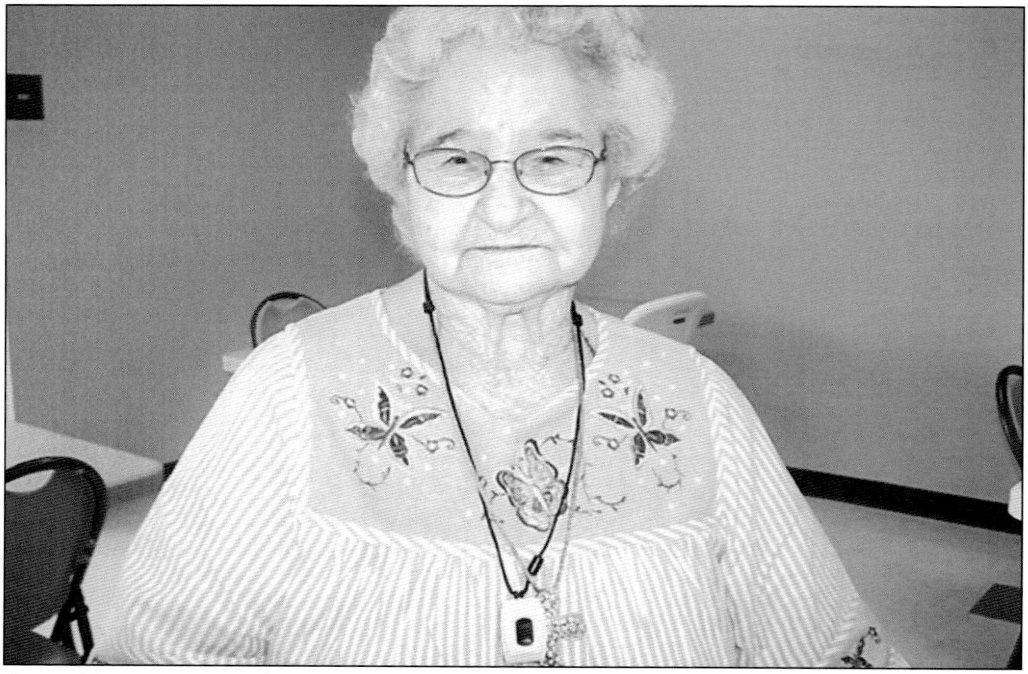

Constable Laura Menard retired in 2014, having served six four-year terms as Ward 5 constable, a job that at times crossed geographical boundaries. Being a civil servant is still all in the family, as Laura's daughter Barbara Broussard is the current justice of the peace. (Author's collection.)

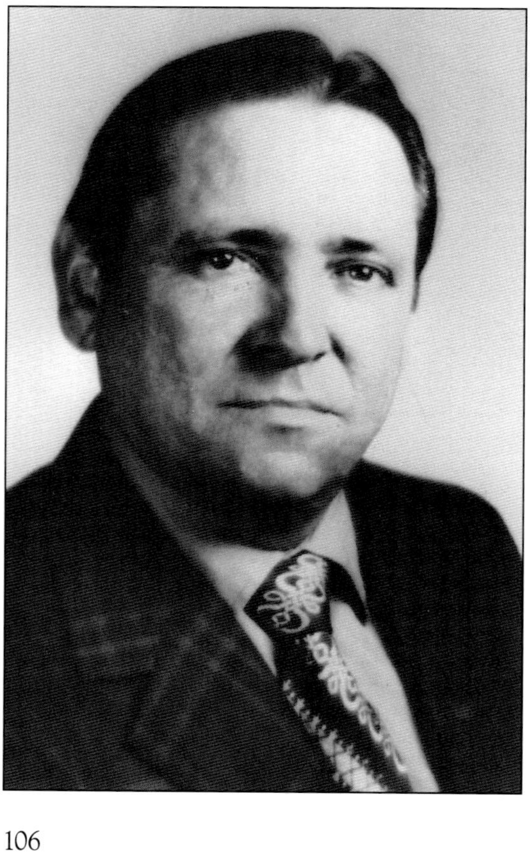

Lloyd Girouard served as a police juror from 1967 to 1969. In 1973, Girouard headed the Lafayette Parish Department of Registrar of Voters. Before entering the political arena, he ran a local Broussard bar. (Lafayette Parish Clerk of Court Louis J. Perret.)

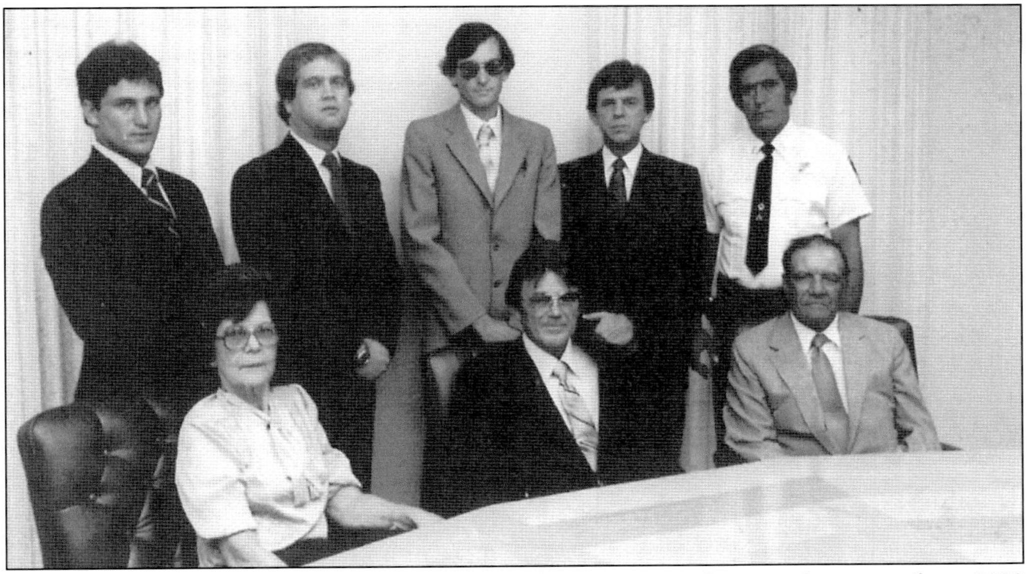

Leroy Miguez, a town grocer for 45 years, served two terms as Broussard mayor—from 1982 to 1986 and 1986 to 1990. He was also elected as an at-large councilman in 1994. A major accomplishment under his watch was the creation of districts as representation for the African American community. Pictured here are, from left to right, (first row) Annette Broussard (town clerk), Mayor Leroy Miguez, and Chief of Police Harold Romero; (second row) council members Mark St. Marie (youngest member to serve), Chuck Billeaud, James Choplin, Charlie Landry, and Sid Broussard. (Mark Ste. Marie.)

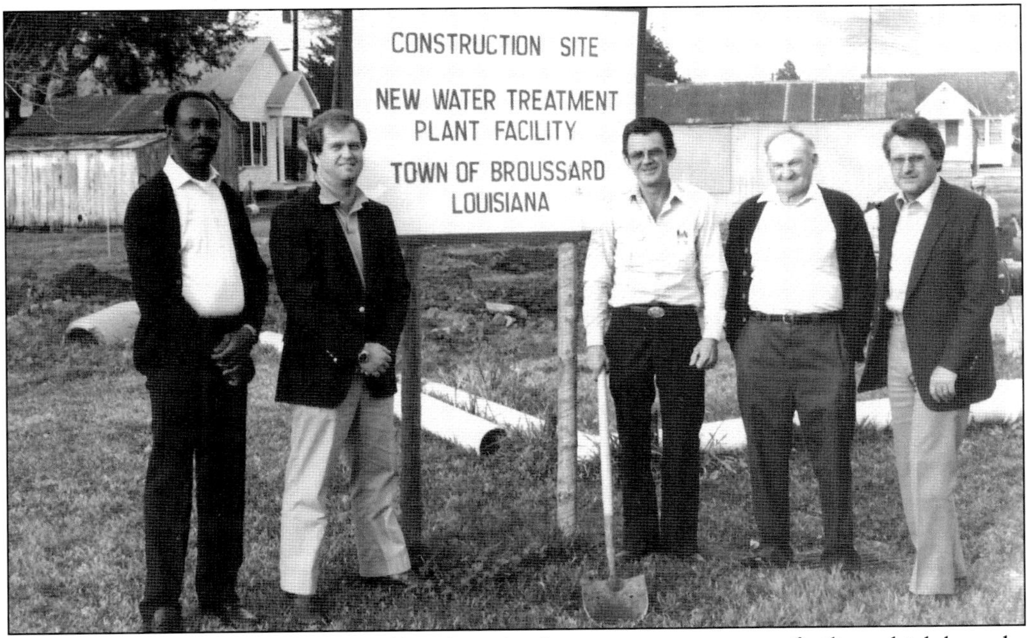

The Town of Broussard held a ground breaking for the new water-treatment facility, which brought its water standards up to federal regulations during Mayor Leroy Miguez's administration in the early part of 1982. From left to right, councilmen Harold Johnson, Chuck Billeaud, Mayor Leroy Miguez (holding shovel), George Choplin, and Burton Duhon check out the construction site, which was across from the old Broussard Middle School on Madison Street. (Maxine Duhon.)

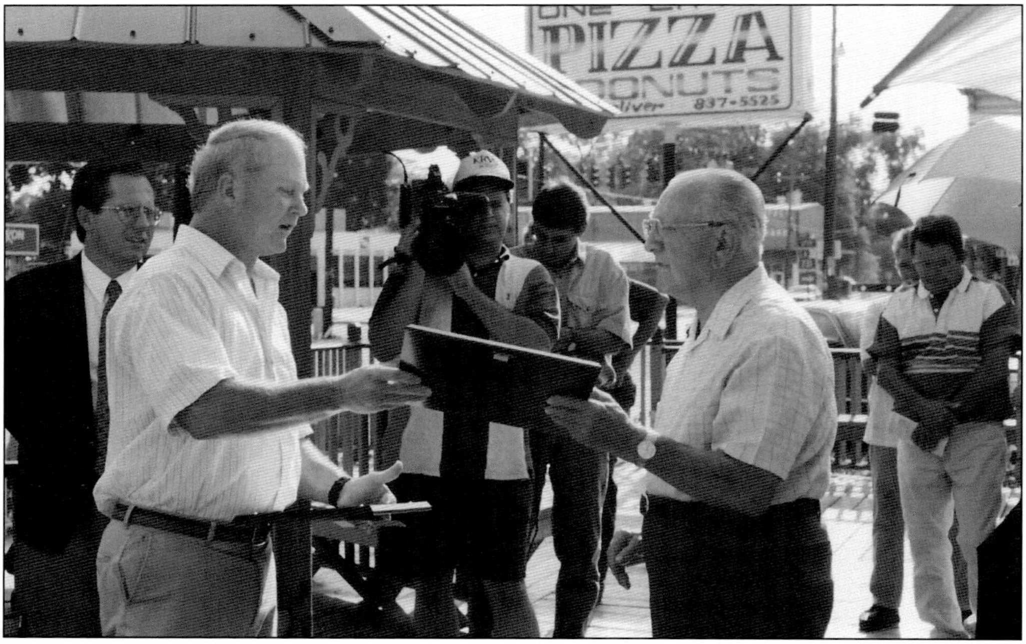

Former mayor Charles A. "Boy" Girouard (right) is pictured here accepting a dedicatory plaque for his years of service from 1966 to 1982 from Charles E. Langlinais. The original plaque hangs on the exterior of Broussard City Hall. (Eula Bodin.)

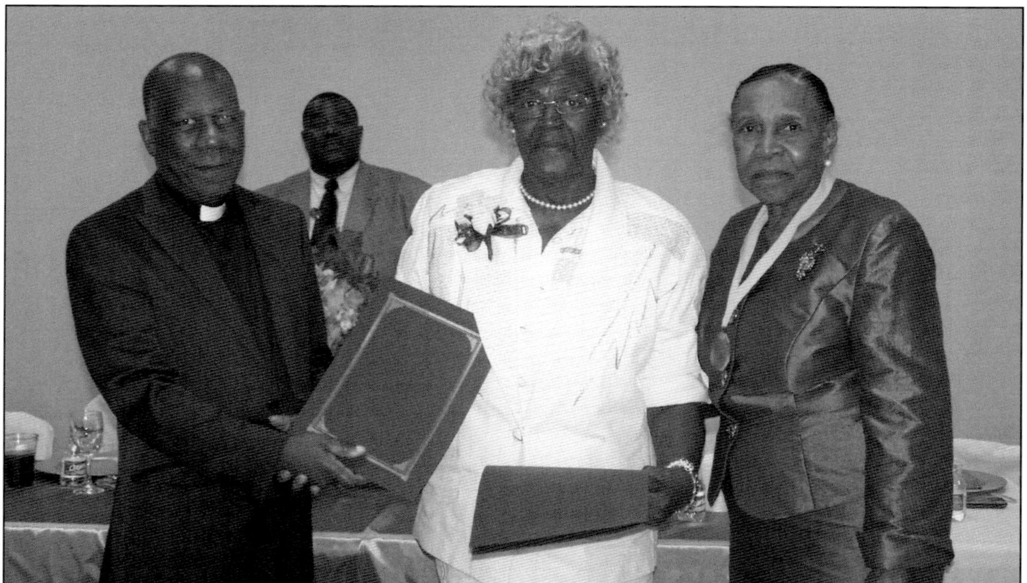

Gertrude Nickerson Batiste, a parishioner of St. Joseph's Church and alumna of old St. Joseph's School, lives in the Anita St. Julien Home, one of the town's historic houses. She is the first African American woman to serve as District 4 councilwoman. When it comes to volunteering, Batiste has a big heart, whether sitting with the sick or delivering commodities to less-fortunate citizens. Brother Justice Crowder, Order Friars Minor, and Margaret Green Guidry, retired educator, present Batiste with the Mother Katherine Drexel Society award for exemplary church and community service. (Author's collection.)

Walter St Julien Comeaux Jr. served as a city councilman from 1972 to 1976 and became the first Lafayette Parish president in 1984. Comeaux's most noteworthy accomplishment was his oversight of funeral homes. There was a time when the owners felt they could no longer provided ambulance service to the community. He met with Richard Zuschlag and Roland Dugas, and they established and trained the first EMTs in the state of Louisiana; returning Vietnam veterans with medic experience provided their initial source of manpower. The result was an ambulance company—Acadiana Ambulance, today's leader in its field. (City of Broussard archives.)

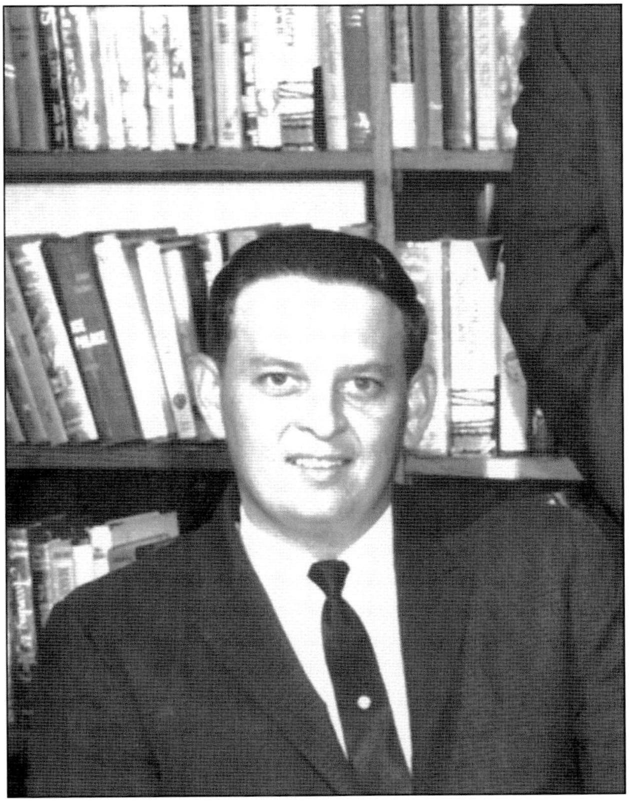

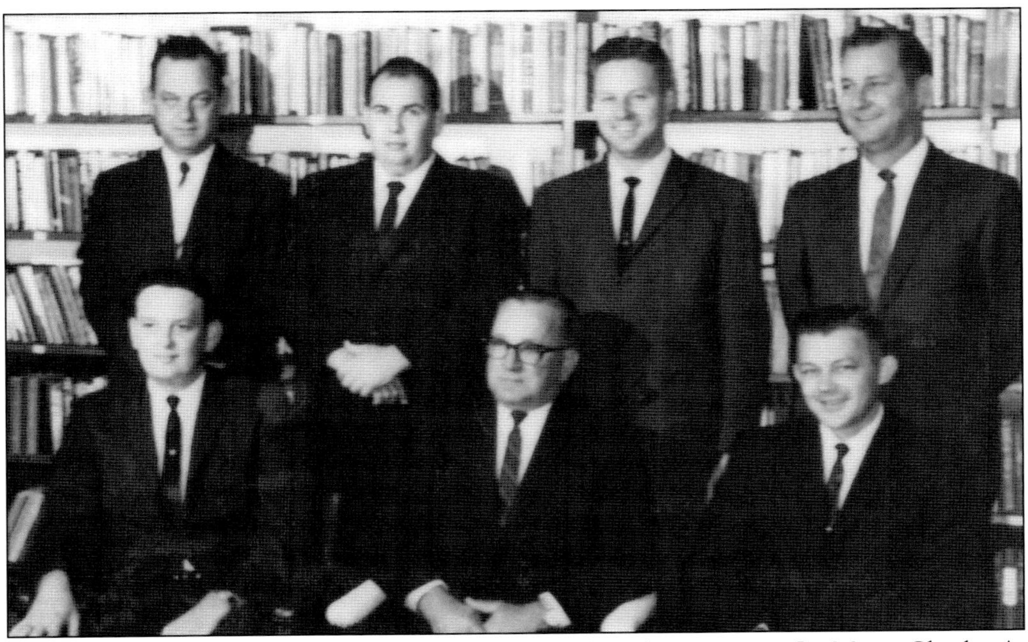

Pictured here in 1966 are, from left to right, (first row) Walter Comeaux Jr., Mayor Charles A. "Boy" Girouard (1966–1982), and Leroy Miguez; (second row) Clarence Smith, Roland Laurent (city engineer), Ramon Billeaud, and Louis Edward Billeaud. (Lafayette Parish Clerk of Court Louis J. Perret.)

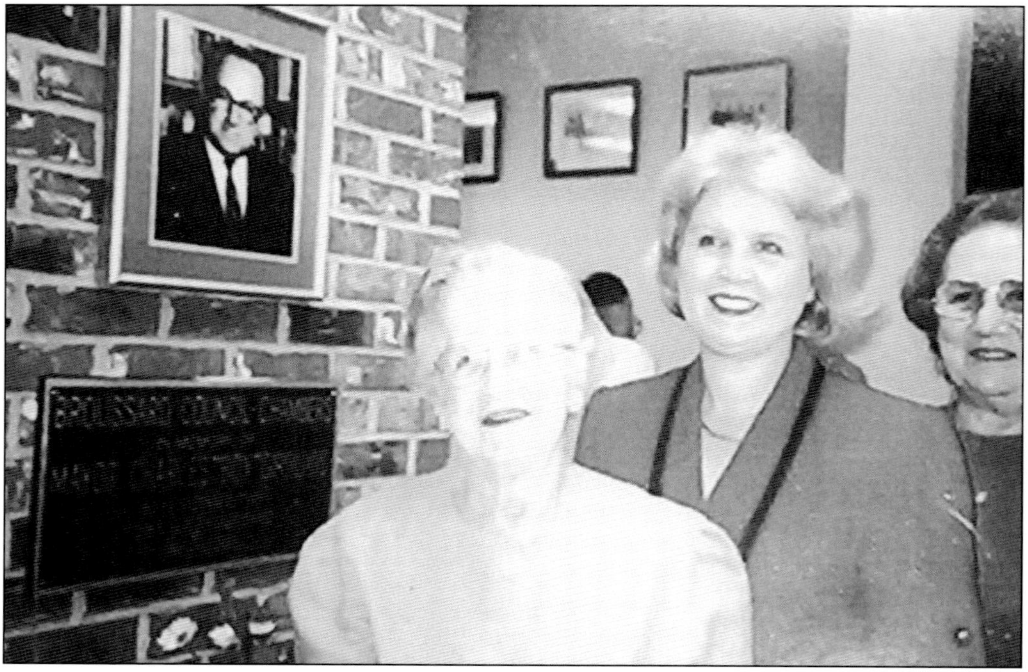

Attie Talbot Girouard is seen here with her niece at the dedication of the new Broussard City Council chambers. It was dedicated in memory of Charles A. "Boy" Girouard, who was a four-term mayor of Broussard, from 1966 to 1982. (City of Broussard archives.)

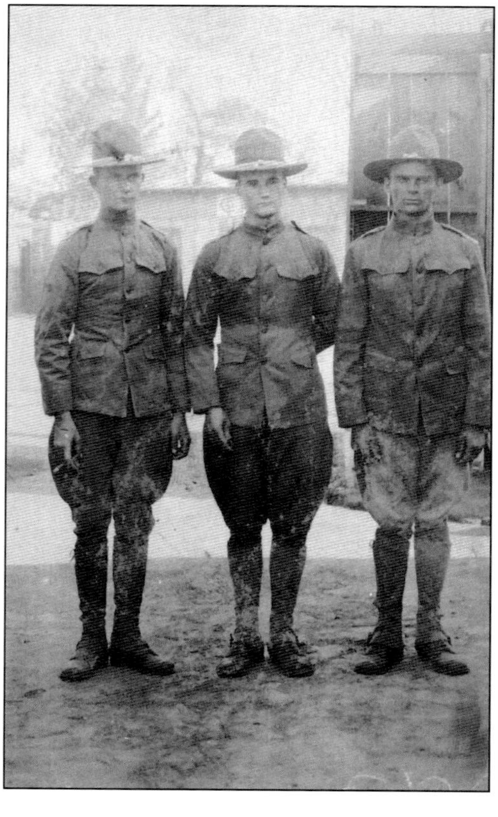

World War I veteran Gaston Gondron (center) poses for the camera with a couple of his Army buddies. Gondron was a dairy farmer in the downtown area of Broussard; his granddaughter Carolyn Gondron Langlinais is married to six-term mayor Charles E. Langlinais. (Jim Gondron.)

Joseph Huval served in the US Army during World War I. He and his wife, Lorena Landry Huval, reared a large family, invested in property, and raised cattle and sugarcane in Broussard. Huval founded Evangeline Maid Bread in 1919 and opened his first bakery in 1937 on Simcoe Street in Lafayette. Their youngest daughter, Mary Helen Guchereau, was the model whose face is on every loaf of Evangeline Maid Bread, one of the top-selling breads in Acadiana. (Lafayette Parish Clerk of Court Louis J. Perret.)

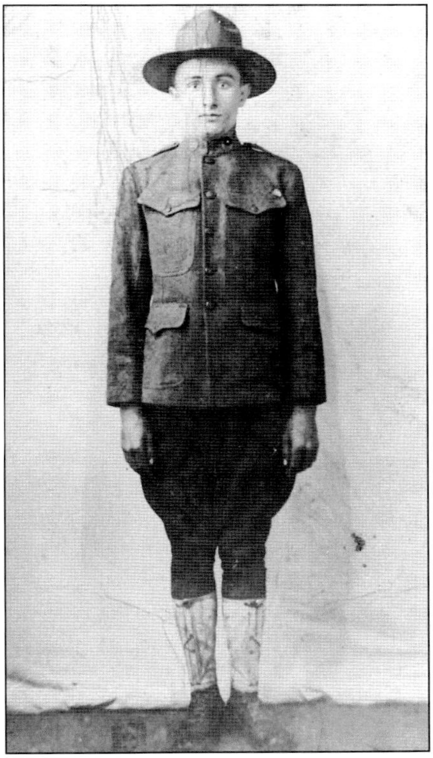

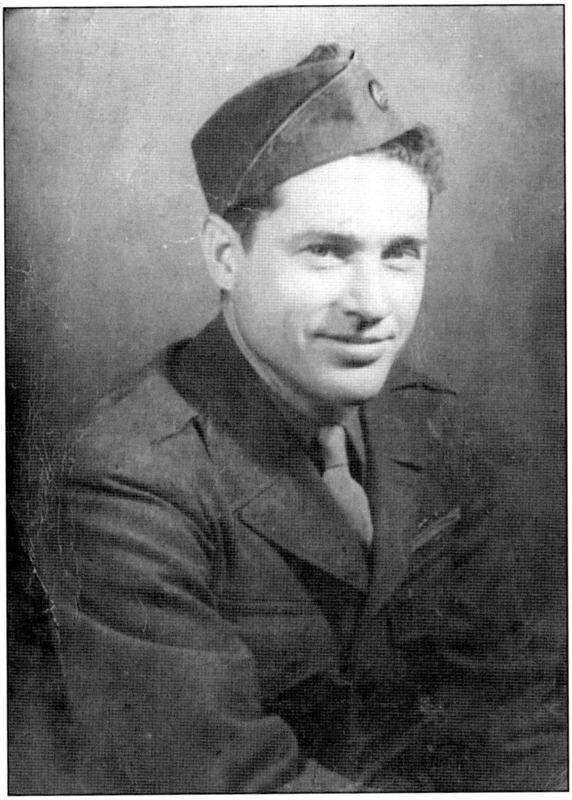

Pvt. Alexander P. Choplin was among thousands of young soldiers from Lafayette Parish who proudly answered the Selective Service Act call to service during World War II. Choplin made the ultimate sacrifice and was killed in action in 1945. He left behind his namesake, Alexander Choplin Jr., who was five years old. (Alexander "Brother" Choplin.)

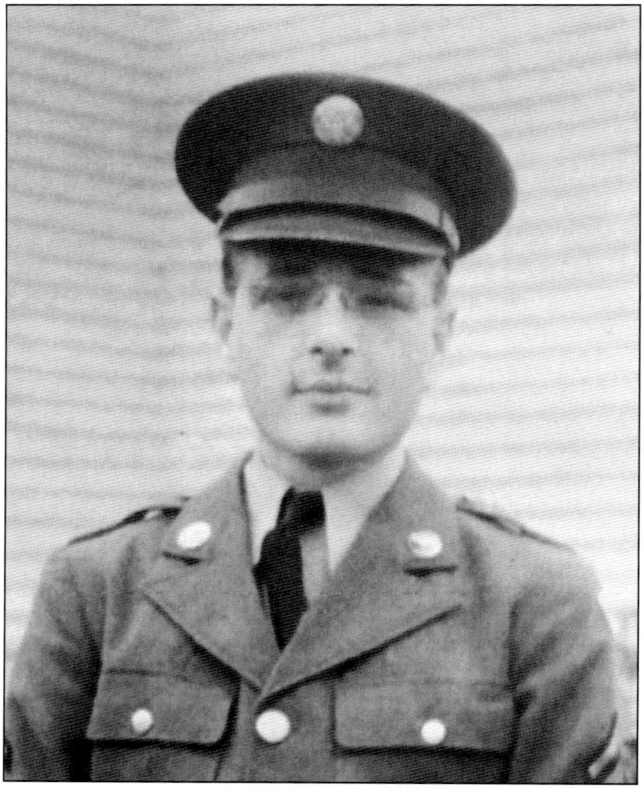

Eugene Edward Soulier Jr., the son of E.E. Soulier, a Broussard dentist, served in the US Army during World War II. After the war, Soulier Jr. returned to Broussard, where he operated an independent insurance agency. (City of Broussard archives.)

On April 8, 1945, Pvt. Henry Langlinais (third in line on the right side) marches with the 35th Infantry Division from Camp Campbell, Kentucky. The unit is taking part in a parade held in Chicago, Illinois, honoring Pres. Harry S. Truman. (Henry Langlinais.)

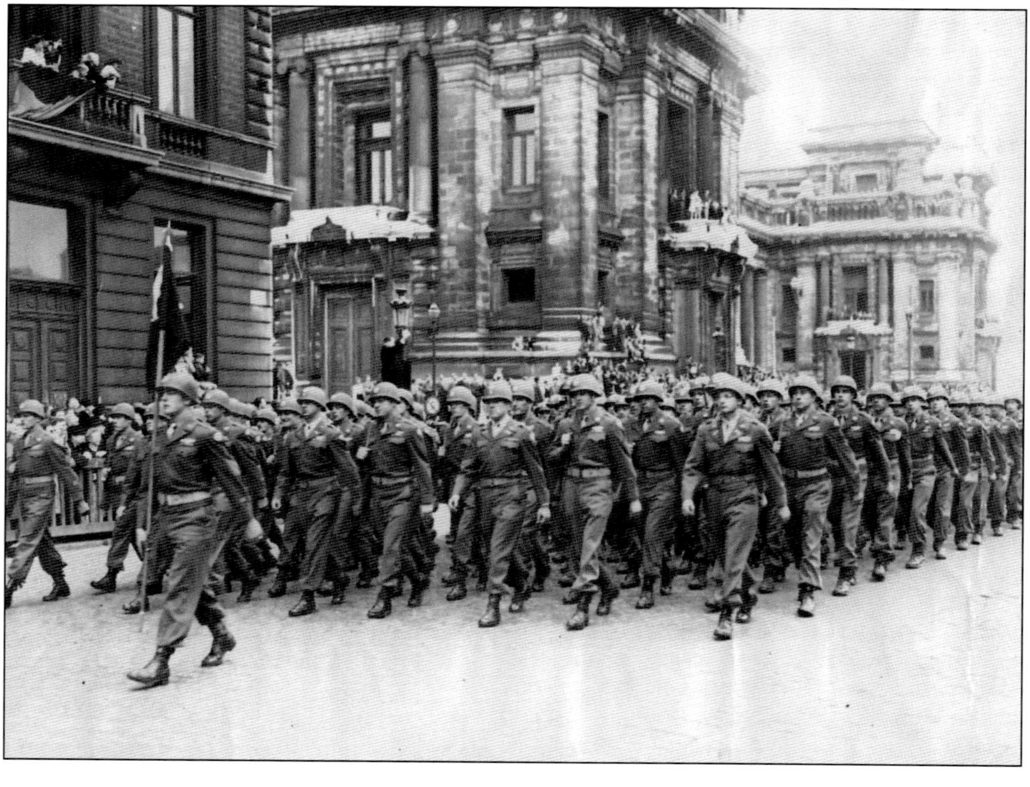

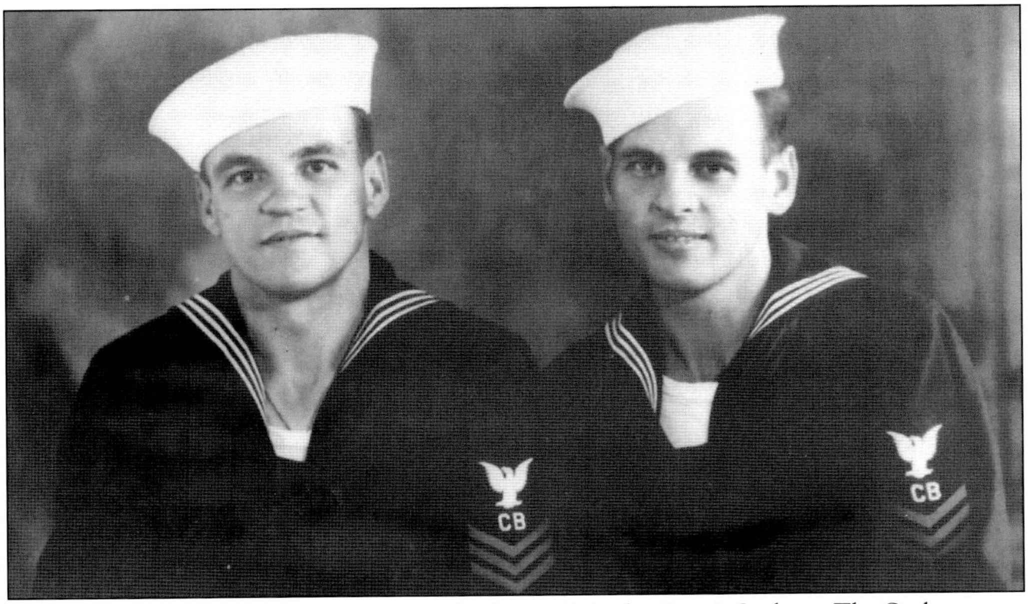

Lloyd and Walter Comeaux were among the first to join the Navy's Seabees. The Seabees were organized in 1942 to serve as engineers during World War II. (Lafayette Parish Clerk of Court Louis J. Perret.)

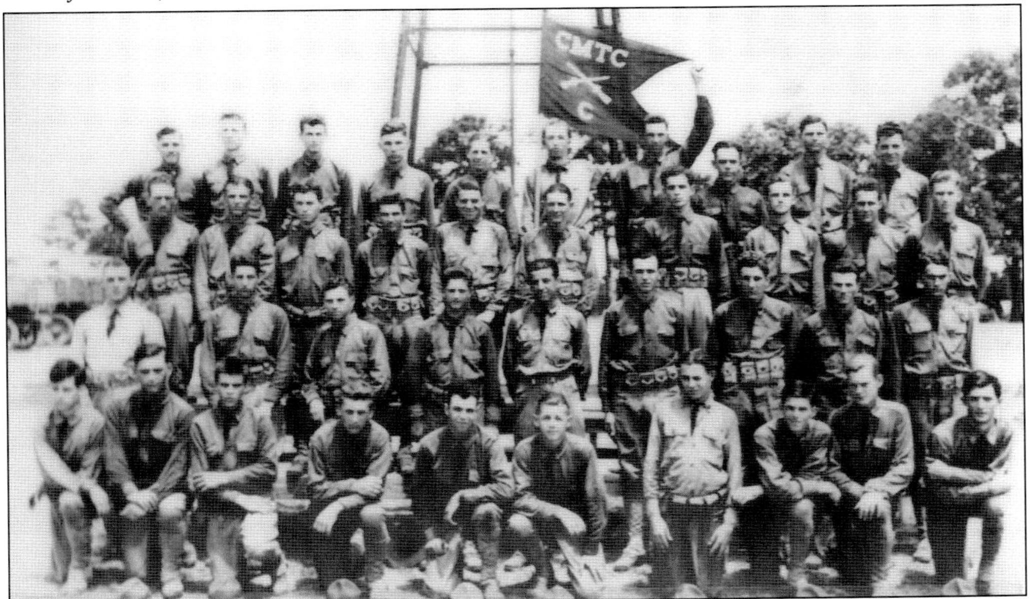

Camp Beauregard in Pineville, Louisiana, was a training and mobilization center dating back to World War I; these Broussard soldiers with Company C, 3rd Platoon, were in training in 1928. They are, from left to right, (first row) ? Burley, ? Broussard, Paul Miguez, ? Guigrioy, Smith Yersier, ? Barrouse, Sergeant Eliot ?, and ? Wimberly; (second row) ? Verret, Blaise Reaux, George Comeaux, ? Smith, ? Broussard, ? Arceneaux, Maxie Girouard, Cyrus Vincent, and ? Breaux; (third row) Rene Theriot, David DeLaureal, ? Hobby, ? Gregory, ? Louison, ? Harris, ? Leblanc, unidentified, Tom Reaux, and ? Love; (fourth row) Sgt. D.K. Ryan, ? Hart, Willis Delana, ? Calligan, unidentified, ? Henry, Maurice St. Julien, ? Poussan, ? Quirk, and ? Richard. (Lafayette Parish Clerk of Court Louis J. Perret.)

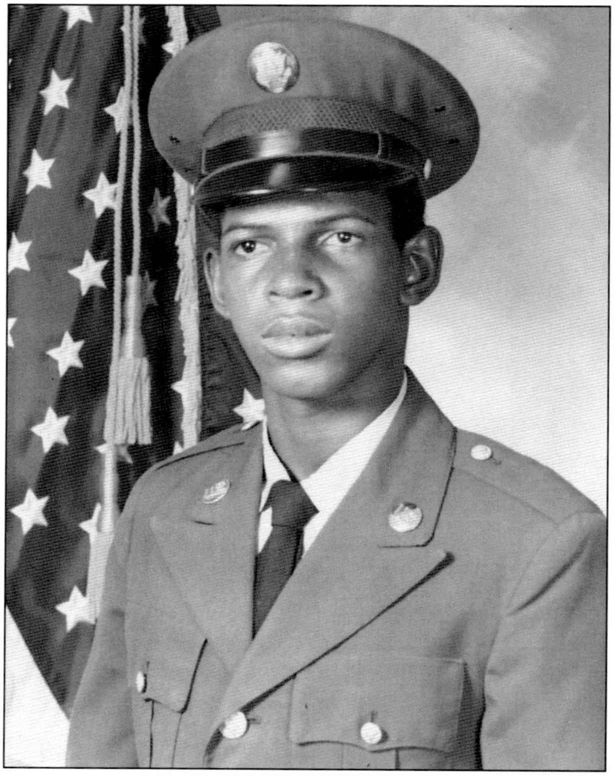

Russell Flugence, a three-time Golden Glove champion (1973–1975), enlisted in the Army after high school graduation in 1975. Flugence attained the rank of specialist fourth class while serving in Swanson, Germany. Following his military tour, Flugence pursued a career with the postal service and in his spare time plays competitive tennis. He finished sixth in the 2011 United States Tennis Association National Senior Tournament. (Russell Flugence.)

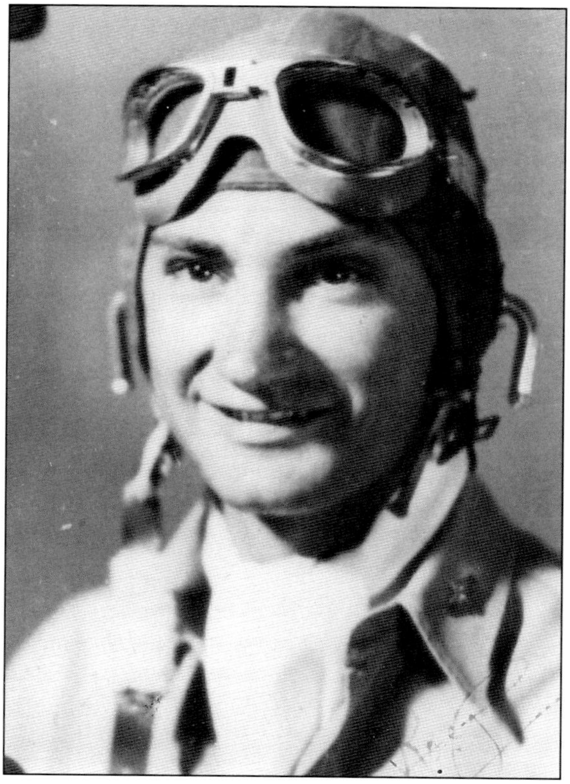

LeeRoy Gondron loved aviation and proudly served in the Army Air Corps, which played a combat role with the Army during World War II. Following his return to civilian life, Gondron settled down on the family farm, married Margaret Morvant, and bought a small herd of dairy cows. (Jim Gondron.)

Francis Newton Leblanc was a man who literally walked all over the world. Newton, raised in the Leblanc community, lived near an aviation viewing area. He lied about his age, enlisting in the Army like his older brother Joseph Leblanc, one of hundreds of soldiers forced to undergo the Bataan Death March in the Philippines. Newton was attached to the 751st Field Artillery Battalion in Germany. After the war, he followed his brother in becoming a petroleum engineer and traveled with his wife, Clara Leblanc, all over the world—except England. Business took them from the North Pole to the South Pole and Australia. He loved walking through the different villages and towns. (Author's collection.)

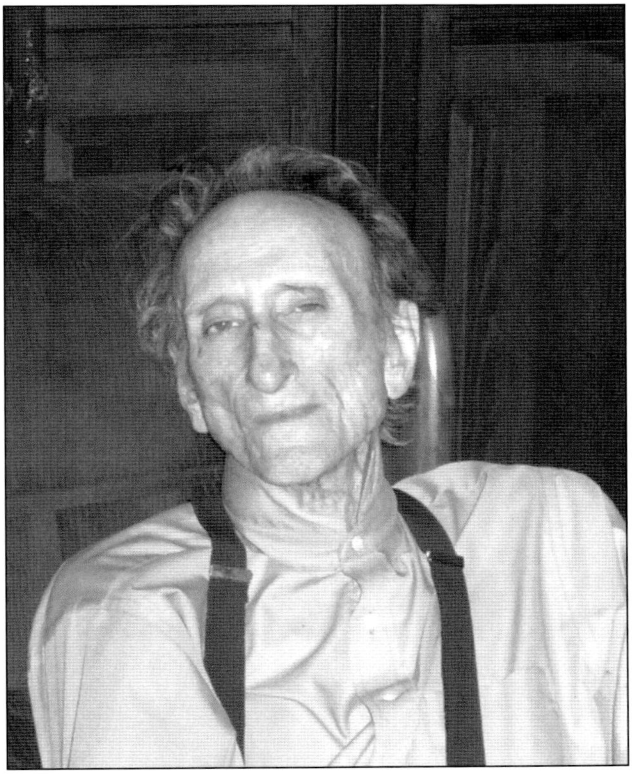

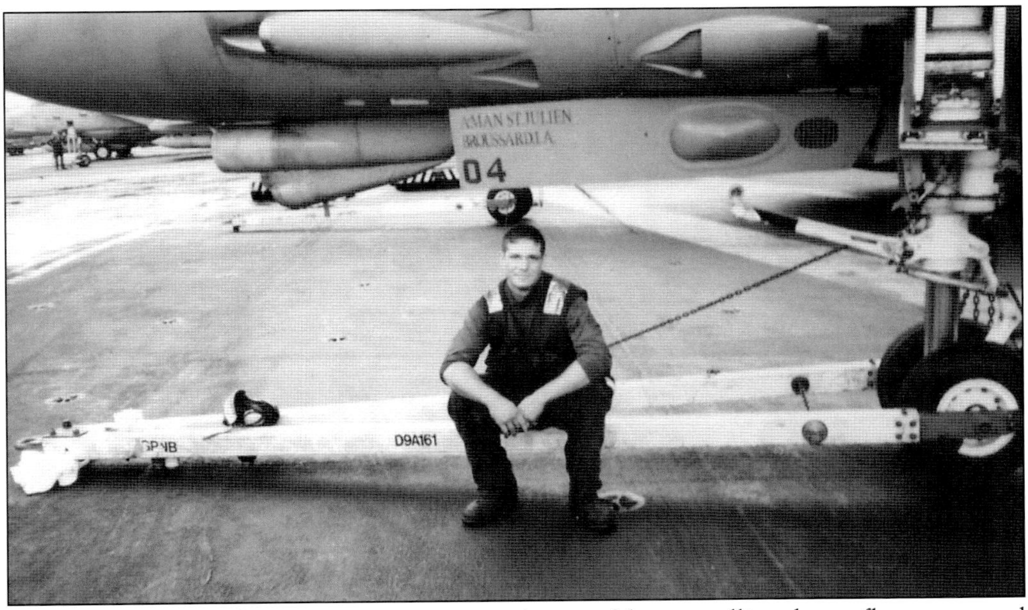

Airman Steven St. Julien was serving a six-month tour of duty patrolling the no-fly zone around Iraq from aboard the USS *Enterprise* aircraft carrier out of Norfolk, Virginia, and was headed back to the United States when news arrived of the Pentagon bombing placing the country officially at war in September 2001. St Julien's name appears several times, along with the bomber pilot's name, on the doors of the landing gear of an F-14, the first planes to bomb in Afghanistan. (Patrick St. Julien.)

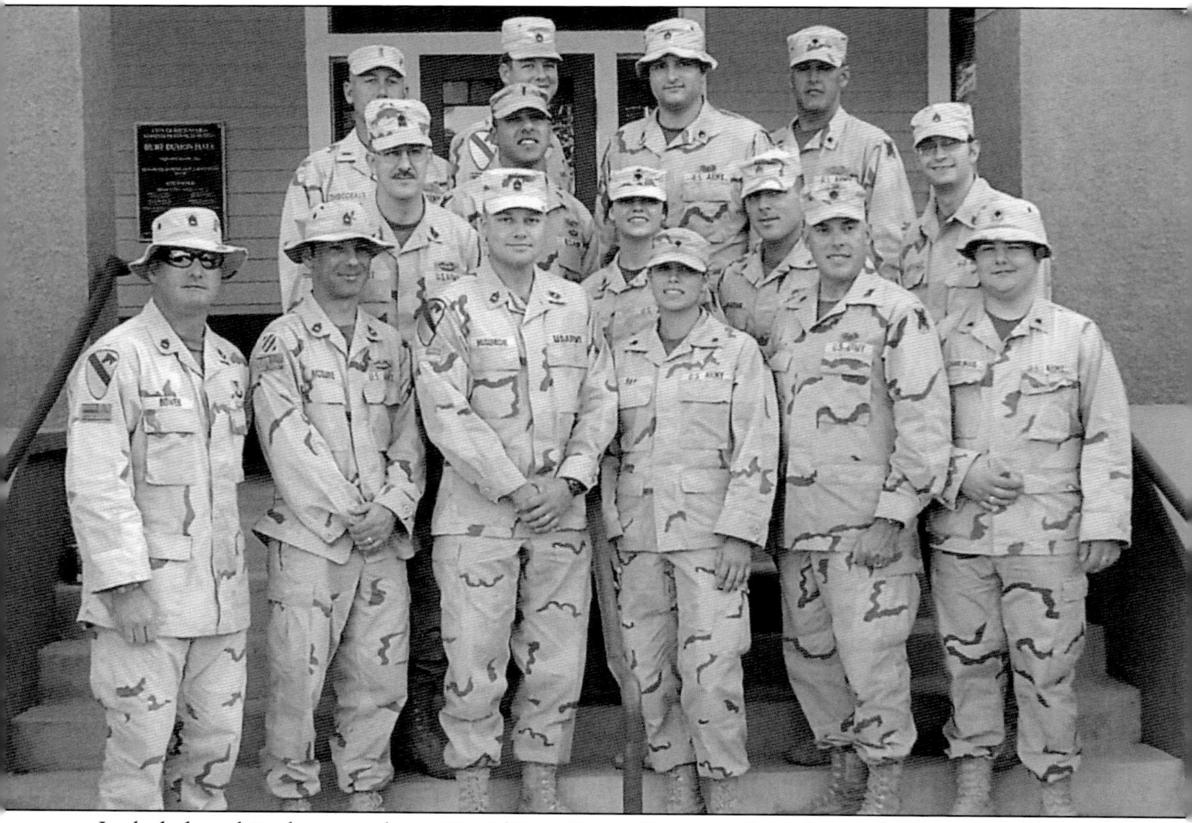

Included in this photograph are David Langlinais (first row, far right) and Selina Ray (first row, center), a former unit supply specialist. Both served with the Louisiana National Guard 256 Infantry Brigade Combat Team in Iraq at Camp Liberty. When the 256th arrived at Camp Liberty, the group changed the name to Camp Tigerland. Langlinais is the son of Charles E. Langlinais, who is currently serving his sixth term as mayor of Broussard. Ray is the daughter of Claude and Brenda Ray, owners of Claude's Cabinets and Millworks in Broussard. (Carolyn Langlinais.)

Eight

Town Ball and Other Fun

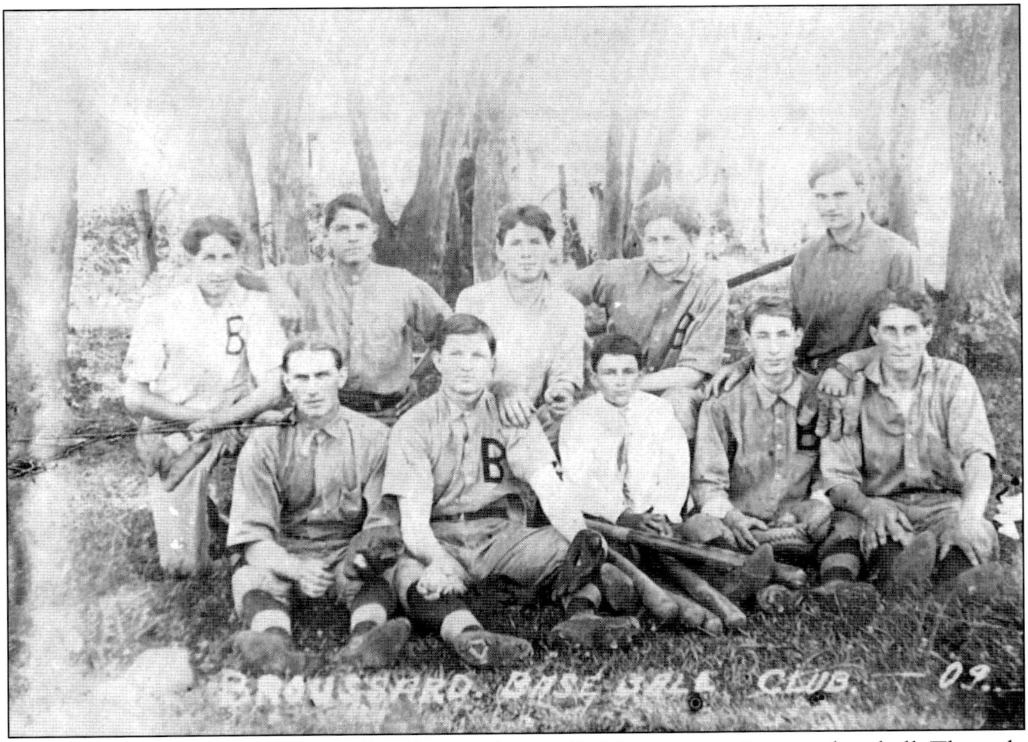

It was evident as far back as 1903 that America's so-called favorite pastime was baseball. The only team members identified in this photograph are Frank Girouard Sr. (back row center) and Charles Reaux (front row, right). These Class C ballplayers were at the top of their game. (Lafayette Parish Clerk of Court Louis J. Perret.)

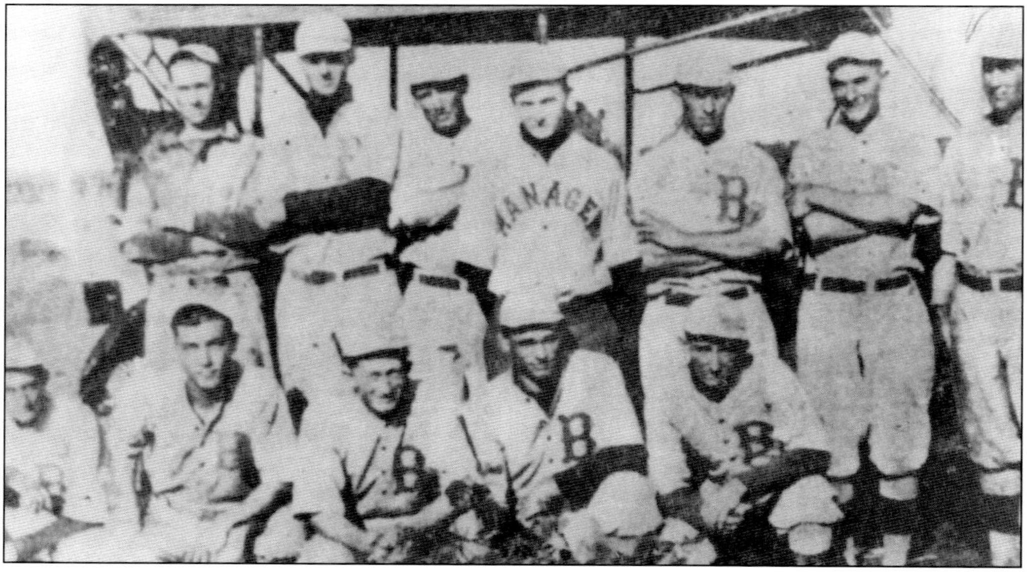

Small-town baseball teams mirrored the social fabric of the surrounding community's economic and political structures. These players from Broussard Baseball Club are, from left to right, (first row) Gilbert "Bert" Broussard, Curley Richard, Charles K. Langlinais (catcher), F.T. Olivier (pitcher), and George Stromer (catcher); (second row) Eric St. Julien, Ray LeBlanc, Frank Girouard, Dr. Eugene E. Soulier (team manager), Pep Dupuis, Walter Billeaud, and Boone LeBlanc. (Lafayette Parish Clerk of Court Louis J. Perret.)

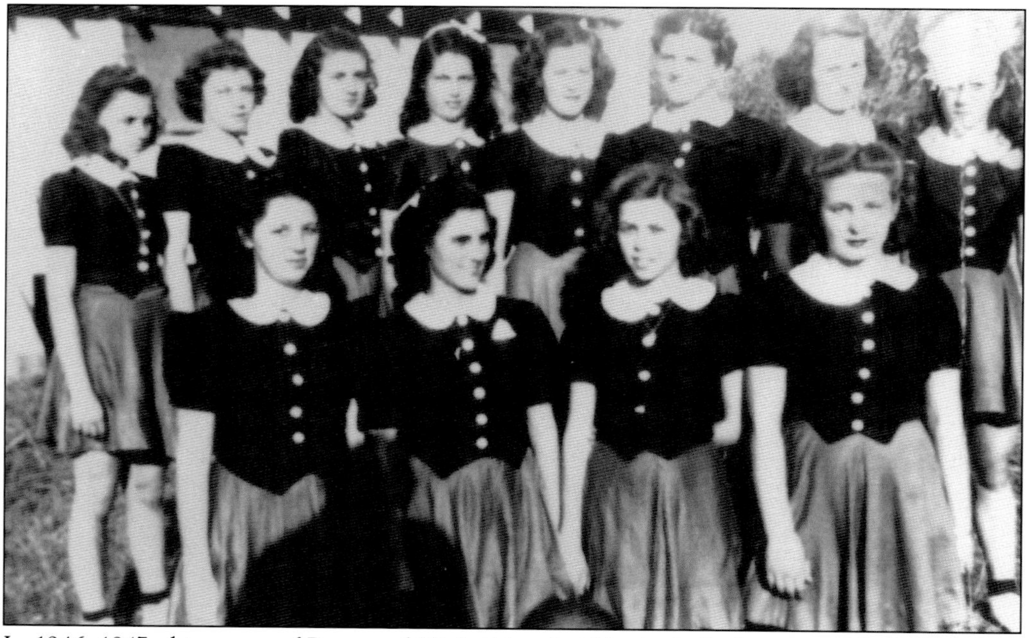

In 1946–1947, this group of Broussard High School girl basketball players was the last team to play prior to the high school department closing in the effort to consolidate public high schools in Lafayette Parish. Among those pictured are Lucille Landry Smith, Ethel Hollier Morvant, Melba Miller Dubois, Lillian Guilbeaux Dugas, Lorraine Ledoux, Lou Patin Beam, Maggie Garber Hebert, Sylvia Leblanc Langlinais, Leona Ducrest, Yvonne Yongue, and coach Ruby Roseberry Duhon. (Lafayette Parish Clerk of Court Louis J. Perret.)

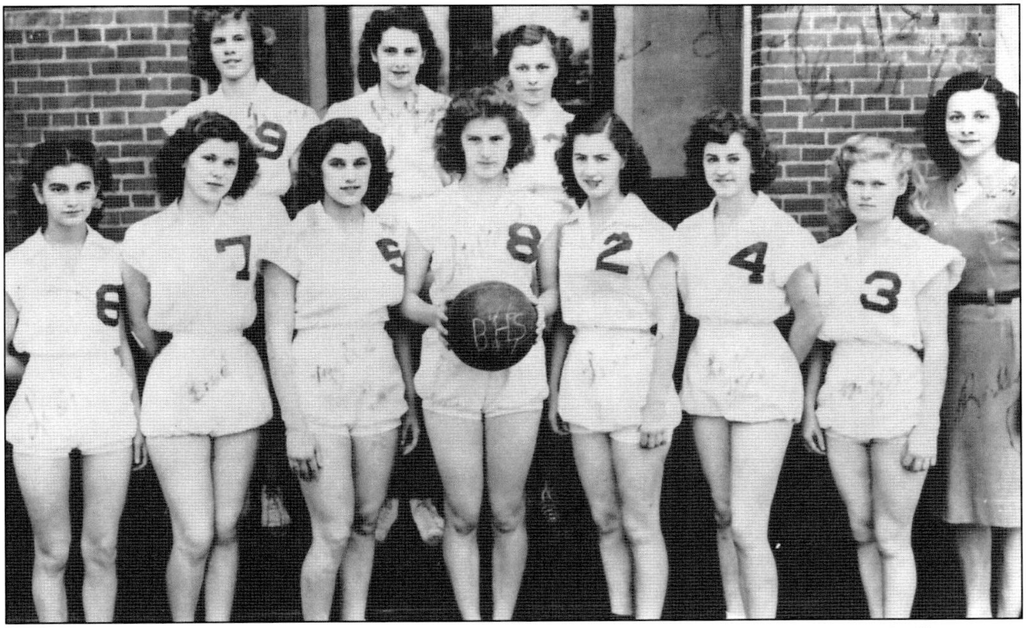

In 1946–1947, these players dressed in white uniforms were the last girls' basketball team at Broussard High School, prior to the consolidation of Lafayette Parish public high schools. Pictured are (front row), from left to right, Lucille Landry Smith, Ethel Hollier Morvant, Melba Miller Dubois, Lillian Guilbeaux Dugas, Lorraine Ledoux, Lou Patin Beam, Maggie Garber Hebert, and coach Ruby Roseberry Duhon; (back row) three unidentified. (Lafayette Parish Clerk of Court Louis J. Perret.)

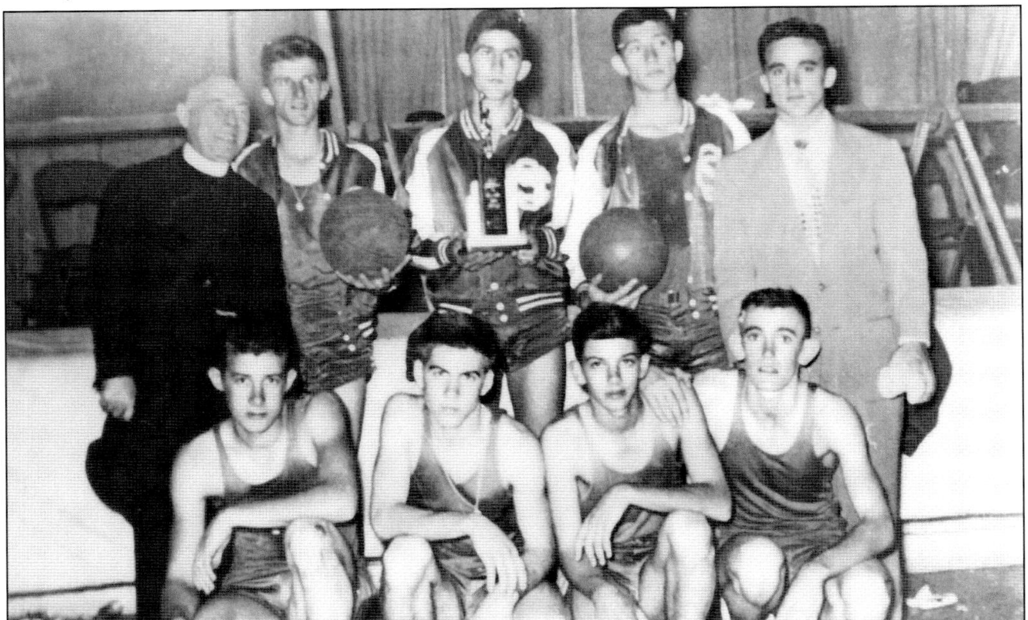

The boys' basketball team from St. Cecilia High School won the 1951 district championship. Pictured here are, from left to right, (first row) Fernest Guilbeau, Edmond Dugas, Edward Bonin Jr., and Clifford Viator; (second row) Fr. P.G. John Kemps, Johnny Billeaud, Harry Patin, Ned Armentor, and coach Perry Dugas. (Lafayette Parish Clerk of Court Louis J. Perret.)

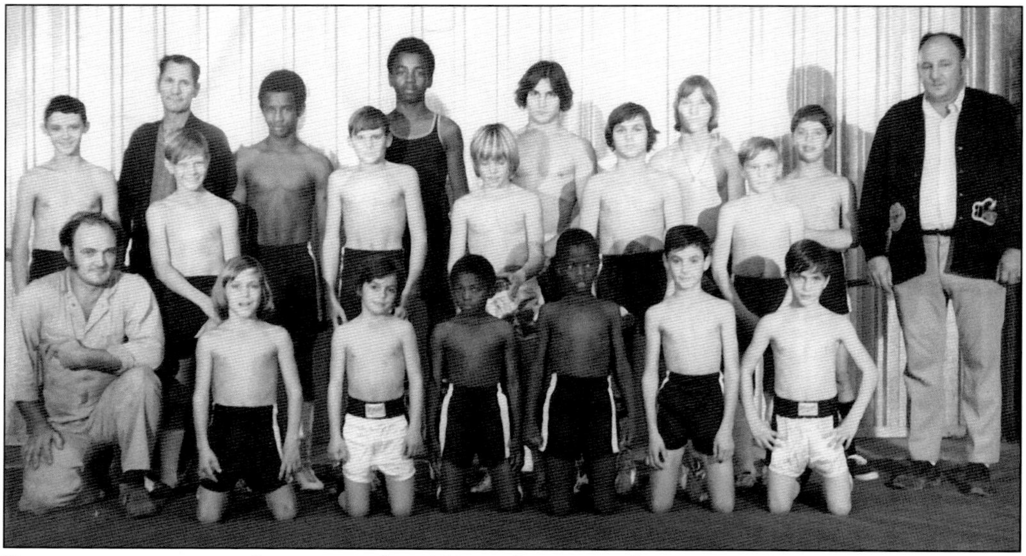

Boxing was a very popular sport in the 1950s and 1960s, with young pugilists wanting to emulate superstar idols of the era such as Rocky Marciano and Floyd Patterson. Russell Flugence, one of the fighters (first row, third on left), fought for the Broussard Boxing Club. (Russell Flugence.)

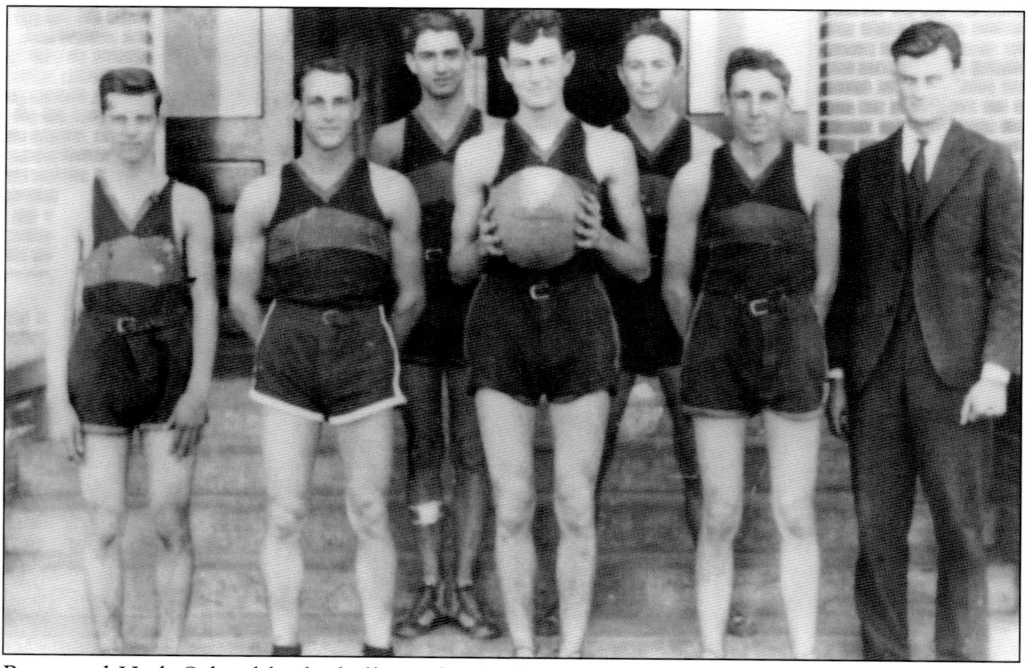

Broussard High School basketball coach Charlie Delana (right) is pictured with 1930 team members, from left to right, Ralph Romero, Thomas Reaux, Abel Guidry, Willis Delana, George Dupleix, and Maxie Girouard. In later years, Girouard made a name for himself on the Evangeline League baseball team. (Lafayette Parish Clerk of Court Louis J. Perret.)

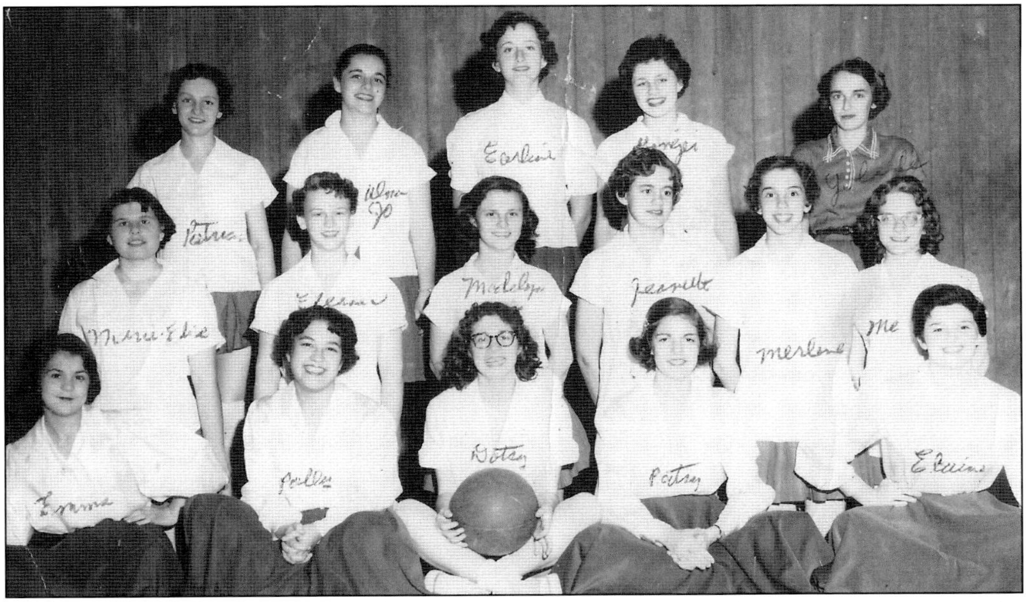

The St. Cecilia School Basketball players, cheerleaders, and coach are pictured during the 1954–1955 school term. They are, from left to right, (first row) Emma Lee Girouard, Polly Billeaud, Dotsy Bernard, Patsy Caffey, Elaine Comeaux; (second row) Marie Elise Cousson, Eleanor Duhon, Madelyn Duhon, Jeanette Mouton, Mereline Girouard, and Velma Langlinais; (third row) Patricia Bonin, Alma Jo Billeaud, Earline Chauvin, Virginia Wall, and coach Yolanda Gondron. (Velma L. Reaux.)

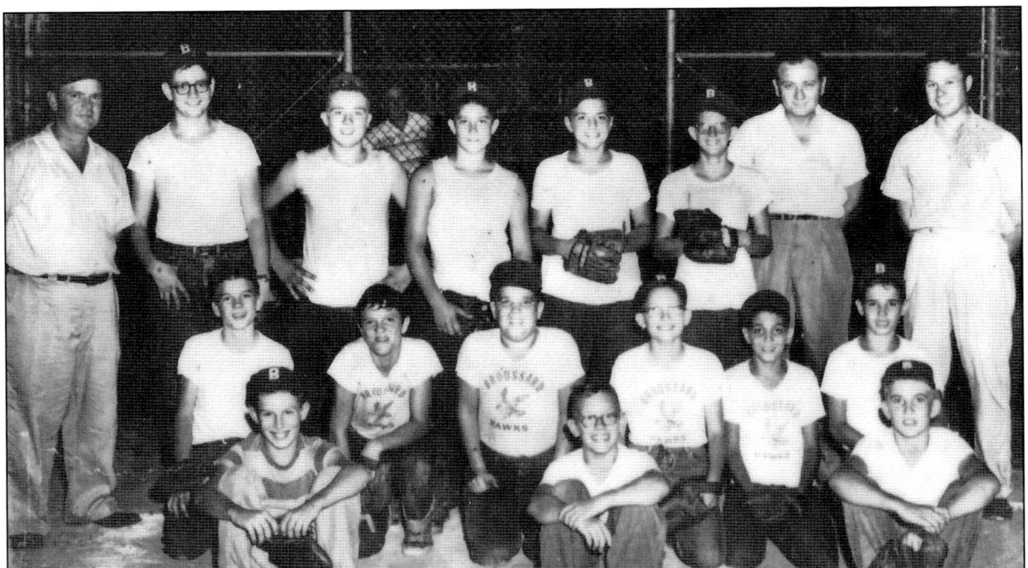

The Broussard Hawks C League Champions of Lafayette Youth Baseball are shown here in 1959. Pictured are, from left to right, (first row) Gil Malagarie, Leo Donald Malagarie and Ronnie Patin; (second row) Gene Dugas, Curley Vallot, Gerald Boutte, Eddie Maslife, Raymond Boutte and Jimmy Garber; (third row) coach Austin Landry, Eddie Duhon, Mackey Soulier, Louis Bernard, Bill Morvant, Charlie Reaux, and sponsors Maxim Soulier and Raymond Billeaud. (Lafayette Parish Clerk of Court Louis J. Perret.)

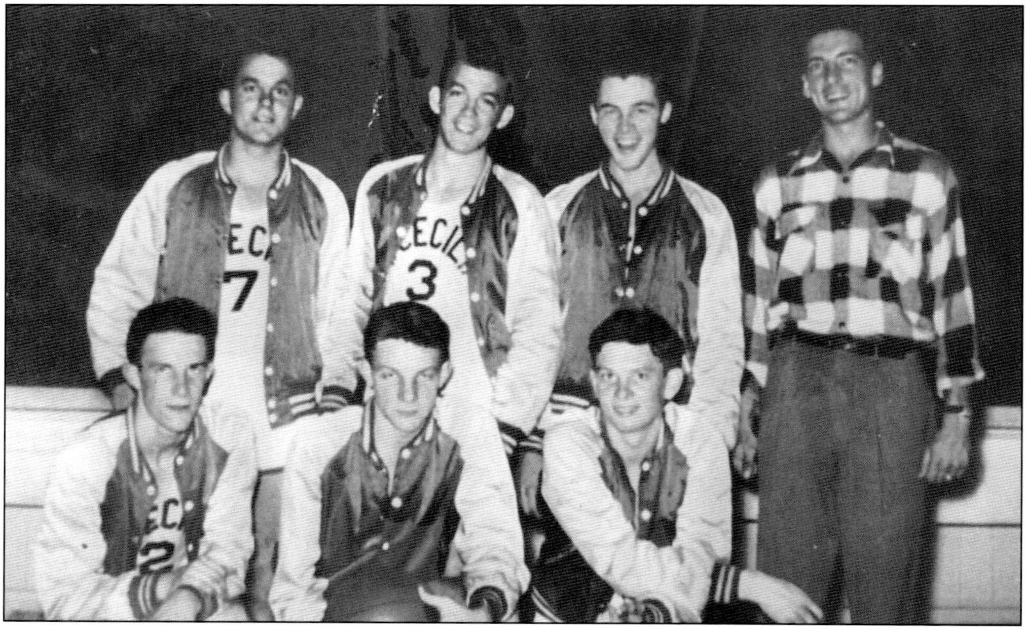

Members of St. Cecilia High School basketball team in 1954 pictured here are, from left to right, (first row) Ronnie Reaux, Neil Reaux, and Walter Comeaux; (second row) Tommy Hollier, Blaise Armentor, Kenneth Emmer, and coach Donnie Pontiff. In his teenage years, Neil worked for Billeaud Grocery delivering groceries to the customers' homes on his big red bicycle. (Velma L. Reaux.)

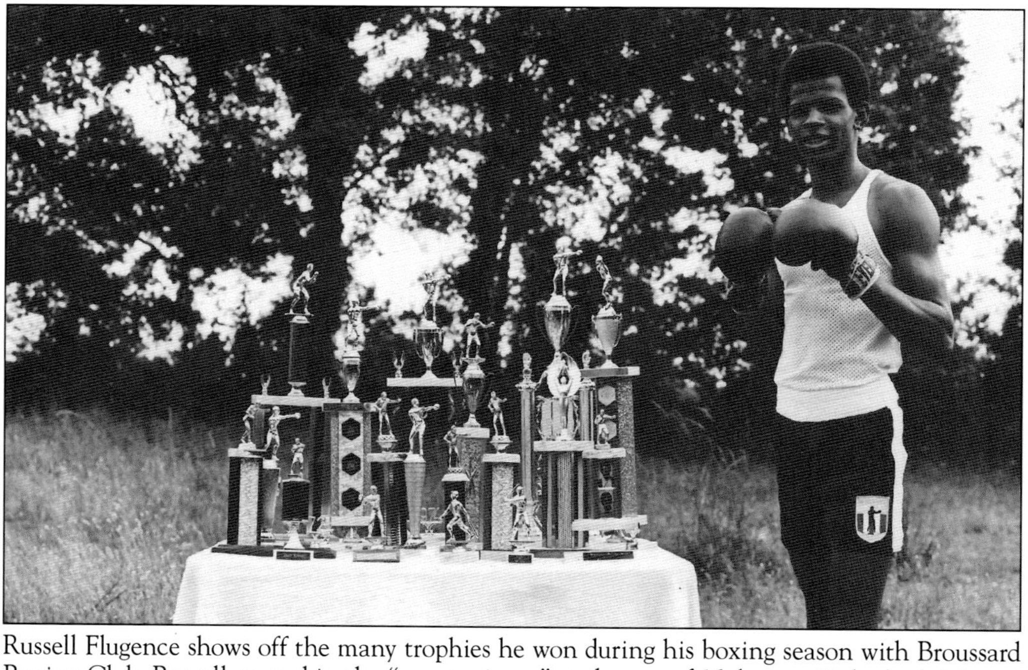

Russell Flugence shows off the many trophies he won during his boxing season with Broussard Boxing Club. Russell started in the "sweat science" at the age of 16; by age 18, he had defeated Leo Harmon from Crowley in 1973, Horace Brooks of Sunset in 1974, and Donnie Leger from Rayne, Louisiana, in 1975. These days, Russell Flugence competes in National Senior Tennis games and ranks sixth in the 53–59 age group. (Russell Flugence.)

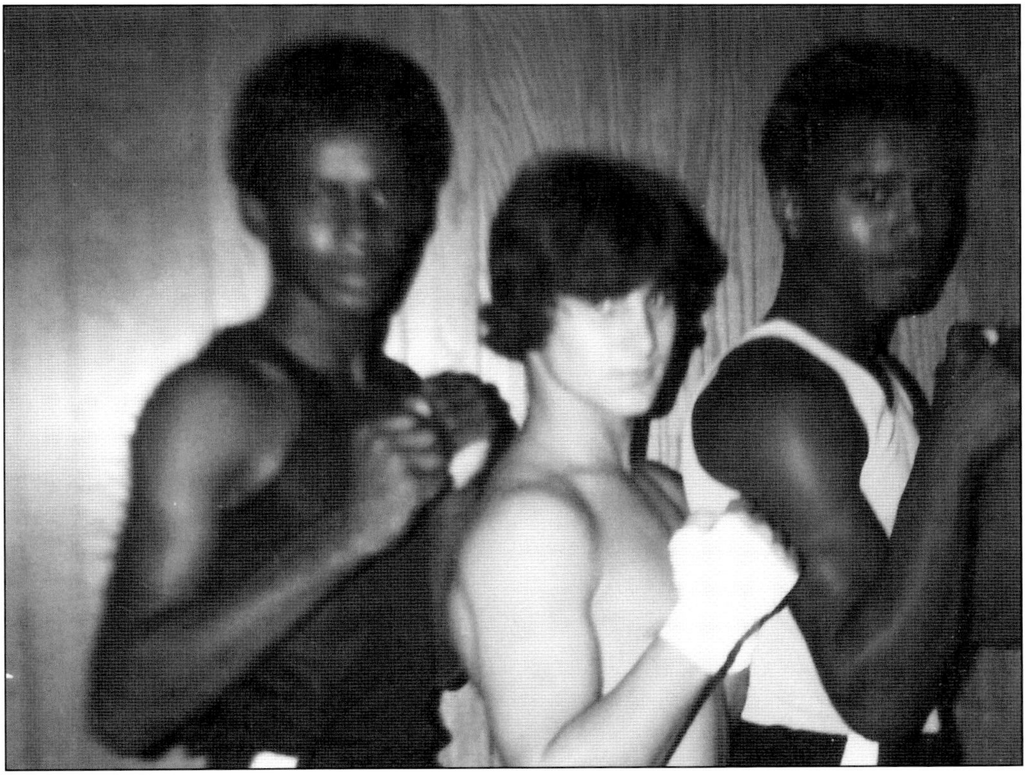

Mark Ste Marie (center), a member of the Broussard Boxing Club, excelled in the fight game as a three-time Louisiana Golden Gloves boxing champion, rarely losing a bout. He is pictured with fellow boxer Russell Flugence (left), and an unidentified boxer. Ste. Marie earned another type of award in 1995—the Carnegie Hero Fund Commission medal honoring his heroic efforts that saved a Texas man from a fiery car crash. (Mark Ste. Marie.)

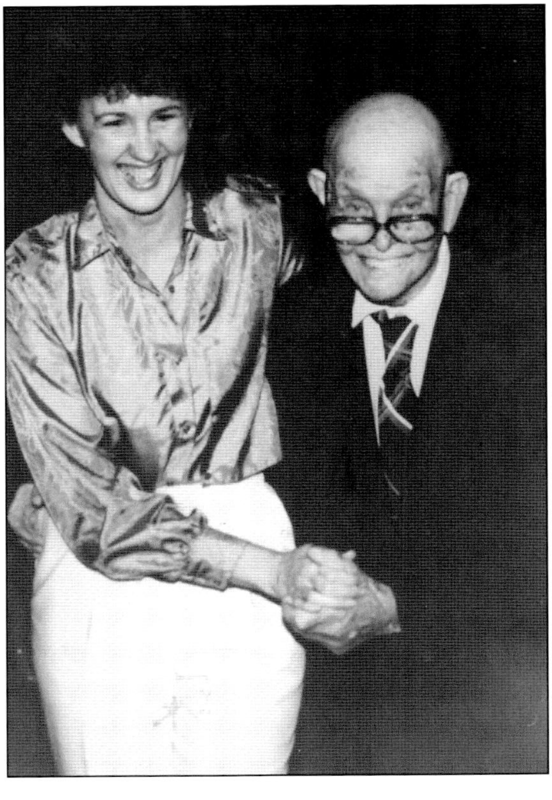

Willie Garber, a World War I veteran, is pictured here dancing with his great-niece Linda Garber at the American Legion Hall. Willie, a chicken and watermelon farmer from Broussard, will always be remembered as a great polka dancer. His goal was to outlive his brothers, and he did, passing at age 97. (Lafayette Parish Clerk of Court Louis J. Perret.)

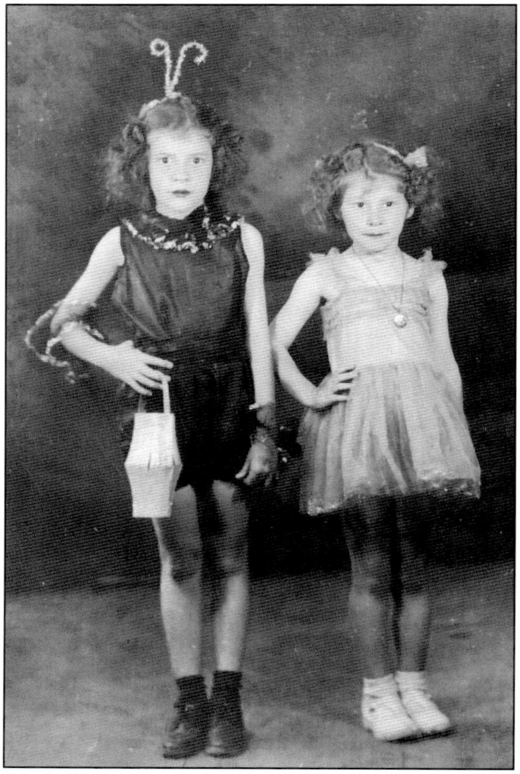

Nella Guilbeau (Miguez), left, and her sister Hazel Guilbeau (Bourque) were the daughters of Ernest and Laurence Guilbeau of Broussard. Nella married Lee Roy Miguez, who served twice as mayor of Broussard, from July 1982 until December 1990. Hazel married Raymond Bourque Sr., an engineer for B.F. Trappey Company, maker of hot sauce and other Cajun products. (Hazel G. Bourque.)

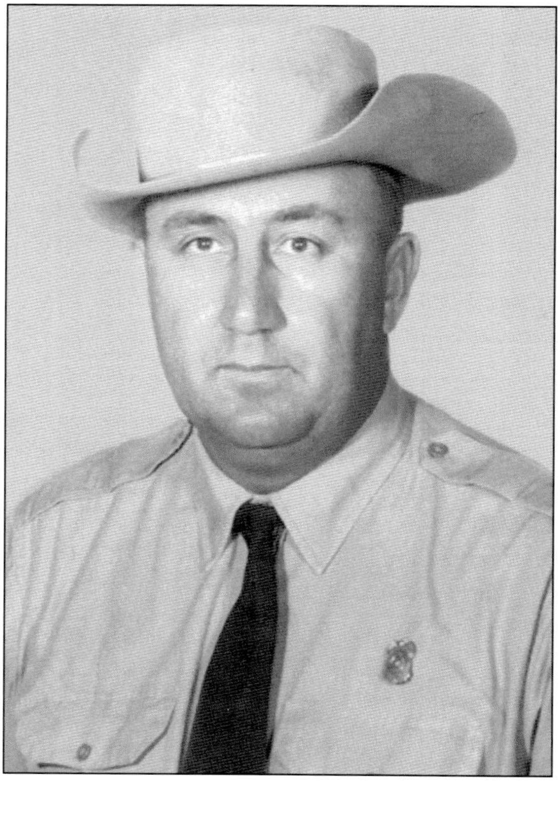

John "Gus" Guilbeau wore many hats during his lengthy career starting in 1943, serving with the US Army 81st Cad Division. Guilbeau took on a new role in 1954 as a law enforcement officer and firefighter for the town of Broussard back when the town's population was just 900 people. Guilbeau loved children and drove a school bus from 1973 to 1988. Coaching and umpiring baseball in the 1960s and 1970s was yet another way Guilbeau gave back to the community. (Darnell Guilbeau.)

Euclide "Euc" St Julien, son of Gustav St. Julien, former Lafayette clerk of court, is seated between Eugene Labbe Sr. (left), a St. Martinville practicing attorney, and John Reaux Sr., who served as a bookkeeper for Martial Billeaud Mercantile and the US Post Office. Euc was appointed to fill in Gilbert St. Julien's one unexpired term as mayor of Lafayette. The three families represented in this photograph are connected through marriage. This image taken when the Woodmen of the World Insurance Company used to have a marching band. (Courtesy Lafayette Parish Clerk of Court Louis J. Perret.)

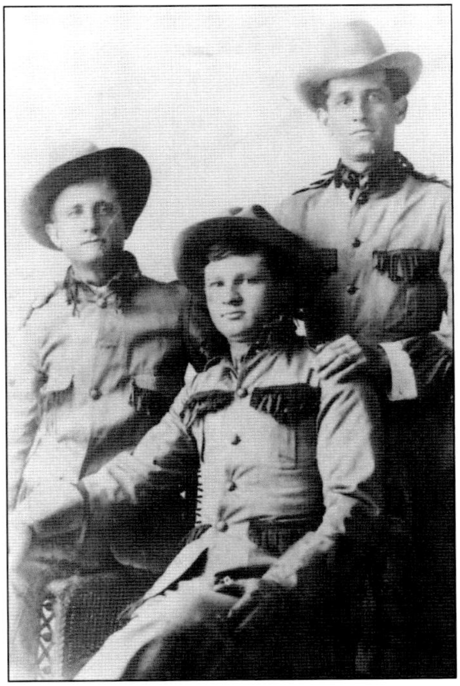

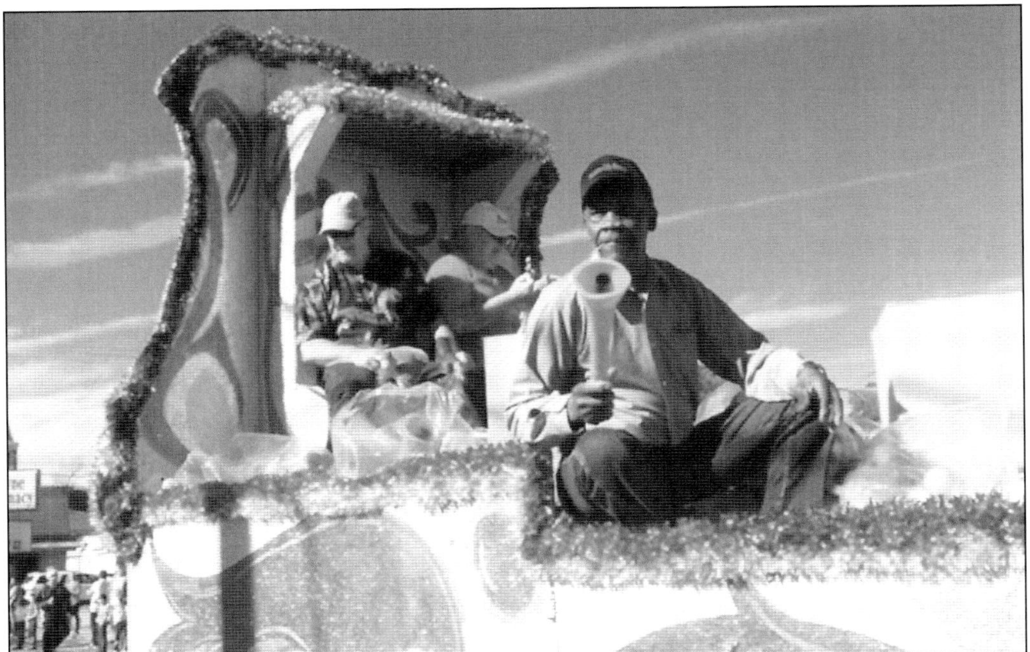

Broussard District 4 city councilman Harold Johnson has plenty to toot his horn about as he rides in an annual Broussard Christmas Parade. Johnson retired from the Lafayette Parish School System, having served as a custodian at Broussard Negro Elementary, which became Katherine Drexel Elementary and was desegregated in 1970. In addition, no one can lay claim to serving more years on the Broussard City Council: Johnson had a total of 20 years uninterrupted service. He was 53 at the time he first decided to run, when only a handful of mom-and-pop businesses occupied the community. (Author's collection.)

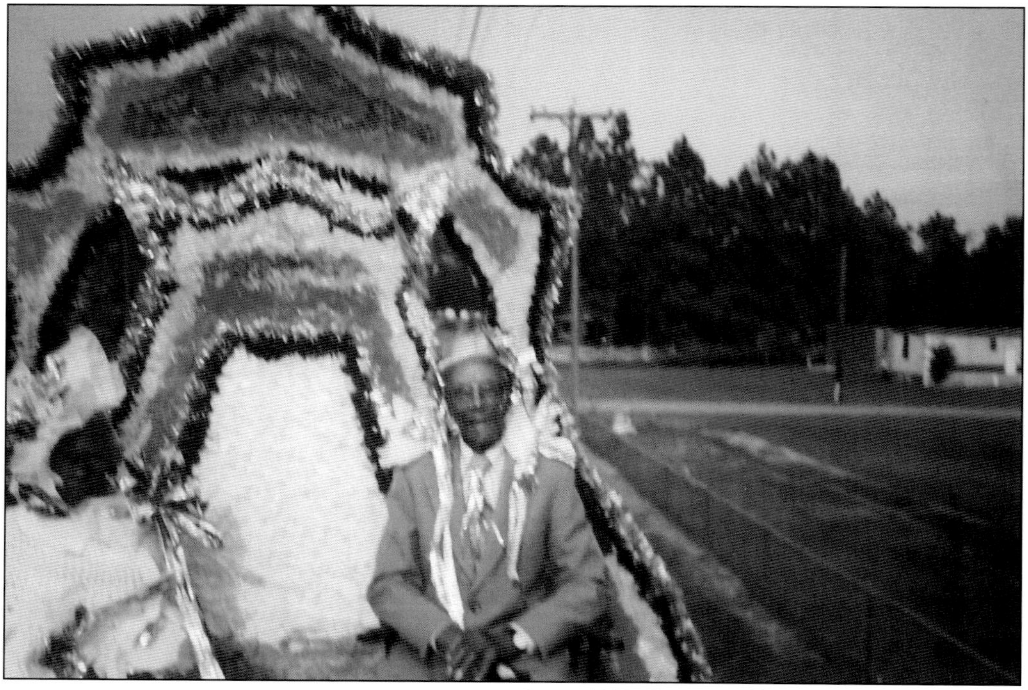

Since 1970, Broussard has celebrated the Christmas season with an annual parade rolling through downtown. Chosen as reigning royalty over the festivities in 1970 were King Lucien Brown and Queen Eldize Adams. In this image, the couple represents St. Joseph Church parish as its two eldest African American citizens. (Roy Brown.)

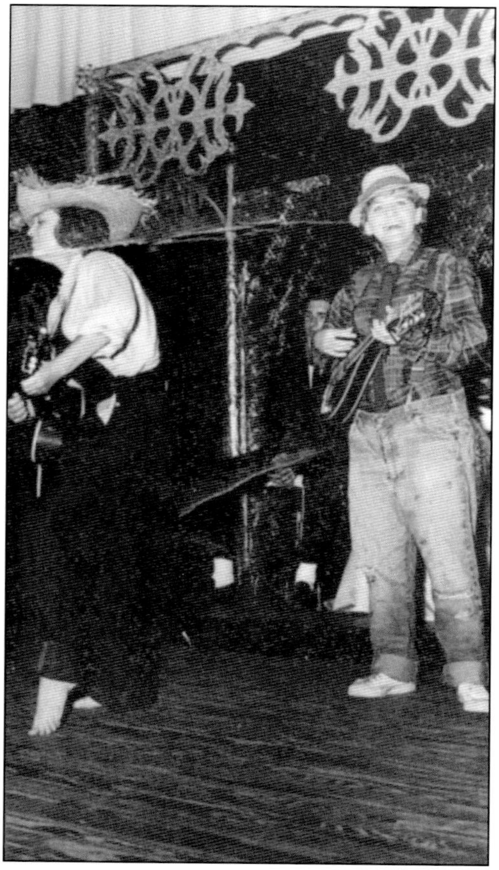

St. Cecilia School's gymnasium was the scene for many annual plays, part of the pageantry, and other festivities that took place annually during the Broussard Community Fair. In November 1964, Dolores Howard (left) and Catherine Trahan (right) participate in a Western-themed production. The man in the background is not identified. (Catherine Romero Trahan.)

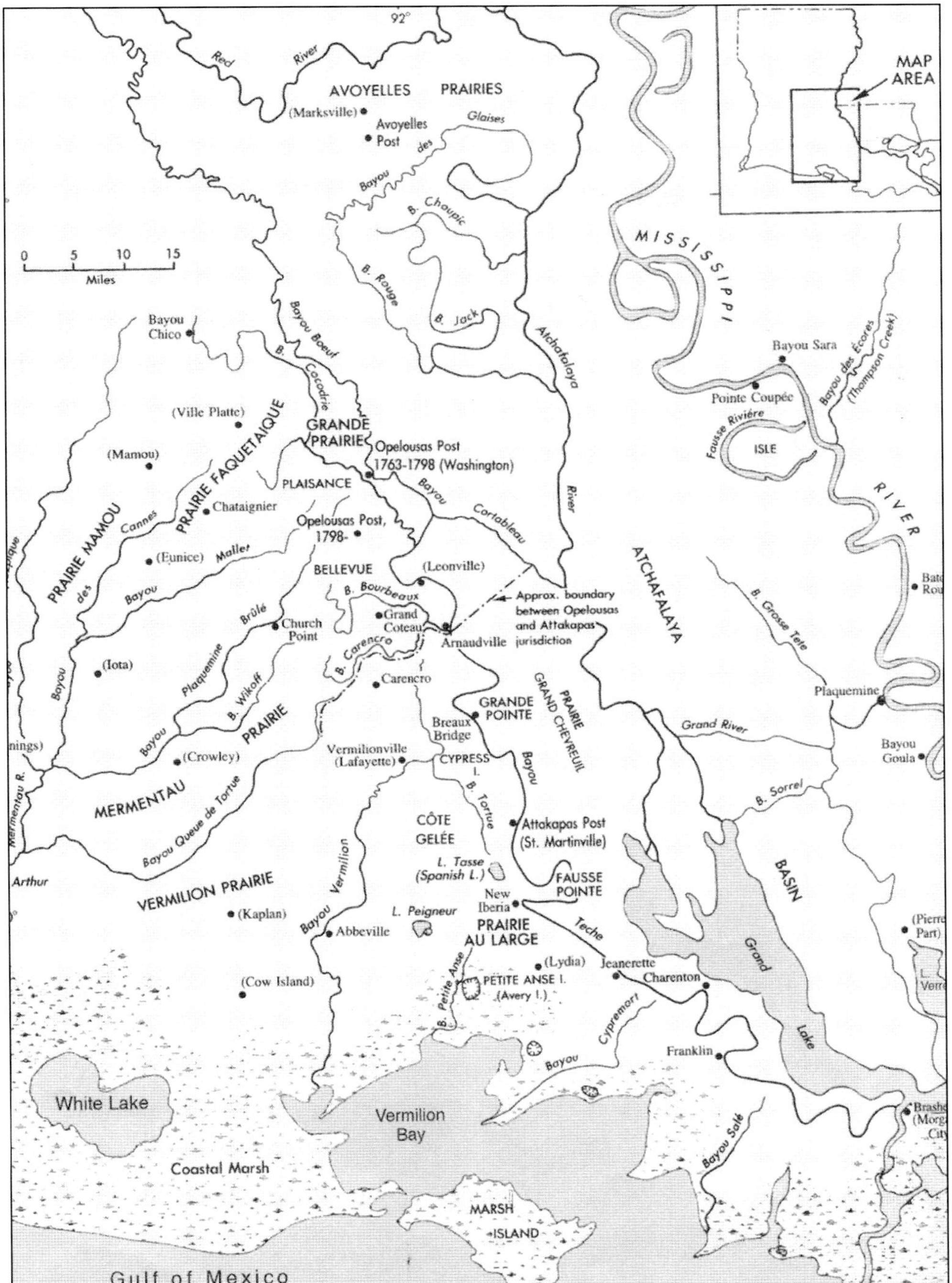

This book tells a story of the Acadian émigrés' contributions in colonizing one of the first Acadian settlements in mid-18th-century Louisiana. Pictured here is a map showing Côte Gelée, which was part of a Spanish land grant. Côte Gelée means "frozen ridge." At Fausse Point, located on the Bayou Teche near Jeanerette, is the location where New Acadia Project will be exploring in 2015, searching for the unidentified graves of Joseph "Beausoleil" Broussard, Alexandre Broussard, and the many other émigrés who settled near Côte Gelée in 1765. They lived solitary lives and died undocumented deaths. (Acadiansingray.com)

Discover Thousands of Local History Books Featuring Millions of Vintage Images

Arcadia Publishing, the leading local history publisher in the United States, is committed to making history accessible and meaningful through publishing books that celebrate and preserve the heritage of America's people and places.

Find more books like this at
www.arcadiapublishing.com

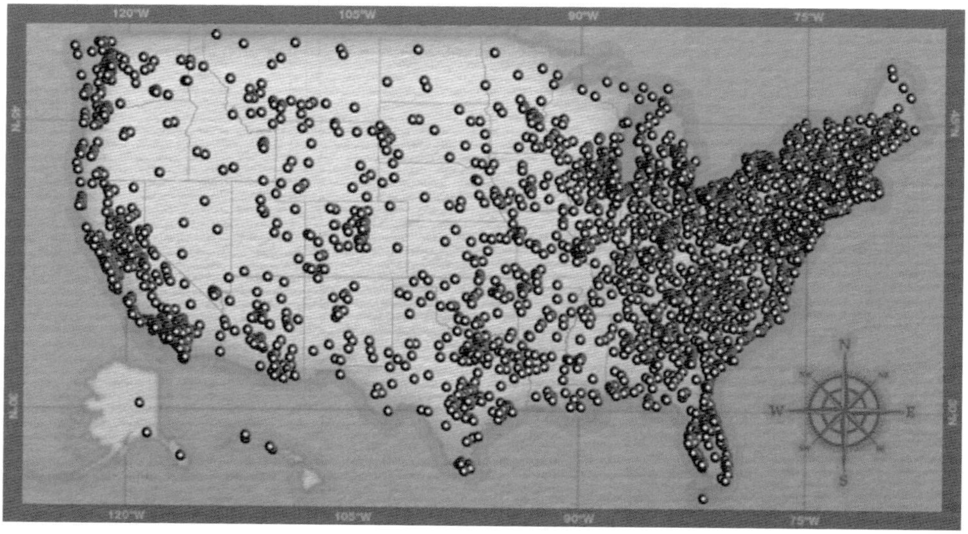

Search for your hometown history, your old stomping grounds, and even your favorite sports team.

Consistent with our mission to preserve history on a local level, this book was printed in South Carolina on American-made paper and manufactured entirely in the United States. Products carrying the accredited Forest Stewardship Council (FSC) label are printed on 100 percent FSC-certified paper.

MADE IN THE USA